PRECARIOUS LIVES

Forced labour, exploitation and asylum

Hannah Lewis, Peter Dwyer, Stuart 2-87 LEW
and Louise Waite

First published in Great Britain in 2015 by

Policy Press
University of Bristol
1-9 Old Park Hill
Bristol BS2 8BB
UK
t: +44 (0)117 954 5940
tpp-info@bristol.ac.uk
www.policypress.co.uk

North America office:
Policy Press
c/o The University of Chicago Press
1427 East 60th Street
Chicago, IL 60637, USA
t: +1 773 702 7700
f: +1 773-702-9756
sales@press.uchicago.edu
www.press.uchicago.edu

© Policy Press 2015

British Library Cataloguing in Publication Data
A catalogue record for this book is available from the British Library

Library of Congress Cataloging-in-Publication Data
A catalog record for this book has been requested

ISBN 978 1 44730 690 0 hardcover

Cover design by Qube Design Associates, Bristol
Front cover image kindly supplied by www.istock.com
Printed and bound in Great Britain by CPI Group (UK) Ltd,
Croydon, CR0 4YY
Policy Press uses environmentally responsible print partners.

Contents

List of tables and figures

Tables

Figures

Acknowledgements

A large number of organisations and individuals in the Yorkshire and Humber region and beyond facilitated access to potential interviewees. We are grateful to over 400 contacts made at refugee support organisations, drop-ins and advice services for supporting the research. Special mention goes to the organisations and individuals who contributed rooms for meetings and interviews or shared their insights and contacts with us: Abigail Housing, ASSIST, Asylum Seekers in Kingston upon Hull, British Red Cross (Refugee Services), Kate Smith, Open Doors, The Poppy Project, Positive Action for Refugees and Asylum Seekers, Northern Refugee Centre, Rachel Mullan-Feroze, Solace, Sheffield and Doncaster Conversation Club, and Women Asylum Seekers Together.

We would like to thank our advisory group for their valuable guidance: Bill Adams, TUC Yorkshire and Humber; Anne Burghgraef, Solace Surviving Exile and Persecution; Jon Burnett, Institute of Race Relations; Charlotte Cooke, The Refugee Council; Gary Craig, University of Durham; Jane Holgate, University of Leeds; Said Rahim, Leeds Refugee Forum; Ben Rogaly, University of Sussex; and Mariam Tola Williams, Yorkshire and Humber Refugee of the Year 2010.

We are grateful to David Brown at our partner organisation Migration Yorkshire for support throughout the project. Many thanks also to Mike Kaye, Don Flynn and Klara Skřivánková who gave feedback and advice at various points during the project. We are grateful to Calum Carson for research cluster support that helped the smooth running of the research. We would like to thank the Economic and Social Research Council (ESRC) for funding the research on which this book is based.

We thank all of the participants who agreed to be interviewed for this project: refugees and asylum seekers who spoke out about their experiences, and the practitioners working in refugee organisations, migrant advocacy, migrant worker organising, anti-trafficking advocacy and support, policy-makers and civil servants who provided valuable views and insights that informed our approach to research and analysis.

Finally, we would like to thank our families and friends for supporting us so much during the writing of this book. We could not have finished without you.

List of abbreviations

A2	Accession 2
A8	Accession 8
EEA	European Economic Area
EU	European Union
ILO	International Labour Organization
IMF	International Monetary Fund
IOM	International Organization for Migration
JRF	Joseph Rowntree Foundation
NASS	National Asylum Support Service
NINo	National Insurance number
NRM	National Referral Mechanism
TCN	Third country national
TNC	Transnational corporation
UN	United Nations

Glossary

NB: The first time these terms are mentioned in the text they are highlighted in **bold**.

Asylum
A form of protection given by a State to a person who is unable to seek protection in his/her country of citizenship and/or residence owing to a fear of being persecuted for reasons of race, religion, nationality, membership of a particular social group or political opinion.

Asylum seeker
Someone who has made a claim for asylum, and is awaiting determination of his/her case.

Asylum support
The national support system in the UK for dispersed asylum seekers, formerly known as 'NASS' (National Asylum Support System). This can include housing and financial support depending on individual circumstances provided under Section 95 of the Asylum and Immigration Act 1999.

Case resolution
The case resolution process was set up by the Home Office to grant or remove unresolved cases of those who claimed asylum before April 2007. Claims were dealt with by the Case Resolution Directorate at the UK Border Agency (UKBA). Grants of 'indefinite leave to remain' were given but without the entitlements of 'refugee status' to those with a positive outcome.

Deportation (also known as 'removal')
The removal of a person who is not a national by the state from its territory to another country or territory after refusal of admission or termination of permission to remain.

Destitution
The situation of lacking the means to meet basic needs of shelter, warmth, food, water and health for a variety of reasons.

Detention
The restriction on the freedom of movement through physical confinement in a detention centre.

Dispersal
The system to provide accommodation to asylum seekers in towns and cities around the UK, introduced in the Immigration and Asylum Act 1999.

Forced labour
The International Labour Organization (ILO) defines forced and compulsory labour as 'all work or service which is exacted from any person under the menace of any penalty and for which the said person has not offered himself voluntarily'.

Home Office
The Home Office is a UK ministerial department that leads on immigration and passports, drugs policy, crime policy and counter-terrorism.

Human trafficking
The recruitment or transportation of people by threat or coercion in order to have control over another person for the purpose of exploitation.

Informal economy
Refers to the diversity of economic activities that are not regulated by the state, whether self-employment in unregistered enterprises, wage labour in unprotected jobs or unwaged labour in the household economy.

International Labour Organization (ILO)
An international organisation of the United Nations (UN) comprised of representatives of governments, employers and workers whose role is to devise and oversee international labour standards such as workers' rights, health and safety, child labour and equality.

International migrant
A non–UK national who comes to live in the UK. Migrants include asylum seekers, refugees, European Union (EU) and non-EU migrants.

Irregular migrant (sometimes known as 'undocumented' or 'illegal' migrant)
Someone who enters or remains in a country without legal permission from the state, either because they entered clandestinely without permission, or because they entered in another visa category and have stayed after their visa entitlement expired.

Labour exploitation
Usually used to define situations of one or more of the following kinds of practices: low or no pay, long hours, insufficient breaks, broken promises, bullying, or contravention of labour rights.

Precarity
The concept of precarity has three main dimensions: the rise of insecure forms of employment; a wider feeling and experience of insecurity; a platform to mobilise against insecure and exploitative work.

Refugee
According to the 1951 Geneva Convention, a refugee is a person who because of a well-founded fear of being persecuted for reasons of race, religion, nationality, political opinion or membership of a particular social group, is outside their country of nationality and is unable or, owing to such fear, is unwilling to avail themselves of the protection of that country; or a stateless person, who, being outside of the country of former habitual residence for the same reasons as mentioned before, is unable, or, owing to such fear, unwilling to return to it.

Refused asylum seeker
Someone who has applied for asylum and who has been refused; the Home Office uses the term 'failed asylum seeker'.

Regularise
To give legal status to irregular migrants without documentation, including permission to work.

Remittances
Broadly defined as any transfer of money from migrants living in the UK to beneficiaries (for example, family or dependants) residing in other countries, typically the migrants' country of origin.

Section 4 support
Section 4 of the Immigration and Asylum Act 1999 gives the Home Office power to grant support to some destitute asylum seekers whose asylum application and appeals have been rejected, and who meet one of five narrow criteria: taking steps to leave the UK; being unable to leave because of physical impediment or a medical reason; if there is no viable route of return; if granted permission to proceed to judicial review of their asylum claim; or because provision of accommodation is necessary to avoid breaching their human rights.

Slavery
A system in which people are treated as the physical property of someone else, held against their will and are either forced to work by that person, or sold to others for the same purpose.

United Kingdom Border Agency (UKBA)
Formerly the Borders and Immigration Agency (BIA), and before that, the Immigration and Nationality Directorate (IND), part of the Home Office. The immigration section of the Home Office is still commonly referred to as UKBA, but the agency was abolished and split into two organisations as of 31 March 2013: UK Visas and Immigration (UKVI) and Immigration Enforcement.

Introduction: the return of slavery?

"You say to [a] European you are an asylum seeker, they don't look at you like a normal person. You are savage, you are nothing like a human, they are not going to speak even with you.... Before Great Britain went to India, Africa and brought here slaves by force – the gun. Now the policy has changed.... They go the slaves way, as before, but without the force.... If I have a shop and I have three illegal workers my work is sweeping the floor, washing the dishes, kind of job that English people don't like to do.... I'm illegal, instead of paying me £6.50 an hour, you know they are going to give me £3, then the cost of that shop, it's come down. And that shop can give *you* a cheaper food – that's good for this society. That's the slavery of this country...."

The words above were spoken to us in anger by 'Alex',[1] a man we interviewed in late 2011 who was living and working in the UK without the legal right to reside in the UK. Alex was a **refused asylum seeker**, someone whose application to the UK government for protection from persecution as a refugee under international law has been rejected. He had agreed to speak to us as part of a study into **forced labour** among **asylum seekers** and **refugees** in the UK that is the focus of this book.

Based on international law, forced labour involves a situation in which a person is forced to work or provide a service under the 'menace of any penalty' and for which they have not offered themselves 'voluntarily' (ILO, 1930, Article 2). Forced labour cases are deemed to be distinguishable from more generalised forms of **labour exploitation** by the existence of various forms of coercion by one or more persons on the worker who at the same time lacks a 'real and acceptable alternative' to the abuse involved (ILO, 2005, p 21). As this book will demonstrate, while forced labour is often conflated or confused with **human trafficking** – the coercive transit of people for the purposes of exploitation – not all forced labour results from trafficking, and those responsible for deceptive border crossings may or may not be directly linked to subsequent exploitation (Flynn, 2007; van den Anker, 2009).

Alex's story was one of 30 testimonies we collected from people who had all made claims for **asylum** in the UK between 1999 and 2011. In Alex's case, like many others we encountered, the government's refusal of his asylum application had left him destitute with no legal recourse to public funds or permission to work. Penniless, homeless and focused on survival, Alex managed to stay with a friend while doing cash-in-hand jobs in pizza takeaways. Yet having told his various employers about his immigration status, all had then taken advantage of his vulnerable status and lack of options to profit from his precarious labour by paying him far less than the National Minimum Wage. Reflecting on his experiences of working in different fast food outlets for extremely low pay, Alex explained how he and other refused asylum seekers like him were being turned into modern-day 'slaves', trapped by the UK government in a situation of enforced vulnerability to exploitation by state-sanctioned denial of basic rights to employment, housing, or welfare.

In this book we provide new evidence showing how forced migrants like Alex – whether refugees, asylum seekers or refused asylum seekers – end up in forced labour in the UK. Although it is widely recognised that the lives of many asylum seekers and refugees in the UK are characterised by poverty, social exclusion and **destitution** (see, for example, Bloch, 2004; Phillips, 2006; Craig et al, 2007; Crawley et al, 2011), there has been very little research into their working experiences, and even less documenting their experiences of exploitation at a time of growing evidence of migrant labour exploitation in general (Anderson and Rogaly, 2005; Craig et al, 2007; van den Anker, 2009).

Our book details asylum seekers and refugees' struggles to subsist in predominantly low-skilled and low-wage settings often outside of 'formal' employment relations, whether making or serving fast food, doing domestic or care work, cleaning or working in factories, packing goods or processing food. In so doing we reveal normally hidden lifeworlds characterised by liminal work spaces that serve to protect exploiters as migrants attempt to evade encounters with those who 'police' such spaces. In particular, we demonstrate how all of the asylum seekers and refugees we interviewed experienced forced labour practices as defined in UK and international law (ILO, 2012a) at some point while in the UK, with the majority experiencing such practices across multiple jobs.

The most common of these forced labour practices were: the non-payment of wages where migrants were either forced to work for 'no pay' or their promised wages were withheld in part or whole; being forced to work excessive overtime beyond the limits prescribed by UK law under some form of threat or penalty; and deception about levels of remuneration and/or the nature of the work to be undertaken and the abuse of vulnerability by an employer or third party deliberately using the precarious immigration and labour market status of a refugee or (refused) asylum seeker to exploit them as workers. We explain how these forced labour practices are often combined with other forms of coercion and entrapment, such as threats of denunciation to the authorities or actual physical acts of violence and restriction of movement, to produce severe exploitation of forced migrants in the UK.

A central claim of this book is that severe labour exploitation – including forced labour – among certain **international migrant** groups residing in the UK is structured and sustained by an exclusionary UK immigration policy. We argue that far from being coincidental, labour exploitation among migrants is intimately connected to an increasingly draconian immigration policy regime that purposefully restricts the rights of newly arriving migrants, whether from the newest member states of an enlarged European Union (EU), or the growing humanitarian disaster zones of the Global South. We make this argument through an in-depth analysis of the wider structures and processes of neoliberal labour markets, immigration and welfare policies, and migrant trajectories. In short, we argue that *asylum policy and forced labour are linked*, and that such a relationship is enmeshed in a broader picture of *modern slavery* being *produced* through neoliberal globalised working conditions in the UK economy.

These findings are significant for four main reasons. First, forced labour is now a *criminal offence* in the UK since 2009/10, and is not only a violation of a person's basic human rights enshrined by European and United Nations (UN) Conventions, but is widely interpreted as contravening international law. In other words, even migrants with irregular status should be protected from forced labour. Second, forced labour is an extreme form of abuse and exploitation that not only harms those affected, but also serves to violate fundamental labour rights and standards for all workers that in turn generates downward pressure on wages and conditions through what is known as the 'race to the bottom'. Third, while there is heightened political and public interest in tackling all forms of modern **slavery**, as illustrated by the current UK Coalition government's draft Modern Slavery Bill, existing government policy appears to be part of the problem. Finally, the fact that forced labour is happening to asylum seekers and refugees is particularly worrying both because of the numbers of people potentially open to exploitation and the fact that they are forced migrants who are seeking protection from the UK state from persecution elsewhere. The issues we highlight thus extend beyond the individuals we interviewed.

In this introductory chapter, we situate the main arguments and evidence of the book within the current political climate and policy debates on migrants, labour market exploitation and the relationship to forced labour. We begin by discussing the historical background to the recent emergence of the UK government's commitment to 'tackling modern slavery in all its forms' with the launch of its draft Modern Slavery Bill in 2013 (Home Office, 2013a). We argue that the government's approach to the eradication of slavery and forced labour is flawed due to its limited focus on prosecution and criminalisation which diverts attention away from the fundamental role that asylum and immigration policy plays, in combination with a deregulated labour market, in reproducing migrant exploitation. We then briefly outline our study of forced labour among asylum seekers and refugees in the UK, setting out how and why we chose to explore these issues before providing synopses of subsequent chapters of the book and the key arguments they contain.

Modern slavery and the UK

Slavery is not new to these shores. From 1562 until the 1800s, Britain was at the heart of the Transatlantic Slave Trade, its slave ships transporting a mass of forced labourers bought or stolen mainly from the West coast of Africa to the Caribbean cotton and sugar cane fields of the British colonies (see Fryer, 1984; 1988; Rodney, 1972; Williams, 1944). The Slave Trade was a state-sponsored economic system backed by Royal Charter of 1585 and dependent on the direct involvement and material and moral support of the Crown itself. It formed part of the hugely profitable 'triangular trade' in which British manufacturing products were sent to the African coast to pay for slaves who were then transported to the Americas and sold to plantation owners; the sugar produced by African hands was then exported back to Britain for resale.

African slavery, as the seminal works of Williams (1944) and Rodney (1972) proved, not only produced the prosperous UK slave port cities of London, Bristol and Liverpool, but was also integral to Western capitalist development and African underdevelopment more generally. While the scale of this system remains open to conjecture and debate, tens of millions of Africans became subject to a 'brutal and inhuman stem of chattel slavery [that] involved the removal of individual freedom and rights and the allocation of enslaved Africans as property; the transition

—

4

of human beings into economic units' (World Development Movement, 2007, p 6). Millions died in the process. Peter Fryer, in his classic book, *Staying power: the history of black people in Britain*, paints a vivid picture of the unspeakable horrors of African enslavement:

> The Africans bought by the European slave-traders were mostly very young: healthy, able-bodied young men and women between the ages of 15 and 25. Cargoes often included a proportion of children, but people over the age of 30 were almost always rejected. The young men, young women and children were branded like cattle, then carried across the Atlantic, the men in chains in the hold for 20 hours out of the 24. Of those transported in British ships, between one in four and one in twelve perished on the way. It was taken for granted that, of those who survived the "middle passage" one in three would die, of dysentery or suicide (a form of resistance) in their first three years in the New World. Those first three years were the "seasoning" or acclimatization period. The survivors were set to work under the whip to produce "white gold" for their white masters. Flogging – in Jamaica with a 10ft cart-whip – was routine punishment for almost every offence, and was inflicted on girls, women, boys and men alike. The slaves were grossly underfed, as both an economy and an attempt, rarely successful, to break their spirit. (Fryer, 1988, pp 10-11)

Yet, as Fryer intimates, the unbreakable spirit of enslaved Africans underpinned their heroic and continuous resistance to enslavement, their struggles gradually joined by European abolitionist movements that successfully campaigned for the abhorrent trade to cease (Drescher, 2009). The British Parliamentary abolition of slavery in 1833 took place at a time of general abolitionist progress across European states and their colonies, and was progressively outlawed in most countries by the time of the 1948 UN Universal Declaration of Human Rights, which stated that 'No one shall be held in slavery or servitude; slavery and the slave trade shall be prohibited in all their forms'.

Sadly, despite the centuries of struggle to rid the world of slavery, growing evidence suggests it is alive, well and flourishing in the contemporary era across the globe. On receiving the 2014 Best Picture Oscar for the film '12 Years a Slave', director Steve McQueen dedicated his award to 'all the people who have endured slavery, and the 21 million people who still suffer slavery today' (Suebsaeng, 2014).

This figure comes from the **International Labour Organization's** (ILO, 2012b) latest estimate of people trapped in forced labour across the globe with the overwhelming majority (18.7 million, that is, 90 per cent) exploited in the private economy. It is widely believed that this figure is a conservative estimate given the often hidden nature of the problem.

Although mostly concentrated in the so-called 'slavery super centres' of India, Pakistan and Brazil (Bales, 2004), modern-day slavery in the UK was brought dramatically to public and political attention by two tragedies involving Chinese migrants during the 2000s. In June 2000, 58 Chinese were found dead through asphyxiation in the back of an airtight tomato lorry at Dover, the last stage of a horrific 10-week journey by train, truck, horse and cart often under armed guard by the criminal gang of traffickers who held the migrants' documents and luggage as surety (Macleod, 2000). If they had survived, they would have almost certainly been subjected to bonded labour in the underground economy in order to pay off their £20,000 debt to the traffickers. Then, in February 2004 came the Morecambe Bay disaster when 23 Chinese migrants – all irregular immigrants, that is, without formal legal entitlement to work or residence in the UK – drowned in treacherous tides as they picked cockles for just £5 a bag under the supervision of their Chinese 'gangmaster' (*The Guardian*, 2005; Pai, 2008).

These tragedies part-fuelled a growing body of research into migrant labour exploitation and forced labour in the UK. Much of the early focus of research in the UK was on the 'trafficking' of mainly women and children for the purpose of commercial sexual exploitation (Kaye, 2003; Skřivánková, 2006; Andrijasevic, 2010). In 2005, Anderson and Rogaly (2005) published what would become a landmark study, showing how migrant workers from Asia, Africa, Latin America and Central and Eastern Europe working in construction, agriculture, care and cleaning sectors in the UK were engaged through a bewildering array of subcontracting chains and agents that made safeguarding their basic human and labour rights difficult in general, and in some cases led to forced labour. Migrant domestic and care workers have been particularly identified as at risk of forced labour due to the highly unequal power relations between employer and worker, and the relative invisibility of their workplaces behind closed doors (Anderson, 2007; Oxfam and Kalayaan, 2008; Gordolan and Lalani, 2009; Clark and Kumarappan, 2011; Lalani, 2011).

Growing evidence and pressure to tackle these issues has prompted government action. Marking the 200th anniversary of the parliamentary abolition of the slave trade within the British Empire in March 2007, former Prime Minister Tony Blair argued that the government needed to 'acknowledge the unspeakable cruelty that persists in the form of modern day slavery ... such as bonded labour, forced recruitment of child soldiers and human trafficking – and at its root is poverty and social exclusion' (Blair, 2007, p 2). Subsequently, the Labour government introduced a flurry of new laws, regulations and cross-border initiatives aimed at combatting organised 'people trafficking' and gaining control of so-called 'gangmasters' – labour agents who provide large numbers of workers, typically migrants, including those with 'irregular' status, to labour-intensive industries for employment in exploitative conditions that often amount to forced labour.

This policy framework has been continued by the Conservative-Liberal Democrat Coalition government (2010–15), and is embodied in the Coalition's draft Modern Slavery Bill, published in December 2013 (Home Office, 2013a). Proposals within the Modern Slavery Bill, which cover England and Wales only, include tougher sentencing for those convicted of forced labour offences; the creation of a 'modern slavery commissioner' with responsibilities for monitoring the work of government and law enforcement agencies; establishing a legal duty on specified public authorities to report potential victims of trafficking; a company commitment in which employers pledge not to use slave labour and measures to ban persons convicted of trafficking offences from holding a gangmaster's licence; strengthening border controls to detect victims and their traffickers; and increasing support for victims. In her foreword to the Bill, Home Secretary Theresa May made clear the government's belief that tackling forced labour meant fighting mafia-like crime through further criminalisation and an extension of policing powers and immigration controls:

> This is organised crime perpetrated by criminal gangs with links all over the world. They have the ability to move money and people without recourse from one end of the globe to the other. We need law enforcement at every level, from the National Crime Agency to local forces to be engaged in relentlessly pursuing and disrupting these groups. Stopping these organised crime groups at their source will result in more arrests, more prosecutions, but most importantly, more people released from slavery and more prevented from ever entering it in the first place. I want a strong message to go out to any individual or group involved in the enslavement of victims; you will not get away

with it, we will catch you and you will go to prison for a
very long time. (quoted in Home Office, 2013a)

While this crackdown on modern slavery has created a welcome
spotlight on the issue, our research suggests that the modern slavery
discourse and its particular framing of forced labour as a purely 'criminal'
act, perpetrated by a villainous cast of underworld characters on helpless
victims, is deeply problematic, not least because the nature of the
problem, its scale and scope, and its root causes, are all framed within
a narrow 'law and order' framework that excludes the government's
own immigration and labour market policies from consideration. In
this book we argue that the government's approach to tackling forced
labour among migrants will not only fail to help many victims, but
will arguably worsen the situation because it does not address the root
causes of forced labour among migrants we have identified in our
research. The Immigration Act 2014, introduced in parallel to the draft
Modern Slavery Bill, will most likely render migrants in the UK even
more vulnerable to exploitation by further reducing their rights, access
to resources and support, thus driving them deeper underground and
further into the strengthened hands of their abusers.

Freeing markets, closing borders: forced migrants and the hyper-precarity trap

Tackling modern slavery in the UK, especially among forced migrants
who often make unsuccessful claims for asylum, first requires an
understanding of what makes such migrants particularly vulnerable
to forced labour. Like McKay et al (2009), we are less persuaded by
orthodoxies that explain the exploitation of migrants as primarily
a product of individual factors (limited language competence or
qualifications, for example), but rather are drawn to explanatory
frameworks that deploy a political economy lens to explore the role of
structural factors. Yet we remain sensitive to agentic factors, as Chapter 5
in particular will reveal, with our discussion of the 'migrant project'. In
general terms, we adopt Giddens' structuration theory that creates an
analytical space for both structure *and* agency (Giddens, 1984). In this
book we argue that forced migrants' susceptibility to labour exploitation
does not derive primarily from criminals and unscrupulous employers,
but from the interaction of three particular processes.

The first relates to the advance of neoliberal globalisation (Herod,
2000) and its associated processes of deindustrialisation and the
flexibilisation of labour markets (Peck et al, 2005) that have strongly

eroded working-class and labour movement power, and are widely held to have underpinned the rise of insecure and casualised employment relations over the past 30 years (Cumbers et al, 2008). Arguably, these processes have combined to create two-tier labour markets in many countries, in which well-paid, skilled and highly protected employment is contrasted with flexible, low-skilled work routinely undertaken by marginalised groups including vulnerable migrants (Barbieri, 2009). A glance around neoliberal migrant-receiving states such as the UK reveals that those who work in the lower echelons of the labour market are commonly in precarious work characterised by short-term employment, few social protections, experiences of discrimination and economic insecurity in workplaces lacking collective representation or control over wages or conditions where employers evade labour standards to maximise profit in response to global competition.

The second basis of susceptibility to labour exploitation for forced migrants is their *socio-legal status* – principally the 'stratified rights' they enjoy as part of their structured exclusion from mainstream society, that has long been an integral feature of the UK's asylum, immigration and borders regime (Craig, 2007; Morris, 2001). This results in a situation whereby different subgroups of migrants experience widely divergent rights and entitlements to residency, work and welfare, depending on their specific immigration status (Vertovec, 2006; Dwyer et al, 2011). Current policies at best provide limited, highly conditional support for some, while simultaneously promoting the destitution of others, for example, refused asylum seekers. While refugees and other **irregular migrants** who receive leave to remain in the UK have permission to work and are theoretically able to find employment or access benefits, they experience one of the highest rates of unemployment of any group in the UK (Bloch, 2002) as they face formidable structural barriers in accessing employment and benefits related to delays or mistakes in **Home Office** documentation, limited English language skills, a lack of UK work experience or references, and non-recognition of qualifications awarded in other countries (Bloch, 2004; Hurstfield et al, 2004; Dwyer, 2008). Evidence suggests that these factors have been influential in forcing increasing numbers of asylum seekers and refugees into severely exploitative labour conditions as individuals try to meet their basic needs (Dwyer, 2008; Burnett and Whyte, 2010). Fear of detection and **deportation** shapes daily life for those with temporary, precarious or non-existent rights to residence, further disciplining individuals' susceptibility to exploitation. This fear is considerably accentuated for forced migrants who risk return to persecution, torture, and forced labour (Lewis, 2007; Kibreab, 2009; Bloch et al, 2011; Bloch,

2013). But as we show in Chapters 4 and 5, 'deportability' (de Genova, 2002) relates not only to the actual risk of *deportation*, but is constituted in a lived experience of state enforcement of border controls. For example, in the UK, the policing of 'illegal migrant workers' results in certain workplaces being targeted for raids by immigration officials, heightening the sense of insecurity that inhibits resistance and collective action for those working without papers (Burnett and Whyte, 2010).

The final set of processes that render forced migrants vulnerable to exploitation in the UK relate to their own micro-level experiences and circumstances that can erode individuals' abilities to enter and negotiate decent work and/or to leave highly exploitative employment. As Hynes (2010, p 966) argues in her analysis of child trafficking, there can be multiple and clustering 'points of vulnerability' linked to factors both prior to arrival, such as previous experiences of exploitation, loss of parents and so on, and after arrival in the UK, including, 'negotiating the immigration and asylum systems, the overarching environment of deterrence of new arrivals into the UK, accessing services, mistrust and disbelief of accounts provided'. The role of labour market intermediaries can be key here in the multi-placed exploitation of migrants (see, for example, Mahdavi, 2013). As Geddes (2011) states, these intermediaries could be kin or kith who enable/facilitate migration at the start, who themselves may be linked to (or be one and the same as) smugglers or traffickers, and labour recruitment agents or gangmasters in destination countries that recruit low-skilled temporary labour. At each point of the chain, there is the potential for migrants to be forced, coerced or otherwise presented with an absence of acceptable alternatives but to submit to an exploitative situation.

The glue that holds this web together may frequently be indebtedness. At the extreme end of the indebtedness spectrum lies trafficking and debt slavery, but smuggling costs are also often very high and can result in a patchwork of debts being owed to various third parties and thus ongoing relationships with each after border crossings (Triandafyllidou and Maroukis, 2012). Debt may be an aspect, not only of non-trafficked irregular migration (as with smuggling), but also of perfectly legal migration. This may originate from debt incurred to finance migrants' journeys, some from money borrowed in order to augment **remittances** to families back home and/or finance family reunification, and some may emerge from paying high fees for arranging legal movement and organising employment. In this way, states' immigration policies may create and promote migrant indebtedness. What is particularly vital in understanding the notion of 'exit' from a particular 'forced labour' situation is the recognition that workers' perceptions of their own obligations to support families or honour debts (O'Neill, 2011) are 'powerful disciplining mechanisms which can very effectively be harnessed to the cause of exploitation' (Phillips, 2013b, p 8).

When combined, this myriad of processes generates what we call *hyper-precarious* migrant lives. In a literal sense **precarity** refers to those who experience precariousness, and is generally used to describe lives characterised by uncertainty and instability, a description that clearly resonates with the lifeworlds of asylum seekers and refugees who experience forced labour (Waite, 2009). Precarity has become an increasingly influential conceptual frame for capturing the rise in insecure employment emerging from the globally prevailing neoliberal labour market model (see, for example, Bourdieu, 1998, 1999; Dorre et al, 2006; Fantone, 2007) as well as wider feelings and experiences of insecurity beyond the labour market which are indicative of a generalised societal malaise (see, for example, Neilson and Rossiter, 2005). What our empirical research on the working lives of asylum seekers and refugees in the UK suggests more generally is that migrants journeying through and around various immigration and socio-legal statuses while under serious livelihood pressures are at risk of entering the labour market at the lowest possible point in their effort to secure work. These constraints on migrants can combine with 'unfreedoms' in labour market processes to create situations of '*hyper*-precarity' (discussed further in Lewis et al, 2014, forthcoming). For any one individual, aspects of socio-legal status, migration context and gender relations compound to create multi-dimensional insecurities that contribute to their necessity to engage in, and close down exit from, severely exploitative, and in some cases, forced labour. In this reading of the problem, criminalising the perpetrators while further tightening immigration controls and deregulating labour markets treats the symptoms while exacerbating the causes of forced labour.

Forced or unfree labour?

A second argument we make in this book is that asylum seekers and refugees are not protected from existing exploitation because of how forced labour itself is legally and ideologically conceptualised. We follow a number of scholars in finding that forced labour has been narrowly defined and conceptualised and to some extent decoupled from wider debates about exploitation and the wider paid labour market (see, for example, Lerche, 2007; Kagan et al, 2011). The introduction of the concept of 'exploitation' into forced labour debates is not without its critics. While many would accept that there are significant problems with exploitation within the paid labour market, the focus of such debates is broadly about substandard living and working conditions. This is qualitatively different from forced labour where, as noted, 'coercion' or the 'threat of menace' is the key to successful prosecutions of forced labour in the courts. While a narrow definition of forced labour can be defended where the primary purpose is enforcement, in this book we see such a neat distinction between forced labour and highly exploitative working conditions as unhelpful due to both the complex factors and processes that render asylum seekers and refugees vulnerable to forced labour and the alternative meanings and interpretations of coercion excluded by the ILO approach.

We argue that a theoretical way out of this impasse potentially lies in the concept of 'unfree labour' whose influence is growing in development studies and political economy (Phillips, 2013b). Unfree labour situates 'unfreedoms' in opposition to 'free' labour, characterised by agreement, or 'free' contractual relationships. This concept is helpful in understanding the highly constrained choices and lack of alternatives that lead many asylum seekers and refugees to engage in severely exploitative work. The idea also enables an understanding of how contemporary unfreedom differs from 'traditional' forms of slavery that emphasise one person's directly coercive control over another human being. The notion of unfree labour, which can include contractual forms that involve labour being sold for money, also encompasses the preclusion of exit (rather than necessarily situations of coerced entry), and is characterised by harsh, degrading or dangerous working conditions and the violation of workers' labour and human rights. Such debates serve to highlight the blurred boundaries between workers' consent and the coercion that some argue delineate forced labour *per se* from wider exploitation in the labour market (see Chapter 6 for fuller discussions).

The notion of unfree, as opposed to forced, labour is also important in emphasising that migrants are neither passive nor entirely without *agency* (see Chapter 5 and also Sigona, 2012). Notwithstanding powerful structural aspects of unfree labour relations – for example, workers experiencing practices of coercion, menace of penalty and the abuse of vulnerability related to their socio-legal status – it is also critical to recognise the ways that workers *actively resist* poor treatment within unfree labouring environments. In exploring both structure *and* agency we consider how unfree labour situations can be understood as part of the 'migrant project' in relation to migration trajectories across time and space involving extensive transnational social relationships, and not just as an isolated labour situation (Bastia and McGrath, 2011; Mai, 2011; O'Connell Davidson, 2013).

Research presented in this book

The research underpinning this book was generated by the Precarious Lives project funded by the Economic and Social Research Council (ESRC) between March 2010 and December 2012. The overall aim was to gain an in-depth understanding of the experiences of forced labour among asylum seekers and refugees to contribute to ongoing policy and academic debates on the causes of, and solutions to, forced labour in the UK. While existing research had raised the profile of forced labour in the UK in both public and political realms, none had addressed the forced labour susceptibilities of this particular group of migrants. The project therefore set out to investigate the key factors and processes that make asylum seekers and refugees vulnerable to forced labour, and to consider how they might be challenged. We also wanted to explore the ways in which socio-legal status shaped experiences of forced labour and the need to engage in exploitative work, and consider different meanings and interpretations of forced labour. Linked to this was a desire to allow the voices of such migrants to be heard in order that they might inform wider research and debate on forced labour.

Fieldwork was conducted in the Yorkshire and Humber region of the UK in 2011 and 2012. We chose this research site primarily to explore migrant exploitation in a different context to London, which has attracted many studies already. Our previous work in the region also presented us with a range of contacts that would help facilitate the fieldwork. The core empirical data for the research came from 30 interviews with asylum seeker and refugee participants aged 18+ years who were selected on the basis that they had made a claim for asylum in the UK, had experience of work that met descriptions of one or more ILO forced labour indicators and were either residing, or had previously resided in, the Yorkshire and Humber region of England. They comprised 12 women and 18 men, were aged between 21 and 58 years and came from 17 countries in Africa, the Middle East, Central Europe and South and Central Asia. Interviews typically lasted between 2 and 3 hours and involved biographical accounts of migrating to the UK, entering the asylum system and experiences of work guided by semi-structured prompts. To contextualise these in-depth interviews with asylum seekers and refugees and further explore relevant policy/legal issues, a further 23 interviews with key informants (practitioners working in frontline, policy-making, support and advocacy organisations focused on migrant's rights and/ or employment issues) were also conducted. The methodology, access and ethical considerations are discussed further in Chapter 3.

Outline of the book

Following this introductory chapter, *Chapter 2* deploys both global and national lenses to ask why vulnerable migrant workers routinely experience labour exploitation. We deepen our argument – outlined in this chapter – that the UK's neoliberal labour market regime has combined with a damaging asylum and immigration policy to render particular *international migrant* groups hyper-precarious and deeply susceptible to forced labour exploitation. We review literature evidencing migrant workers' exploitation at a global level before focusing on the more extreme exploitation characterised as forced labour. Recent UK governments' attempts to 'manage' migration are then explored, before offering a critical discussion of UK asylum legislation highlighting how restrictive policies have played an important role in creating a complex socio-legal differentiation of migrants' rights that help to facilitate the *production* of forced labour in this realm.

Chapter 3 focuses on the forced labour experiences of the 30 asylum seekers and refugees we interviewed. The first part introduces the conceptual framework of forced labour as defined by the ILO. It then sets out the empirical context for our research into forced labour – the Yorkshire and Humber region of England, UK – and explains how we designed our research approach to address the various practical and ethical challenges we encountered. We then review the types of work, workplaces and sectors our 30 interviewees were engaged in before using the ILO forced labour framework to demonstrate the prevalence and types of forced labour practices across our interviewees. These included formal and informal waged 'jobs' in the labour market, transactional-based work exchanged between both friends and total strangers, and unwaged reproductive labour and forced prostitution in private households. Most of these labour experiences involved one or more of the ILO's 11 indicators of forced labour, with the most common being the abuse of vulnerability of compromised socio-legal status and the withholding of wages. Of three groups we identify – asylum seekers on entry, irregular migrants and trafficked migrants – we found that those trafficked to the UK were in the most exploitative forms of forced labour including domestic servitude, sexual exploitation and care work.

Chapter 4 explores the significance of socio-legal status in structuring the lives of asylum seekers and refugees resident in the UK. It is argued that the limited or non-existent rights to residence, work and welfare that are variously available to migrants at different stages of the asylum process create conditions which help to facilitate entry into and continuation in severely exploitative work. The chapter outlines the typology of the three groups identified by considering the intersection of forced labour and asylum: asylum seekers on entry, irregular migrants and trafficking migrants. Drawing on the narratives of migrant interviewees, the chapter goes on to consider the relationship between both irregular and regular migrant status and susceptibility to labour exploitation, relating compromised rights to work, welfare and residence to lived experiences of 'illegality', destitution and deportability. We argue that employers make instrumental use of precarious immigration status as tool of coercion and control in exploitative labour relation. Importantly discussions in the chapter also show how the legacy of constrained socio-legal status and the criminalisation of those asylum seekers and refugees prosecuted for illegal working produce lasting precarity in the lives of many, even when rights to residence, work and welfare are ultimately acquired.

Although the closing down of space for negotiation of work conditions is common to all the labouring situations outlined in Chapters 3 and 4, in *Chapter 5* we turn our attention to the ways that workers *did* resist poor treatment within such unfree labouring environments. Through a presentation of a more agentic picture of forced migrants' lives – that of the 'migrant project' – it describes how workers negotiated, resisted and rejected their exploitation within unfree labour situations, including examples of nascent solidarity in hidden spaces that allowed for informal and fleeting forms of effective organising. We explore how workers exited from unfree labour situations, drawing a distinction between those who 'ran away' or escaped from confined-coerced forced labour, workers who 'walked away' or changed jobs, and those who were 'pushed away' through the job ending or dismissal from insecure work. The final part of this chapter explores the idea of a continuum of unfreedom and its resonance for discussions of hyper-precarity in Chapter 6.

In *Chapter 6* we reflectively stand back from the 30 human stories to critically interrogate the very meaning and relevance of 'forced labour'. We critique the ILO approach to defining and tackling forced labour and argue that discussing such phenomena in rigid binaries (such as free/forced) is unhelpful. Instead we highlight continuums and processes in migrant labour experiences and in line with recent work (see, for example, Skřivánková, 2010) we suggest that a continuum approach built around the concept of 'unfreedom' is the best way to ensure that the diversity of migrants' experiences of forced labour are considered. We further posit the 'hyper-precarity trap' as an analytical device to show how racialised and gendered migration, work and welfare regimes, and neoliberalism combine to create the 'demand and supply' of migrant forced labourers who are subject to multi-dimensional insecurity and exploitation. We argue that attempts to portray contemporary 'slavery', 'trafficking' or 'forced labour' as exceptional phenomenon undermines an understanding of how such exploitation emanates from broader structural inequalities.

Chapter 7 concludes with a reiteration of our salient findings across the previous chapters before a consideration of the effects of the global financial and economic crisis for hyper-precarious migrants, where we speculate that workplace conditions, if anything, may be worsening. We then discuss suggested interventions for policy-makers, practitioners and campaigners that are deemed useful to reduce exploitative and forced labour. We call for the reinstatement of the right to work for asylum seekers and an unconditional regularisation of all undocumented migrants, including refused asylum seekers. We make the critical point here that refugees and asylum seekers are part of a much larger group of vulnerable migrant workers in the UK whose commonplace exploitation within labour markets is mediated and structured by the interplay of broader gendered, social political, and economic, processes. As such, we suggest a multi-layered approach to tackling exploitation and forced labour that combines a focus on immigration policy solutions and employer sanctions to build and enhance universal rights for *all* migrant workers, together with improving asylum seekers and refugees' mobilisation opportunities and access to information in order to exercise their particular agency and rights. In the current anti-immigrant climate, enormous political obstacles will have to be overcome to achieve these goals. As such, a grassroots movement will need to be built with migrants centre-stage, and we conclude by examining the potential of social movement unionism through examples such as the Justice for Domestic Migrant Workers campaign.

Note

[1] Throughout the book interviewees are referred to using a preferred pseudonym of their choice to protect their identities. This is explained in Chapter 3.

2

Structuring forced labour: neoliberal labour markets, immigration policy and forced migration

Introduction

Although migration is as old as humanity, it is regularly portrayed as an exceptional event outside the norms of everyday life with the migrant routinely constructed as the problematic 'Other' (Rapport and Dawson, 1998; Anderson, 2013). However, major waves of international migration have been an ever-present feature of previous centuries. These include the enslavement and transatlantic trafficking of African people, the flow of indentured labour into Europe and European colonies from India, China and Japan, the European colonisation of much of the planet, mass emigration to the United States, and post-Second World War immigration into the Global North. All of these waves have been inextricably connected to the development of capitalism, colonialism and imperialism (Cohen, 1987), and many have been closely associated with forced migration (Marfleet, 2006; Castles and Miller, 2009). Today large numbers of people are migrating, but understandings of movement, frequently framed by xenophobic political discourses, tend to portray contemporary migration as exclusively international and one-directional (that is, from the 'poor' Global South to the 'rich' Global North) and motivated by a desire to access jobs and welfare unavailable back 'home'. The reality is different, with South–North migration flows broadly equal to South–South and North–North movements (Standing, 2011), and the majority of the world's one billion migrants moving within their own national borders (UNDP, 2009). The estimated 214 million migrants crossing international borders in 2009 migrated for multiple reasons that counter simplistic economic rationales for mobility (UN DESA, 2009). In recent decades receiving countries in the Global North have faced increasingly diversified and complex migration streams, and are encountering highly disparate groups of *international migrants* within their borders. These include both high and low skilled labour migrants, refugees, trafficked persons, undocumented persons, students and migrants motivated by family reunion, marriage or lifestyle decisions. This complexity highlights how the clumsy generic term 'migrant' triggers a host of further definitional debates and categorisations (see, for example, Anderson 2013). Migrants can be variously differentiated by classifications based on nationality, ethnic origin, migration pathway, immigration status and/or temporal dimensions concerned with length of stay and types of movement.

Questions concerned with how and why large numbers of migrants living in the UK invariably find themselves working at the bottom of labour markets in low-paid precarious work (Standing, 2011) are of great relevance to this book. In the opening chapter we outlined the key argument, that the UK's neoliberal labour market regime has combined with a draconian asylum and immigration policy to render particular international migrant groups hyper-precarious and deeply susceptible to forced labour exploitation. This chapter deepens this approach by focusing on the policy context that underpins the labour market exploitation of migrant workers in the UK regardless of their particular migrant status. The chapter begins by discussing how neoliberalism has played a central role in the generation of precarity and migrant labour exploitation, reviewing literature evidencing migrant workers' exploitation at a global level before focusing on the more extreme exploitation characterised as forced labour. Given the book's focus on the labour exploitation of asylum seekers and refugees, the next section of this chapter provides a critical discussion of recent UK immigration and asylum legislation to argue that restrictive policies have played an important role in creating a complex socio-legal differentiation of migrants' rights that help to facilitate the *production* of forced labour in this realm. The conclusion of the chapter briefly explains how the politico-economic and policy contexts (noted in Chapter 1 and subsequently developed here in Chapter 2) provide both the basis for the empirical analyses we present in Chapters 3-6 and also inform our argument that asylum seekers and refugees should be considered as part of the migrant worker spectrum.

Neoliberalism and the rise of migrant labour exploitation: from a global to a UK context

At the contemporary global scale, it can be said that vulnerable migrant workers experience commonplace labour exploitation mediated and structured by the interplay of broader political, economic, social and gendered processes (Taran and Geronimi, 2003). Central to these processes has been the emergence of neoliberalism. Neoliberalism, although nebulous as a political theory, is associated with a package of policy measures that coalesce around a belief in free trade, market liberalisation and deregulation, fiscal austerity and privatisation. Neoliberal forms of international economic integration have reshaped traditional ways of working and living (Stiglitz, 2002). Connections between global economic change and related labour market transformations are an important explanatory framework for understanding severe exploitation and forced labour in the workplace. An important backdrop to the story of neoliberalism's emergence is the erosion in the political and industrial power of the working class since the world capitalist crisis of the 1970s. This enabled the dominant assertion of neoliberal ideas that aim to flexibilise global labour markets and restore the conditions for profitable growth (rf Harvey, 2005).

In the industrialised capitalist societies of the Global North, governments have used state power to restore management's 'right to manage' the labour process, while abandoning the post-Second World War commitment to full employment and universal welfare in favour of wholesale privatisations that have directly attacked workers' collective power by undermining trade unionism (Martin and Ross, 1999). These same governments have simultaneously worked with transnational corporations (TNCs) and multi-lateral institutions such as the International Monetary Fund (IMF), The World Bank and the World Trade Organization to impose neoliberal structural adjustment policies of privatisation and liberalisation using the conditionality of debt relief and aid to achieve their aims (Bush, 2007). In this perspective, therefore, globalisation is intimately connected to neoliberalism as a complex process of market transnationalisation in which capital has developed an unprecedented level of mobility principally through the organisational strategies of TNCs and the constitutive power of states (Radice, 2000; Harrod and O'Brien, 2002).

As a result of these neoliberal policies, those who work in the lower echelons of labour markets in the Global North are likely to face: uncertainty over the continuity of employment; a lack of individual and collective control over wages and conditions; limited or no social protection against unemployment, and discrimination; and insufficient income or economic vulnerability. This vulnerability in low-wage economies is 'part of a larger international trend in labour relations in which employers increasingly evade and violate labour standards to maximise profit amid globalized competition' (McLaughlin and Hennebry, 2010, p 1). Global supply chains and subcontracted agency labour (Fudge and Strauss, 2014) enable corporations to organise production across borders, generating an enormous supply of labour in competition for jobs and a deterioration in wages and conditions, conditions which may also apply to national supply chains.

The concept of *precarity* is being increasingly deployed as a way of understanding intensifying and insecure post-Fordist work in late capitalism. In a literal sense, precarity refers to those who experience precariousness. It is generally used to refer to people whose lives are characterised by uncertainty and instability, a description that clearly resonates with the experiences of asylum seekers and refugees who experience forced labour. Within the academic literature three important dimensions of precarity have been identified. First, a rise in insecure employment emerging from the globally prevailing neoliberal labour market model is said to render *particular* groups vulnerable to exploitative and insecure working conditions (see, for example, Bourdieu, 1998, 1999; Dorre et al, 2006; Fantone, 2007). Second, engagement with the concept of precarity as something more than a position in the labour market (Neilson and Rossiter, 2005) has sought to encapsulate how precarious employment affects, and is also intertwined with, other areas of life, such as household dynamics, individual circumstances, and welfare provision (Barbier, 2002). Here, precarity resembles ontological insecurity (Giddens, 1990; Neilson and Rossiter, 2008), and is seen by Ettlinger (2007) to be an enduring feature of the human condition found within all micro-spaces of everyday life. Butler takes a similar stance, viewing widespread precariousness as deriving from oppressive everyday governmentality (Butler, 2004), and more recently as a response to differential exposure to the violence and suffering that emanates from socio-political contexts (Butler, 2009). The third dimension is the use of precarity as an idea to mobilise struggles against exploitation.

Given this book's empirical focus on migrant labour exploitation, we find the concept of precarity most useful as a term through which to explore labour conditions, while acknowledging the profoundly destabilising effects of precarious work on broader lifeworlds. Migrants are differently placed and positioned within these environments according to immigration stratification, and this helps structure and consolidate notable migrant hierarchies that may emerge around racial, ethnic, national and gender identities. Such hierarchies have *purpose* within the liberal-capitalist order. Differential emplacement and hierarchies enable employers to play different migrant groups off against each other in the interests of driving down wages and working conditions, and make it easier for employers to choose cheaper and more compliant workers. As Wills et al (2010, p 6) state, 'migrant workers are attractive to employers precisely because they are migrants'. Evidence suggests these employer choices may further be racialised. Model (2002) found a fairly consistent racialised cross-national hierarchy of discrimination reflecting established prejudices and stereotypes in London, New York and Toronto. Within the UK, for example, many employers now favour A8/2 (Accession 8/2) migrants due to their clearly legal status, and this has displaced other low-paid non-EU migrants from jobs. The knowledge of this competitive selection in turn ensures a flexible and motivated workforce. Indeed, the 'project' of neoliberalism itself in exalting individualism in everyday spaces (Giddens, 1991; Beck and Beck-Gernscheim, 2003; Bondi and Laurie, 2005) attempts to make migrant workers into self-managing and disconnected individuals compliant to the whims of capital.

At the international institutional level, the UN and ILO have long been concerned about how to effectively protect the rights of internationally mobile workers, as mobility often has an impact on migrants' status and their attendant privileges in their new locations. The ILO Conventions on Migration for Employment (No 97, ILO, 1949) and Migrant Workers (No 143, ILO, 1975) collectively call on member states to ensure that 'legal' migrants and their families have equal treatment and rights to work and social security as their own nationals, and that all migrants have protections from abusive conditions. The ILO's Committee on the Freedom of Association has also repeatedly ruled that undocumented migrant workers are equally entitled to fundamental trade union rights as enshrined in their core labour standards. 'Decent work', understood as 'access for all to freely chosen employment, the recognition of fundamental rights at work, an income to enable people to meet their basic economic, social and family needs and responsibilities and an adequate level of social protection for the workers and family members' (Solidar, 2010, p 7), has been central to the ILO's conceptual framework since 1999. The notion of decent work has also been built into the UN Millennium Development Goals and the EU's social agenda.

The UN is also a significant international player in the pursuance of migrant worker protections. The UN International Convention on the protection of the rights of all migrant workers and members of their families (UN, 1990) reinforced ILO standards on legal rights, equality of treatment and trade union activities, and also recognised the particular need to protect vulnerable, undocumented migrants. However, recent efforts by the UN and ILO to promote the contribution, role and rights of migrant workers in the world economy is countered by clear evidence that many member states are moving in the opposite direction (Solidar, 2010). The first global UN High Level Dialogue on Migration and Development in 2006 resulted in the creation of the Global Forum on Migration and Development, an intergovernmental and, crucially, *non-binding* dialogue process between UN member states with some consultation of civil society organisations. The Forum identified the need to promote multi-lateral approaches and international cooperation, to expand legal opportunities for migration (especially for low-skilled workers), to protect migrant rights, to develop gender-sensitive migration policies, and to create decent work opportunities in migrants' home countries to reduce migration pressures. This process led to the second UN High Level Dialogue on Migration and Development in October 2013. The efforts of global bodies like the UN have partly been driven by a failure of certain nation states to ratify and observe the various ILO labour standards and UN Conventions on migrant workers. Tellingly, although to date 46 states have ratified the 1990 UN Convention (who, as 'sending states', see the Convention as an important vehicle to protect their citizens abroad), no EU member state has signed up.

In the UK context, although migrants have long underpinned the low-wage economy of many cities, this dependency has grown dramatically in recent years (Burnett and Whyte, 2010; McLaughlin and Hennebry, 2010; Wills et al, 2010). For many employers looking to cut labour costs and to establish or maintain a competitive advantage, migrant workers offer a cheaper and more compliant alternative to local workers (MacKenzie and Forde, 2009), particularly for those looking to employ people to do the 'dirty, dangerous and dull' (Favell, 2008, p 704) jobs at the lower end of the labour market. Migrants, especially new arrivals, are seen as being harder workers, more loyal and reliable, and prepared to work longer hours due to their lack of choice and limited understanding of their rights. This intensifies competition and offers employers the pick of the 'best' migrant workers (McDowell, 2008; McDowell et al, 2009). As such, a growing body of work in the UK details the clear connections between migrants and exploitation in its various forms (Anderson and Rogaly, 2005; Craig et al, 2007; van den Anker, 2009). As later discussions in this chapter note, much recent research on such UK migrant exploitation has concentrated on the constrained position of certain groups of migrants, including Chinese people (Pai, 2008; Kagan et al, 2011) or on employment sectors, including meat processing (EHRC, 2010) and the food industry (Scott et al, 2012). Immigration policy and insecure immigration status is further known to provide environments conducive to exploitation by employers (Dwyer et al, 2011) and the lack of, or highly conditional, access to legal work and/or welfare is also important in rendering migrants who have few other choices susceptible to exploitation. The group of migrants seen as quintessentially vulnerable in this regard are undocumented or *irregular migrants* (Bloch et al, 2009; McKay et al, 2009; Valentine, 2010; Sigona, 2012). Accurate numerical measures of undocumented migrant populations are self-evidently difficult to obtain; the mostly commonly circulated estimate in the UK comes from Gordon et al (2009) who suggested a central estimate of 725,000 undocumented migrants in the UK at the end of 2007. A portion of this population is refused asylum seekers.

There is clear evidence in the literature that various groups of migrants feature significantly in precarious landscapes of low-paid labour markets rife with exploitation. The next section outlines how *extreme* experiences of forced labour are at the acute end of a broad spectrum of migrant exploitation.

Extreme exploitation: forced labour

As noted in Chapter 1, despite the 'abolition ' of slavery in the 19th century, evidence from academics and campaigners in the last decade indicates that modern forms of slavery continue to exist in the UK. Many studies are finding that *migrant workers* are particularly vulnerable to extreme exploitation. The noted vulnerability of migrant workers should not, however, obscure instances where *non-*migrants may experience forced labour (for example, the case of the Connors family subjecting British homeless men to forced labour). Geddes et al (2013, p 4) make the important point here that 'forced labour needs to be approached as an issue of worker rights and criminal justice rather than reduced to a trafficking or immigration issue'. Much of the early focus of research in the UK, however, was on the 'trafficking' of mainly women and children for the purpose of commercial sexual exploitation (Kaye, 2003; Skřivánková, 2006; Andrijasevic, 2010). It is important to acknowledge here that trafficking and forced labour are often unhelpfully framed as synonymous. Flynn (2007) and van den Anker (2009) both highlight that not all forced labour results from trafficking, and those responsible for deceptive border crossings may or may not be directly linked to subsequent exploitation.

In this sense, Anderson and Rogaly's (2005) landmark UK study was sensitive to these trafficking/forced labour definitional problems. Their study drew on the testimonies of a variety of migrants from Asia, Africa, Latin America and Central and Eastern Europe working in the construction, agriculture, care and cleaning sectors. They show how migrants are engaged through a bewildering array of subcontracting chains and agents, which makes safeguarding their basic human and labour rights difficult, and that these combine to result in treatment of workers that can amount to forced labour in some cases. As they demonstrate, jobs in these sectors are highly time- and place-bound, and therefore insecure and flexible, making migrant workers compliant employees who may be more willing than relatively fixed 'local' workers to move within the UK for short-term employment.

A number of important initiatives followed this pioneering study. In April 2009 the Joseph Rowntree Foundation (JRF) launched a multi-pronged programme of work to evidence forced labour in the UK and to identify interventions aimed at eradicating it. The emerging research from this programme details many different aspects of forced labour including a focus on work sectors (fisheries, catering and hospitality; see Allamby et al, 2011); the food industry (see Scott et al, 2012); and findings that extend the Equality and Human Rights Commission's inquiry into conditions in meat and poultry processing (EHRC, 2010). Other JRF-funded studies have highlighted forced labour experiences among particular nationality groups (Chinese; see Kagan et al, 2011), and the importance of issues linked to immigration status (Dwyer et al, 2011), business (Lalani and Metcalf, 2012; Allain et al, 2013), regulation and enforcement (Balch, 2012) and media coverage (Dugan, 2013) alongside a wide-reaching review of the scale and scope of forced labour in the UK (Geddes et al, 2013). The think-tank the Centre for Social Justice (CSJ) (set up by Conservative politician Iain Duncan Smith in 2004) also produced a broad-based report in 2013 entitled *It happens here* that set out to expose modern slavery alongside 80-plus recommendations to a range of stakeholders.[1]

Another important corpus of UK evidence has been presented about forced labour in domestic and care work sectors. This interest in migrant domestic and care workers is due to long-standing mobilisation against abuses and mounting evidence that these workers (often, but not always, women) have suffered the most extreme forms of labour exploitation within the highly unequal power relations between employer and worker that exist in private domestic work settings. Employment and immigration precarity are strongly compounded in migrant domestic work spaces due to the complex interaction between the tied nature of domestic work, the sector's inferior employment rights, the isolation of workers, the particular role of immigration status and specific gendered and racialised vulnerabilities of migrant workers (Anderson, 2000; Hondagneu-Sotelo, 2001; Ehrenreich and Hochschild, 2003; Frantz, 2008; Parreñas, 2008). UK studies have repeatedly shown widespread physical, psychological and sexual abuse and intensive labour exploitation of migrant domestic workers within a wider setting of control, coercion, and employer impunity (Anderson, 2007; Oxfam and Kalayaan, 2008; Gordolan and Lalani, 2009; Clark and Kumarappan, 2011; Lalani, 2011). Furthermore, a number of in-depth journalists' accounts have deepened knowledge of forced labour in the UK, such as Gupta's detailed stories of five 'modern-day slaves' (2007) and Pai's exploration of the lives of undocumented Chinese migrants (2008).

Migrant workers are recognised as a group more likely to experience 'aggravated' (Foti, 2004) conditions of precarity and forced labour. However, there remains a need to further examine both the labour market position of particular migrants (asylum seekers and refugees in this instance), and the relationship between immigration status and migrants' rights to residence, work and welfare. Many of the approaches to precarity outlined do not adequately account for the role of compromised socio-legal status in compounding precarity for migrants. Through our focus on asylum seekers and refugees labouring in the lower and often hidden sectors of the neoliberal UK labour market we are interested in how the relationship between migration and work may create particularly extreme variants of precarity (see Chapters 6 and 7) where significant vulnerabilities and possibly forced labour and/or unfreedoms abound.

Dichotomies and distinctions: the complexity of contemporary forced migration

Following the First and Second World Wars, millions fled their homelands in search of sanctuary while others were variously displaced, deported or resettled. In Geneva in July 1951 the international community adopted the Convention relating to the Status of Refugees (later amended by the 1967 Protocol), and this remains the key legal document in defining a 'refugee', their rights and the legal obligations of states towards them. A refugee is a person who,

> Owing to a well-founded fear of being persecuted for reasons of race, religion, nationality, membership of a particular social group or political opinion is outside the country of his nationality, and is unable to, or owing to such fear is unwilling to avail himself of the protection of that country, or to return there, for fear of persecution. (UN Convention relating to the Status of Refugees [1951], Article 1A(2))

Global refugee numbers have fluctuated over recent decades; numbers declined from 18 million in 1990 to under 14 million in 2005, only to increase to nearly 16 million by the end of 2012. The location of these refugees is regionally concentrated, with developing countries currently hosting around 80 per cent of the world's refugees (UNHCR, 2013). While refugees are part of the migrant spectrum, they are subject in most countries to very different policies and systems of reception, welfare, service provision and justice from migrants who enter under different categories.

The Geneva Convention enshrined a fundamental principle in the regulation of migration – that of an *exceptionalist* discourse of the refugee migrant. It embodies the regulatory apparatus to manage refugee migration as *distinctive* from economic migration. Related to this is the consideration of refugee migrants as 'forced' migrants, and economic migrants as 'voluntary' or 'unforced' migrants. Many states therefore see the separation of 'forced' refugees from 'voluntary' economic migrants as fundamental for effective asylum and immigration policies. Indeed, it has been suggested that refugees and asylum seekers raise very different theoretical and conceptual issues to other migrants (McDowell, 2008).

Yet in recent years there has been concern that the Convention-defined reasons for forcing refugees to seek protection are 'out of date' (Marshall, 2011) and inadequate for understanding the complexity of factors that impel forced migration in the contemporary world. Much of the problem lies in distinctions within the category of forced migration; 'these distinctions, like the term "forced migrant" itself, are artefacts of policy concerns, rather than of empirical observation and sociological analysis' (Turton, 2003, p 2). There are no essential or natural links between people who migrate and the categories used to refer to them (Malkki, 1995, 1997), and this is the bedrock of debates around the inadequacy of migrant categorisation that are particularly crystallised in discussions about forced and economic migration.

Diverse and multiple reasons beyond political persecution often underpin contemporary 'forced' migration with mobility rarely due to one distinctive event/process (Castles, 2003). Is a migrant fleeing state fragility and economic collapse within a country to ensure their livelihood/survival (a movement that might, coincidentally, be a result of damaging Western imposed neoliberal policies) any less a forced migrant compared to the classic refugee seeking protection from political persecution? Most migrants make decisions to leave in response to multifarious reasons that may combine 'elements of both compulsion and choice' (Turton, 2003, p 9) and 'voluntary and involuntary movements do not exist as wholly separate and definable entities' (Zimmermann and Zetter, 2011, p 339). It is therefore now fairly uncontroversial to accept that the reasons compelling migrants to flee may fall outside the narrow Convention-defined reasons for forced migration.

Commentators have responded to the impulse to categorise and describe complexities underpinning migration in different ways. Some have identified continuums of choice along voluntary to involuntary (van Hear, 1998) or proactive to reactive dimensions (Richmond, 1994). Others prefer to discuss the 'migration-asylum nexus' (Castles, 2003, 2007) or 'mixed-flows' and associated 'mixed motive migration' (UNHCR, 2007). All these approaches acknowledge that people who end up in asylum and refugee systems may have multiple reasons for leaving at a particular time and make use of any available pathway they can to reach safety.[2] Such understanding helps decouple forced migration from involuntariness and a complete absence of choice and/ or agency. The victim and agency-stripping discourse seams dangerously through the Refugee Convention and the forced/voluntary migration dichotomy. Strong arguments can and should be made against this tendency. In contemporary conditions it is impossible to,

> Imagine migrants as divisible into on the one hand, those who were driven to move by forces beyond their control or who were forcibly moved for purposes of exploitation by 'traffickers'; and on the other hand, those who exercised agency, choice, and control over their own migration, including those who entered into a partnership with "smugglers" to make an unauthorized border crossing. (O'Connell Davidson, 2013, p 2)

Within the EU, migration policy has developed with the twin aims of boosting territorial security and coordinating a more stringent 'managed migration' system for migrants entering member states from outside Europe. Although the 1993 Maastricht Treaty embedded free movement for nationals of EU member states within Europe, migration and, critically, asylum-related immigration from *outside* the EU were never central to the EU's integration objectives (Joppke, 1998). This dichotomous approach to migration – free movement for EU citizens on the one hand and the development of 'Fortress Europe' and the 'migration state' (Hollifield, 2004) for third country nationals (TCNs, that is, migrants from nations beyond the EU) on the other – set the tone for development of a common approach to immigration policy within the EU (Geddes, 2008). December 2005 saw the EU adopt its 'Global

Approach to Migration'. Focused on Africa and the Mediterranean, it was designed to build a common and strengthened border regime to reinforce security, create a single approach to managing international protection and asylum, and organise selective regular migration to meet European labour market needs while providing development aid to some non-EU countries to help them manage their emigration flows.

Asylum, 'illegal' immigration and selective (numerically small) highly skilled labour migration are therefore at the forefront of developments within EU migration policy. Meanwhile more numerous, low-skilled migration is largely omitted. The EU has also set out in several EU Regulations and Directives common agreed minimum standards for the care of asylum seekers across member states. However, questionable cooperation at the supra-national EU level has arguably given member states a policy arena in which to legitimise and extend exclusive elements of national policy to deter forced migrants from entering Europe (Dwyer, 2005). Additionally, Frontex, the EU coordinating agency for external border security, has a clear mandate to restrict migration flows. Such restrictive immigration policies have led to calls for all governments to ratify and observe the various UN and ILO rights and standards that seek to protect migrants (Castles, 2002; Solidar, 2010).

Facing ever-more constrained migration channels and tighter border controls, some non-EU migrants are forced to seek out unauthorised routes of entry, often relying on 'professional smugglers' (Andreas, 2004). Such migrants include asylum seekers who, faced with deterrence policies, experience restricted access to the asylum process that necessitates irregularity of entry and stay (Jordan and Düvell, 2002; Bloch et al, 2011). Reliance on smugglers is often dangerous and regularly incurs significant fees that can embroil the migrant in a lengthy relationship of indebtedness with the smuggling network (O'Connell Davidson, 2013). Trafficking (the coercive/forced transit of people for purposes of exploitation) is also an important element. However, the line between trafficking and smuggling is frequently blurred. What begins as a 'smuggling' arrangement may subsequently become 'trafficking' if the migrant is coerced into severe labour exploitation or forced labour (Friman, 2011).

'Managed migration': immigration policy in the UK

In an era of increasing global mobility the UK has become home to a diverse range of migrant communities. Part of this story is an increase in recent decades in the numbers seeking refuge. The period 1995-

2003 saw in excess of half a million people apply for asylum in the UK (Dwyer, 2005). Overall, asylum applications in the UK increased from 1987 to 2011[3] but have played a declining role in overall migration since 2004, as part of a trend across Europe and not in response to the restrictive targeted policies outlined above (Blinder, 2013). Another part of this story is around EU enlargement; in 2004 over one million A8 migrants (from eight new accession countries to the EU: Czech Republic, Estonia, Hungary, Latvia, Lithuania, Poland, Slovakia and Slovenia) entered the UK. Around half of these migrants have since either returned to their countries of origin or relocated elsewhere, but considerable numbers remain (Pollard et al, 2008). These significant migration flows have undoubtedly produced a political backlash with the rise of the neo-fascist and racist British National Party during the 2000s and more recently the anti-Muslim protest group, English Defence League, and the Eurosceptic UK Independence Party. Alongside the heightened international security agenda that emerged in response to international terrorist activities (for example, the USA in 2001, Bali in 2002, Madrid in 2004, and London in 2005), the growth of far right political pressure and anti-immigrant hysteria among certain sections of the British media has been influential in setting the tone for the development of restrictive immigration policies. A detailed discussion of the role of the British state in reacting to different waves of migration throughout the 20th century lies beyond the remit of this book; overall, however, it is hard to avoid the conclusion that much UK immigration legislation has helped to build a racialised notion of 'Britishness' that problematises the presence and settlement of many migrants in the UK (rf Anderson, 2013).

In line with much that preceded it, UK immigration and asylum legislation enacted within the last 20 years has consolidated a long established link between immigration status, welfare entitlement and rights to residence and work (Kofman, 2002; Bloch and Schuster, 2002; Dwyer et al, 2011; Lewis et al, 2012). Successive New Labour governments attempted to use asylum policy to deter entry into the country by excluding asylum seekers from mainstream welfare systems and removing their right to enter paid work while claims are considered (to be discussed later in this chapter). After 2004, following the arrival of significant numbers of migrants, the UK government acted to close entry routes for low-skilled migrants from beyond Europe under the mantra of 'managed migration', which 'became the guiding policy concept shifting the focus of restriction from asylum to migration more broadly through the introduction of the points based system' (Lewis et al, 2012, p 87).

The points-based system consists of five tiers. All migrants from outside the European Economic Area (EEA)[4] must accrue sufficient points based on their education, employment and earnings before being granted permission to enter the UK. In effect, entry and rights to reside and settle are now largely reserved for the 'brightest and best' (Anderson, 2013) skilled migrants who match criteria, based on talent, entrepreneurship, or willingness to invest over £1 million in the UK, specified in Tiers 1 and 2. Tier 3, reserved for unskilled workers, has been suspended from the outset on the premise that all future low/unskilled vacancies will be filled by A8 migrants, thus largely ending the necessity of allowing lower-skilled TCNs to enter for work purposes. Stricter conditions attached to entry for Tier 4 and 5 applicants (students and temporary workers/youth mobility entrants) have also been put in place. With the exception of Tier 1, all applicants must identify a specified sponsor before submitting an application, who must then agree to monitor compliance with immigration rules (UKBA, 2013). The enlargement of the EU and the arrival of A8, and, subsequently, A2 migrants from Romania and Bulgaria, has therefore been 'accompanied by a parallel tightening of immigration controls in relation to other groups' (Wills et al, 2010, p 14).

New Labour's commitment to 'stronger borders' and 'firm but fair' managed migration (UKBA, 2008) found further expression in the Borders, Citizenship and Immigration Act 2009 which sought to 'maximise the benefits of migration and minimise the impacts at local level' (DCLG, 2008, p 5). The Act consolidated the points-based system and introduced new rules that denied TCNs access to social assistance benefits and local authority housing or homelessness assistance prior to attaining British citizenship or permanent residence. It also introduced compulsory periods of 'temporary residence' and 'probationary citizenship' as steps on the way to 'earned citizenship', in effect making permanent residence and access to full welfare rights conditional on migrants from beyond the EEA proving economic self-sufficiency over a number of years.

Elected in 2010, the current Conservative–Liberal Democrat Coalition government is continuing with a restrictive approach to immigration most notably through the introduction in April 2011 of an 'immigration cap' which limits the number of non-EEA skilled migrant workers allowed to enter the UK each year. The aim of the cap is to help the government achieve a target of reducing net migration from the current level of 239,000 to less than 100,000 by 2015 (The Migration Observatory, 2011). It has been accompanied by other restrictions to migrant workers entering the UK, including: the closure of the Tier 1 general route, which had allowed 'highly skilled' non-EU migrants to enter the UK without a job offer; changes to the shortage occupation list limiting it to graduate-level occupations; and a series of changes to student migration policy such as ending the blanket post-study work route, increasing financial and language requirements, increasing restrictions on some international students' rights to work or bring dependent relatives, and increasing the financial requirements for those wishing to bring family members to the UK (The Migration Observatory, 2013). In introducing the new Immigration Bill 2013, Immigration Minister Mark Harper heralded its measures to reduce 'illegal entry' and stop migrants 'abusing public services to which they are not entitled' (Home Office, 2013b, p 1) while also repeating the need for policy to attract skilled migrants. Such pronouncements point to ever-more restrictive future policy as the government looks to deliver Prime Minister David Cameron's pledge to make the rules for new immigrants the toughest in Europe (Cameron, 2013). The aim is clear – to create a hostile environment for migrants to effectively deter them from coming to the UK in the first place (BBC, 2013b; Cameron, 2013).

A further defining feature driving the UK's recent immigration regime is the extent to which 'national security' has emerged as a central preoccupation. Many states are increasingly creating a broad 'security continuum' (Bigo, 1994) that stretches from terrorism to action against crime and responses to migratory flows (Walters, 2004; Amoore, 2006; Guild, 2009). Using the pretext of 'securitisation' (Buzan et al, 1998), it is increasingly implied that the integrity of the nation state and its security can only be assured if migration flows and migrants themselves are closely controlled and monitored; hence the emergence of tools such as the points-based system and the strengthening of immigration law enforcement under the new UK Border Force. Indeed, it is no coincidence that there has been a growth in the **detention** and deportation regime in the UK (Bloch and Schuster, 2005) as a response to the creeping criminalisation of migration. Increased mobility within an expanding EU and openness to a global elite has been matched by greater exclusion of poorer migrants from the rest of the world. Immigration policy has promoted an increasingly securitised, bio-political form of 'carceral cosmopolitanism' (Sparke, 2006). In this sense, borders are not merely markers of territory, but create social distinctiveness for migrants (Zolberg, 1989) through their organisational association with work and welfare, and also their conceptual association with notions of entitlement, belonging and identity (Geddes, 2011). Apart from the noted exception of wealthy and highly skilled migrants, current UK migration policy constructs all other forms of immigration as inherently problematic:

> It has become increasingly clear that the poor are to be excluded. The asylum seeker is no longer imagined as the educated professor, but the illiterate global poor, while workers are to be refused entry or the possibility of settlement if they do not earn enough, and similarly family members now have to not simply be self-sufficient but have a minimum income. (Anderson, 2013, pp 69-70)

Non-EU migrants in the UK are therefore confronted by an immigration regime that stratifies entry, delimits employment and welfare entitlements, and places surveillance and monitoring at its heart. This has the twin purposes of eliminating 'undesirable' unskilled migrants while welcoming 'desirable' highly skilled migrants who can fill vacancies in the higher echelons of the labour market and/or offer financial investment into the UK.

Yet the 'supply' of so-called undesirable migrants is likely to continue as people respond to damaging neoliberal IMF and World Bank policies in the Global South which motivate and underpin the migrants' need to relocate across borders to access work (Wills et al, 2010). In so doing, they will find a hungry demand from employers operating in the neoliberal heartlands of the Global North for cheap migrant workers whose lack of rights make them far more precarious and thus far more exploitable. In the UK, neoliberalism found an influential supporter in the shape of Margaret Thatcher. Throughout the 1980s and most of the 1990s successive Conservative governments deregulated markets, attacked organised labour and public ownership through aggressive anti-union laws and privatisation policies that brought subcontracting to the fore of the economy. Subsequently low-paid, often casualised, service sector work (for example, in retail, catering, hospitality, security, cleaning and care) blossomed on the back of competitive tendering and out-sourcing, as manufacturing and related activities declined (Mittelman, 2000). Today, working experiences in the service sector are increasingly characterised by temporary and insecure employment contracts often associated with the rise of agency-supplied labour (Demos, 2007), alongside a concomitant reduction of wages and rights and increased hours and intensity of work (Munz et al, 2007; Lalani and Metcalf, 2012). It is these kinds of insecure, contemporary working landscapes routinely inhabited by migrants in the UK where neoliberal labour markets and restrictive immigration policy intersect to create conditions in which the severe exploitation of migrants flourish.

UK asylum legislation: deterrence, destitution and the tiering of entitlement

In the UK, asylum and immigration more broadly have been political touchstones for two decades. Feeding on uninformed moral panics about asylum seeker numbers (Cohen, 2002; Lynn and Lea, 2003; Schuster, 2003), successive governments have systematically undermined the basic rights of asylum seekers. Jordan and Brown (2007) argue that the subject of the 'immigrant' was discursively reconstructed, particularly during New Labour's period in office, to de-emphasise notions of refuge and protection and instead bring work and entitlement to the fore for both political and economic motives. This shift involved a double movement in which 'good migrants', largely from the expanding EU (coincidentally ethnically and culturally similar), were allowed entry as hard-working and economically useful supporters of the wider economy (and welfare state) in return for highly contingent, stratified and delimited forms of citizenship and entitlement. In contrast, 'bad migrants', such as asylum seekers, came from poorer countries, had 'dubious' claims, were ethnically and culturally dissimilar and thus a 'burden', and identified as problematic for cohesion. Arguably UK policy-makers have attempted to respond to this 'problem' through more hostile refugee status determination procedures (Gill, 2009). A 'culture of disbelief' (The Glidewell Panel, 1996) that implies widespread abuse and misuse of the asylum system has increasingly pervaded the UK asylum system, resulting in high refusal rates (Zimmermann and Zetter, 2011). Although the UK's vast edifice of civic stratification (Kofman, 2002) shapes the lives of all migrants, we suggest that asylum seekers and refugees are a group who are *particularly* subjectified by their socio-legal status (see socio-legal status discussions in the next subsection).

Several policies contribute to this discursive climate and subjectification of asylum seekers and refugees. Critically, in 2002, permission to work for asylum seekers who had not received an initial decision on their claim within six months was removed as employment was considered a 'pull factor' encouraging unfounded asylum claims (Bloch and Schuster, 2002). Earlier, the Immigration and Asylum Act 1999 created the National Asylum Support Service (NASS) that saw responsibility for the delivery of asylum seekers' basic financial support and accommodation removed from mainstream welfare systems. Initially, a cashless support system provided vouchers set at 70 per cent of basic Income Support, which, in the language of New Labour, was intended to reduce asylum applications by showing that the UK was not a 'soft touch'. Following a concerted civil society campaign, vouchers were abandoned in 2002. However, since 2003, support for refused asylum seekers if they are destitute and temporarily unable to leave the UK is provided under Section 4 of the Immigration and Asylum Act 1999. This has been through a cashless voucher system designed to be deliberately punitive to deter continuing residence in the UK. Most refused asylum seekers do not access **Section 4 support**, however, because they are unwilling to take the stipulated 'reasonable steps' to leave the UK that are required to access it. Estimates of refused asylum seekers without permission to work or access public funds who reside in the UK stood at around 500,000 in 2007–08 and have dropped to 155,000 (British Red Cross, 2010) as large numbers of those who claimed asylum before 2007 have been granted status through a 'case resolution' exercise. Deliberate **destitution** is a state-endorsed policy described in 2003 as a 'deterrent but also as an incentive [to return]'.[5] The Joint Committee on Human Rights (2007) described this as a practice of enforced destitution, examples of which breach the Article 3 threshold of inhuman and degrading treatment.

Restriction has become embedded in UK asylum policy. In 2005 leave to remain for people recognised as refugees was reduced from indefinite to *five years*, open to review at any time. Limited leave embeds temporariness, obstructing the ability of refugees to make decisions about their future, to find work, settle and integrate. Regressive policies such as these have led to the treatment of people that is not only inhumane, but which has also proved ineffective in terms of their policy objectives, as this series of deterrence measures have failed to both deter new arrivals and encourage those already here to return (Williams and Kaye, 2010). There is no evidence that welfare entitlements in the UK act as a pull factor (Bloch and Schuster, 2002). As of the beginning of 2012, the population of refugees, pending asylum cases and stateless persons, made up just *0.33 per cent of the UK's population* (UNHCR, 2012).[6]

Socio-legal status and deportability in everyday life

Socio-legal status refers to the differential rights and entitlements to residency, work and welfare that accrue to different migrants depending on their immigration status (Vertovec, 2006; Dwyer et al, 2011). The use of 'stratified rights' (Morris, 2001) has long been an integral feature of the structured exclusion inherent in much UK immigration policy (Craig, 2007), and a consideration of socio-legal status is crucial to understanding the precarious lives of different migrant groups within the UK. Different subgroups of migrants experience widely divergent rights, depending on their specific socio-legal status. For example, under the broad category of asylum seekers and refugees, five subgroups can be identified, each enjoying a differing matrix of basic rights (summarised in Table 2.1). Readers should note that the term refugee is used in this book to refer inclusively to those with refugee status, humanitarian protection, discretionary leave or any other type of leave.

Denied permission to work and with limited access to highly conditional social security, some *asylum seekers* feel compelled to seek alternative means of income often in informal and unregulated sectors of the economy that shield unscrupulous employers, especially when people need to send remittances to families back 'home' (Crawley et al, 2011) or to repay debts incured in migration (O'Connell Davidson, 2013). A growing body of research demonstrates that thousands of *refused asylum seekers* with no right to work or recourse to public funds remain in the UK (Dwyer, 2005; Dwyer and Brown, 2005; Refugee Action, 2006; Dwyer and Brown, 2008; Smart and Fullegar, 2008; Lewis, 2009; Smart, 2009; Williams and Kaye, 2010). In common with other irregular migrants, refused asylum seekers are therefore likely to be working in highly insecure, temporary, difficult and often dangerous jobs in both the formal and informal labour markets (Düvell and Jordan, 2002; Lewis, 2007), and are particularly susceptible to exploitation including forced labour practices as they try to meet their basic needs (Burnett and Whyte, 2010).

Refugees have permission to work and are theoretically able to find employment or access benefits. However, they face formidable structural barriers in accessing employment and benefits related to delays or mistakes in Home Office documentation, limited English language skills, a lack of UK work experience or references, and non-recognition of qualifications awarded in other countries (Bloch, 2004; Hurstfield et al, 2004; Dwyer, 2008). Refugees experience one of the highest rates of unemployment of any group in the UK (Bloch, 2002), and engagement in severely exploitative labour may therefore be the only viable means of supplementing meagre income from benefits. Furthermore, highly coercive working arrangements previously entered into out of necessity may continue long after refugee status has been secured (Refugee Action, 2006). The ways in which socio-legal status

Table 2.1: The variable rights to residence, work and welfare available to asylum seekers and refugees resident in the UK

Subgroup definition/ status	Right to residence	Right to work	Welfare rights
Asylum seeker: a person who has applied for asylum and whose application has not yet been decided	Yes, while their application is considered and given due process	No (curtailed since July 2002) Can apply to **UKBA** for permission to work after one year if the delay regarding a decision on their initial claim is not their fault	Basic accommodation and public welfare support (set at 70% of the social assistance level[a]) under the UKBA **asylum support** system Must be destitute and willing to accept no choice **dispersal** to a location specified by the UKBA to qualify
Refused asylum seeker: a person whose asylum claim has been refused	No Expected to return to their country of origin	No	Not generally entitled to support UKBA support removed within 21 days of refusal decision Basic shelter and support may be available in limited circumstances (eg unable to leave due to illness/disability, no viable route of return) under Section 4 of the Immigration and Asylum Act 1999, providing the person is taking all reasonable steps to leave the UK
Refugee: a person who has received a positive decision on their asylum claim	Yes Since 2005 all refugees whose status is granted in the UK are given five years' temporary leave to remain; previously they enjoyed indefinite leave to remain	Yes	Access to welfare rights on the same basis as UK citizens

Table 2.1: contd

Subgroup definition/status	Right to residence	Right to work	Welfare rights
Humanitarian protection[b]: a person whose case does not fit the refugee criteria but who is given permission to enter or remain in the UK because they need protection from harm by others	Yes Granted for five years in the first instance	Yes	Access to welfare rights on the same basis as UK citizens
Discretionary leave: a person given permission to enter or remain in the UK who falls outside the Immigration Rules or whose asylum claim has been refused but who cannot be removed on grounds such as ill health or a potential breach of their human rights	Yes Granted for up to three years in the first instance	Variable	Access to welfare rights on the same basis as UK citizens

Notes: [a] Recent research reports that the value of the asylum support has subsequently fallen to 54 per cent of the Income Support rate received by a single adult aged 25-plus in 2012 (The Children's Society, 2013b).

[b] Humanitarian protection and discretionary leave replaced exceptional leave to remain (ELR) from 1 April 2003.

has an impact on individual asylum seekers and refugees' susceptibility to, and experiences of, forced labour are an essential part of ongoing discussions throughout the book.

Linked to constrained socio-legal status is fear of return, or what de Genova (2002) terms 'deportability in everyday life'. This acts as a further powerful disciplining device for forced and irregular migrants that often results in increased susceptibility to exploitation. Such migrants fear not only the loss of face and changes in family relationships confronted by many migrants returning without the status or income expected from migration, but also confront risks of persecution, torture, and other threats to themselves and their families in states known for human rights abuses and conflict (Lewis, 2007; Bloch et al, 2011). Indeed, some refugees are escaping forced labour practices in their countries of origin, such as Eritrea (Kibreab, 2009), which may deepen fear of return. The practice of state enforcement can also have a disciplining effect for individuals and enhance migrants' vulnerabilities (Wills et al, 2010). For example, in the UK, management of immigration and illegal working enforcement results in the targeting of some sectors more than others with raids. This consequently makes certain jobs more risky for those working without papers, pushing workers into more invisible areas of the informal market, and discouraging organisation or action against mistreatment at work (Burnett and Whyte, 2010). The era of 'managed migration' in most developed states – and the UK is no exception – has been accompanied by increased numbers of undocumented migrants, with de Genova (2002) reminding us that the very notion of migrants being 'illegal' is the product of immigration laws. Although many wealthier states publically protest against undocumented migrants, commentators suggest that states also tacitly tolerate such migrants as they comprise a malleable supply of labour that create only limited social and welfare costs (Castles, 2000). These populations are further disciplined through increasingly normalised techniques of state power such as detention and deportation (Bloch and Schuster, 2005; Gibney, 2008). Peutz and de Genova (2010, p 14) consequently suggest that the threat of such state power (if not the actuality) leads to irregularity becoming a 'deeply interiorised mode of being' that inscribes migrants' everyday lives and is utilised by state actors to fulfil disciplining objectives. Yet alongside appreciating such governmentality as a feature of undocumented migrants' lives, we are also concerned here not to construct migrants as entirely without agency or as passive (see Chapter 5; and also Sigona, 2012).

Structuring susceptibility to forced labour

What our empirical research on the working lives of asylum seekers and refugees in the UK suggests more generally – irrespective of national context – is that migrants journeying through and around various immigration and socio-legal statuses while under serious livelihood pressures are at risk of entering the labour market at the lowest possible point in their effort to secure work. These constraints on migrants often combine with 'unfreedoms' in labour market processes to create situations of 'hyper-precarity'. To summarise, neoliberalism has resulted in growing inequality, undermining livelihoods in the

Global South and contributing significantly to the generation of migration to the Global North while also creating the environment of exploitation in low-paid labour markets where many migrants find work. To understand exploitation in countries like the UK, we therefore consider it necessary to link global economic change with transformations in the workplace. The roles of economic dispossession and states' accommodation of large-scale capital in producing unfree labour mobility are similarly recognised by other authors (Cross, 2013; Rogaly, 2008). Phillips and Mieres (2013) point out that forced labour, rather than emerging simply from exclusion or marginalisation, can result from the terms on which certain groups are included in global economic activity. These factors relating to capital–state relationships are what we are referring to when we suggest the need for considering the political economy context of refugees and asylum seekers as working migrants. These situations are in turn compounded by host states denying many non-citizen migrants access to basic social rights and protections. The stratified rights associated with socio-legal status of migrants as noted above (see Chapter 4 for extended discussions) result in structured exclusions being an inherent component within many Northern nations' immigration policies. Aside from the direct outcomes of these curtailed rights to welfare, residence and work, many migrants lack full knowledge of their civil and social rights – particularly of their rights within employment (for example, minimum wage, workplace mistreatment). These situations are especially acute among asylum seekers and undocumented migrants. Access to information about rights and broader access to support and protection are further curtailed for these groups by social isolation, and/or an unwillingness to engage in the public sphere for fear of disclosure to the authorities. There are often few social or economic spaces to meet people from different ethnic enclaves, and hence the acquisition of receiving country language skills (known to be important in forming social networks, employment opportunities and broader protection/rights issues) are limited (Ahmad, 2008).

Conclusion

Within Chapter 1 and this chapter, we have explored the inter-connections between neoliberal work and welfare regimes, asylum and immigration controls, and the exploitation of migrant workers. We have built an argument that migrants are centrally implicated in highly precarious working experiences at the bottom end of labour markets in the Global North, including becoming trapped in forced labour. We have also asserted that there is a gap in studies of migrants and extreme exploitation, in that the susceptibilities of *asylum seekers* and *refugees* to forced labour have not been hitherto extensively subject to empirically grounded research. In order to build a conceptual framework for our argument that asylum seekers and refugees should be incorporated in to the research field of forced labour, we have deployed concepts of *precarity*, *socio-legal status*, *deportability in everyday life* and *unfreedom* as the conceptual pillars underpinning our forthcoming empirical chapters. These concepts make sense of the interactions of forced migration, work and welfare that structure the lives of asylum seekers and refugees experiencing forced labour in the UK.

The specific vulnerabilities of asylum seekers and refugees are discussed more fully in subsequent chapters. Suffice to say here that they form part of the broader group of low-wage migrants who find themselves in a toxic environment in the UK that combines competition among the labouring masses to secure work, with a restrictive set of immigration policies that limit welfare access – and all set within a broader environment that delimits legal protections for migrants. Circumscribed welfare access is thought to be a particular 'push' that leaves migrants more willing to work for low wages in insecure and short-term jobs. An additional set of more individually oriented 'points of vulnerability' that come into play prior to, during and after international migration further compounds this situation (Hynes, 2010). The cumulative effect of these vulnerabilities may disadvantageously position particular migrants in comparison to other fellow migrants who are able to draw on more resources. Such clustering of vulnerabilities for migrants in low-paid sectors of the economy can thus contribute to more marginal and exploitative employment experiences that slide into processes of forced labour in certain cases (Dwyer et al, 2011; Geddes et al, 2013). Our argument – expanded on in Chapters 6 and 7 – is that the concepts explored in this chapter enable us to deepen our understanding of both structural (for example, securitised border regimes, neoliberal casualised labour markets, stratified and compromised socio-legal status) and agentic factors (for example, poverty and debt, low social position, modes of recruitment into employment) that contribute to the *production* of asylum seekers and refugees' susceptibility to exploitation.

Notes

[1] The political influence of this particular report is indicated through Theresa May's (Home Secretary) request for the CSJ to host a series of official evidence sessions as part of the public consultation in advance of her tabled Modern Slavery Bill.

[2] In the UK, for example, people who fled violence and persecution in Zimbabwe include those who were able to enter under the former Highly Skilled Migrant Programme as health professionals, their spouses and dependants, or as students, and some of these later made a claim for asylum.

[3] Asylum applications (excluding dependants) rose from 4,256 in 1987 to a peak of 84,130 in 2002, and then declined to 19,865 in 2011. Asylum applicants and their dependants comprised an estimated 7 per cent of net migration in 2011, down from 49 per cent in 2002, but up from 4 per cent in 2010. In 2011 the UK received 0.41 asylum applicants per 1,000 people in its population, below the European average (0.65 for EU plus Norway and Switzerland; see Blinder, 2013).

[4] The EEA consolidates 25 EU member states and three EEA states (Iceland, Liechtenstein and Norway).

[5] Beverley Hughes, Minister of State, in evidence to the Home Affairs Select Committee, First Report of Session, 2003-04, p 17.

[6] But note the data source weaknesses of collecting accurate information on asylum seekers (see Stewart, 2004).

3

Forced labour among asylum seekers and refugees in the UK

Introduction

In this chapter we focus on the 30 asylum seekers and refugees we interviewed who had experiences of severe labour exploitation and forced labour. Drawing on their own testimonies, we show how all our interviewees experienced forced labour practices in multiple forms and diverse labour settings while working in a wide range of sectors in the UK, for varying periods lasting days, months or many years. The chapter first introduces the conceptual framework of forced labour as defined by the ILO. It then sets out the empirical context for our research into forced labour – the Yorkshire and Humber region of England, UK – and explains how we designed our research approach to address various practical and ethical challenges. We then review the types of work, workplaces and sectors our 30 interviewees were engaged in before using the ILO forced labour framework to demonstrate the prevalence and types of forced labour practices across our interviewees. In the final section, we move beyond identifying practices in isolated moments to emphasise forced labour as a process by considering three case studies of how work situations were intertwined with socio-legal status. This chapter provides a necessary introduction to the more in-depth analysis in Chapter 4 of how socio-legal status and deportability in everyday life (de Genova, 2002) came together to trap our interviewees in *processes* of forced labour that do not necessarily reflect the legal definitions of forced labour flowing from the ILO approach. In so doing we highlight problems and weaknesses of the ILO approach, which are subject to further critical discussion later, in Chapter 6.

Defining forced labour

In Chapter 1 we explained that the ILO's 1930 Forced Labour Convention (No 29) is routinely the starting point when attempting to define forced labour. Since its establishment in 1919, the ILO has dedicated a core part of its mission to eliminating 'forced labour', and its legal definitions and instruments largely underpin current policy and the legislative approaches of international bodies, national governments, and the campaigns of trade unions and non-governmental organisations (NGOs) (Hodkinson, 2005), as well as the analytical frameworks of much academic research. The result has been the creation of a dominant international norm about what 'forced labour' is, outlined in the ILO's Forced Labour Convention, as

> ... all work or service which is exacted from any person under the menace of any penalty and for which the said person has not offered himself [sic] voluntarily. (ILO, 1930)[1]

While this definition remains the cornerstone of the ILO's and governments' understanding of forced labour today, during the past decade the ILO has significantly developed the concept of forced labour by establishing clearer guidelines, indicators and evaluative frameworks on both forced labour and trafficking for the purpose of law enforcement and legislative action. A key driver of this work has been the break-up of the Soviet Union and other socialist blocs, opening up new territories and political space to implement ILO standards. Another factor has been the changing nature of forced labour in terms of the growth of human trafficking into forced sexual exploitation and domestic servitude in particular – not previously imagined within the ILO's forced labour framework – as an accompaniment to globalisation (Maul, 2007).

Two aspects of the 1930 Forced Labour Convention have been revisited more recently and subject to further discussion and clarification (ILO, 2005). First, the central importance of 'coercive work' extracted under the 'threat of menace' has been highlighted as the vital difference between forced labour conditions that may be prosecuted through the courts and wider exploitation in the paid labour market that is routinely characterised by employers failing to obey prevailing labour laws on wages and working conditions. In relation to this issue, the more recent guidelines clearly state that the 'extraction of work or services "under the menace of any penalty" does not mean that some form of penal sanction is applied; the penalty might take the form of a loss of rights or privileges' (ILO, 2005, p 20). Second, the issue of a worker's consent, or voluntariness, to undertake the work on offer has been explored.

Initially at least, the ILO's (2005) focus was to establish guidelines on forced labour and trafficking specifically for the purpose of law enforcement and legislative action. Nonetheless, its deliberations also have resonance when considering the highly constrained choices available to many migrants who are not trafficked, including asylum seekers and refugees, who, in the absence of rights to 'legal' residence, work or welfare, may have few options other than entering into highly exploitative working arrangements in the **informal economy** in order to meet their basic needs. It is noteworthy that vulnerability which the ILO defines as 'any situation in which the person involved has no real and acceptable alternative to submit to the abuse involved' (ILO, 2005, p 21) is seen as a key factor in facilitating forced labour. The complex 'hierarchy of vulnerability' (Gubbay, 1999) that socio-legal status constructs and promotes, as part of wider UK immigration policy discussed in Chapter 2, is therefore highly relevant to migrants' susceptibility to forced labour practices.

The result has been the development by the ILO of *forced labour indicators*, which, as Table 3.1 shows, have expanded from six indicators in 2005 (ILO, 2005) to 11 indicators in 2012, set within a framework for identifying when a person could be legitimately said to have experienced forced labour exacted through a combination of involuntariness and penalty (ILO, 2011, pp 14-15). By using the ILO's six core indicators of forced labour during the fieldwork, we were able to identify particular experiences of labour exploitation under coercive and menaced conditions. These indicators evoked for our interviewees very clear experiences, practices, social relations, feelings and emotions, demonstrating their usefulness for identifying possible forced labour cases as the first step to achieving possible redress and protection (see Chapter 7 for the limits of this).

Table 3.1: ILO forced labour indicators

ILO (2005) 6 indicators	ILO (2012) 11 indicators
Threats of actual physical or sexual violence	Physical and sexual violence
Restriction of movement of the worker or confinement to a very limited area	Restriction of movement
Debt bondage, where the worker works to pay off debt	Debt bondage
Withholding wages or refusing to pay the worker	Withholding of wages
Retention of passports and identity documents	Retention of identity documents
Threat of denunciation to the authorities	Intimidation and threats
	Isolation
	Abuse of vulnerability
	Abusive working and living conditions
	Excessive overtime
	Deception

Experiencing any of these forced labour indicators within the ILO approach, however, does not automatically mean that a person either is, or has been, in forced labour. In order to make this stronger assertion, the ILO (2011) argues that the 11 indicators have to be considered as part of a field of *power relations* in which forced labourers experience involuntariness or coercion under the threat of penalty. To make this evaluation, the ILO has come up with a multi-dimensional understanding of the forced labour process set out in Table 3.2 (ILO, 2011, pp 14-15). In the left-hand column are three possible *moments* of the forced labour relation: *unfree recruitment* (that is, involuntary or coerced entry into the employment relationship); *work and life under duress* (that is, abusive living or working conditions imposed by employer during the employment); and the *impossibility of leaving the employer* (that is, exit from the relationship). When any one of these

Table 3.2: ILO's framework of forced labour moments under coercion

Three possible moments of forced labour	Penalty or menace of penalty to the worker
Unfree recruitment Workers are forced to work for a particular employer against their will, or they are deceived into entering that employment by false promises about the work	**Threats and violence** (physical, sexual or psychological) encompass all forms or threats of punishment that put the worker in a position of subordination to the employer **Restriction of workers' freedom of movement** due to isolation, confinement or surveillance
Work and life under duress May entail an excessive volume of work or tasks beyond what can reasonably be expected within the framework of national labour law, including degrading living conditions, limitations on freedom or excessive dependency on the employer, imposed on a person against their will	**Debt bondage or debt manipulation** and any accompanying threats against a worker or their family members **Withholding of wages or other promised benefits** may be used by an employer to retain a worker longer than agreed **Retention of passport, identity papers or travel documents** are all situations where workers are denied access to their documents on request
Impossibility of leaving an employer When leaving entails a penalty or risk to the worker	**Abuse of vulnerability**, including threats of denunciation to the authorities, is a means of coercion where an employer deliberately and knowingly exploits the vulnerability of a worker to force them to work and/or work in less favourable conditions

moments in the left-hand column is combined with one or more penalties or threats of penalty listed in the right-hand column, it indicates a situation of ILO forced labour.

The ILO has further nuanced these dimensions and indicators by introducing a 'strong' and 'medium' scoring of them. For example, under the 'unfree recruitment' moment, a strong indicator of involuntariness might be the coercive recruitment of the worker through abduction or confinement, compared to a medium indicator of deceptive recruitment through false promises about working conditions (ILO, 2011, p 25). The ILO approach will only acknowledge the existence of forced labour where at least one indicator of involuntariness or penalty is 'strong'. However, we have not applied this scoring system due to reservations about it such as the highly subjective and value-laden process of deciding that some forms of coercion are naturally more powerful than others. The example of deception in recruitment proves this point well. If a worker is unfreely recruited through false promises about their pay and conditions only to find themselves forced to accept them or be excluded from the local labour market due to the power of the employer, this is not deemed to be forced labour because these are only medium indicators. Further limitations of the ILO's forced labour framework and the broader conceptualisation of forced labour *per se* are discussed later, in Chapter 6.

Finding forced migrants in forced labour in the Yorkshire and Humber region

Between March 2010 and December 2012, we interviewed 30 people aged 18 or over with a residential connection to the Yorkshire and Humber region of England who had made a claim for asylum and experienced working situations associated with one or more of the ILO six indicators of forced labour. Yorkshire and Humber is the fifth largest region in England covering 15,408 square kilometres with a mixture of urban and rural working environments, and a wide range of labour sectors including significant agriculture, manufacturing and food industries. It also has a diverse range of migrant populations, including 'new' migrants who have settled over the last decade. Over 80 per cent of the 5.3 million population live in urban areas, with the proportion (8 per cent in 2011) of the resident population born outside the UK slowly increasing (Migration Yorkshire, 2013c). The economy of the region is relatively manufacturing-heavy and business activity-light compared to other regional economies in England. In 2007 the region had more areas of high deprivation than the English average, but less than the North East and the North West of England (Kay, 2009).

We chose this research site for three reasons. First, many studies on the employment experiences of low-paid migrants in the UK are focused on London, and we wanted to explore migrant exploitation outside of this 'global city' in a completely different UK context. Second, in our previous work in the region we had developed a range of contacts that would help facilitate the fieldwork. Finally, the region received significant numbers of Home Office-dispersed asylum seekers between 2000 and 2013 – approximately 35,000-40,000 asylum seekers, a third to a half of whom are believed to have received a positive outcome to their asylum claim and become refugees (Migration Yorkshire, 2013a, 2013c). Additionally, a small number of refugees have been resettled in Bradford, Sheffield and Hull under the UNHCR/UK Gateway Protection Programme (UNHCR, 2011; Migration Yorkshire, 2013c). By the end of June 2013, 2,183 people were being supported on Section 95 (asylum support) in the region while awaiting a decision on their asylum claim (Home Office, 2013c). Although regional figures are not publically available for precisely how many refused asylum seekers currently receive Section 4 support in Yorkshire and the Humber, it is reasonable to assume that the regional share of Section 4 claimants is similar to the corresponding Section 95 cases, leading to an estimated number of 500. A much larger, but unknown population of refused asylum seekers that possibly numbers in the thousands also exists. Without permission to work or access to welfare many are 'destitute' and likely to be staying with friends or supported by charities (Lewis, 2009; Lever, 2012).

Our interest in labour exploitation among asylum seekers and refugees was stoked during previous research and advocacy work that generated anecdotal evidence of refused asylum seekers being trapped in severe labour exploitation following their removal of government support and housing, leaving many destitute. We wanted to explore evidence linking the asylum system to labour exploitation, including forced labour, but our 30 interviewees were not easy to find, let alone talk to. Since 2002 asylum seekers, except in rare circumstances, have been legally prohibited from working, and employment is therefore normally a taboo subject. Asylum seekers and undocumented migrants do not talk about work out of fear that it will undermine their asylum claim/status and/or get them arrested, convicted and deported. Refugee support agencies are reluctant to ask about work because of the potential damage it could do to their clients. So we had to build trust with both refugee organisations and our potential interviewees, and this meant investing a lot of time in outreach among the refugee support networks in Yorkshire and the Humber to explain what we were doing, who we were and, most importantly of all, how we would protect those who agreed to talk to us.

Ultimately we made over 100 visits and met over 400 contacts in refugee and migrant support agencies, drop-ins, refugee community organisations in Yorkshire and the Humber. We left flyers in community spaces and distributed them to front-line service providers. We were looking for anyone who had made a claim for asylum in the UK, who had lived in the Yorkshire and Humber region. We also mined our existing contacts and used 'snowballing' to help gather possible leads. We subsequently met 70 refugees or asylum seekers who either had themselves, or knew someone with, experiences of exploitative work. From this initial cohort we identified 46 people who had direct experiences of one or more of six ILO forced labour indicators, which reduced to 30 after 16 people declined to further participate for practical, ethical or emotional reasons. Our 30 interviewees comprised 12 women and 18 men aged between 21 and 58 years (see Tables 4.1, 4.2 and 4.3 in Chapter 4) and came from 17 countries in Africa, the Middle East, Central Europe and South and Central Asia, as outlined in Table 3.3. Interviews typically lasted between two and three hours and involved biographical accounts of migrating to the UK, entering the asylum system and experiences of work guided by semi-structured prompts. Interviews were audio-recorded and transcribed.

Table 3.3: Asylum seeker and refugee interviewees' countries of origin

Country of origin	Number of interviewees
Iran	4
Zimbabwe	4
Nigeria	3
Uganda	3
Pakistan	2
Ethiopia	2
Democratic Republic of Congo	2
African country[a]	2
Afghanistan	1
Kuwait	1
Iraq	1
Sri Lanka	1
Malawi	1
Estonia	1
Ukraine	1
Azerbaijan	1

Note: [a] The names of two African countries have been withheld to protect interviewee anonymity

—

Central to our approach was an in-depth analysis of biographical timelines to focus on key events in immigration and asylum system journeys and work histories. We analysed labour experiences in terms of drivers or motives behind each work situation, the working conditions in relation to the 11 ILO indicators of forced labour, as well as the ILO definition of decent work and emergent dimensions of unfreedom that contributed to a lack of a 'free' contractual agreement. It was never our express intention to search for prosecutable legal cases of forced labour, partly due to the extremely complex legal issues in this area and partly because we see forced labour as rooted in people's experiences of coercion and unfreedom, irrespective of whether a court finds them to be unlawful or not. Rather, we were interested in 'forced labour practices', that is, 'acts done to a worker by an employer or employment agent that are exploitative and, if severe enough and/or numerous enough, may constitute forced labour' (Scott et al, 2012, pp 4–5).

Ethics

Ethical considerations were paramount as the project involved working with vulnerable individuals. There is a growing amount of literature that addresses ethical issues of research with refugees and asylum seekers (Mackenzie et al, 2007; Hugman et al, 2011), located within a more established field that explores the ethical dimensions of research with vulnerable groups (Clements et al, 1999; Moore and Miller, 1999). As our research involved interacting with individuals who often desired a degree of 'invisibility' –because of undocumented status or desire to stay 'under the radar' due to lacking permission to work – our approach was also informed by work on researching undocumented migrants lives (Düvell et al, 2010).

Three ethical principles – a desire to 'do no harm' to interviewees, informed (ongoing) consent and anonymity – underpinned the fieldwork. It is known that the experiences of trauma in asylum seekers' and refugees' lives can make participating in research a potentially distressing experience (Herlihy et al, 2002). We drew on ideas from a feminist 'ethics of care' (Temple and Moran, 2006) to interrogate our own positionalities vis-à-vis those involved in our research, and in an attempt to develop an open attitude and reflection on methodological and ethical decisions during the research process. An important part of this 'caring' research was to take steps to avoid or minimise discomfort or stress to individuals, and on several occasions we had cause to direct interviewees to appropriate support services. All potential interviewees received a full explanation of the research and were assured of their anonymity in subsequent outputs. To protect the anonymity of our interviewees, identifying characteristics such as place names, specific nationalities and particularly personal biographical information have been removed from any data presented. Throughout the book interviewees arc referred to using a preferred pseudonym of their choice. Written consent was always sought, and re-visited, and interviewees were also made aware of their right to withdraw from the study at any time. We carefully considered the practical and ethical issues associated with paying interviewees (Head, 2009), and decided that asylum seekers and refugees would receive £20 as a 'thank you' for their time and participation *in cash* to avoid replicating the stigma associated with asylum voucher payments. Interviews were conducted in places convenient to the participants, including their homes, support agencies' offices and cafes, and in one case of an individual confined to the workplace, over the telephone. In recognition of discussions recognising how interpreters can actively shape research encounters (Müller, 2007), experienced interpreters from appropriate organisations were made available if requested by interviewees, who were in turn consulted on the selection of the interpreter.

We now briefly review the types of work, workplaces and sectors our 30 interviewees were engaged in before analysing their experiences against the ILO's forced labour framework.

Experiences of severe labour exploitation and forced labour

The 30 asylum seekers and refugees we interviewed told us about a total of 107 separate labour situations they experienced while in the UK. We use the terms 'labour situation' and 'work experience' interchangeably as opposed to 'job', because these were very diverse forms of labour relations. The majority of these labour experiences took place outside 'formal' employment relations and settings, emphasising the hidden nature of these migrants' labour. *Informal waged work* accounted for around 46 experiences where they worked with the expectation of 'cash in hand' with little, if any, verbal agreement or assurances of conditions. Twelve were of a wage-less *transactional nature* where the worker undertook work or service in the belief that they were engaging in an exchange for food, accommodation, clothes or to repay a debt and did not expect or receive a cash wage. A further eight either were forms of *involuntary and unpaid servitude* in which the workers were trafficked into the UK either already in, or for the specific purpose of future exploitation in, a forced labour situation. In contrast, 41 labour situations were traditional 'jobs', entered into as *formal employment* with a recognised employer, workplace and, in theory, a formal wage and National Insurance (NI) contributions.

Types of work

As Table 3.4 makes clear, our 30 interviewees performed a relatively small range of work-based roles during their time in the UK, with three-quarters of the labouring situations dominated by just six types of employment – making or serving fast food, domestic work, factory packing, care work, cleaning, and food processing.

Most work experiences (90) were service-based, compared to agriculture (2) and manufacturing (15). As discussed in Chapters 1 and 2, the connection between low-skilled, low-wage manual work in the UK service economy and migrant workers is now well established (Anderson et al, 2006; McKay et al, 2009; TUC, 2008; Burnett and

Table 3.4: Types of work

	Frequency
Takeaway restaurant worker	16
Domestic worker	14
Packing and distribution operatives	14
Care worker	10
Cleaner in commercial premises	9
Food processing worker	8
Construction worker	6
Shop assistant	6
Various agency and odd jobs	6
Odd jobs	5
Security staff	4
Car wash attendant	3
Hair braiding	3
Agricultural worker	2
Manufacturing machine operative	2
Volunteer	2
Administrator	1
Hotel assistant	1
Underground criminal activities	1

Whyte, 2010; Wills et al, 2010; Standing, 2011; Anderson and Ruhs, 2012). When translated into employment sectors (see Table 3.5), over half of our interviewees' work took place in just four sectors – catering and hospitality (17), food manufacturing, processing and packing (15), domestic work and childcare (14), and health and social care (11). Recent research has revealed a prevalence of forced labour practices in these sectors (for example, catering and hospitality; Allamby et al, 2011; Kagan et al, 2011), the food industry (EHRC, 2010; Scott et al, 2012) and domestic and care work sectors (Clark and Kumarappan, 2011; Lalani, 2011).

Table 3.5: Labour situations by employment sector

	Total
Catering and hospitality	17
Food manufacturing, processing and packing	15
Domestic work and childcare (including forced pregnancy)	14
Health and social care	11
Commercial cleaning	7
Manufacturing and construction	7
Small retail (convenience, electric goods, pet shop, markets)	7
Waste and recycling	5
Transport, packaging and distribution	5
Hair and beauty	5
Car wash and valeting	4
Security	3
Agriculture, forestry and fishing	2
Voluntary and charity sector	2
General agency work	1
Real estate	1
Underground criminal activities	1
Overall total	107

However, when each experience is analysed further in Table 3.6, the overarching dominance of the food industry (broadly defined) is apparent, with *44 out of the 107* work experiences located at some point within food production, distribution and consumption supply chains. This reinforces findings elsewhere that highlight the centrality of precarious work within the food industry (Dolan and Humphrey, 2000;

Table 3.6: Labour experiences along the food and drinks supply chain

Producer end		Consumer end	
Potato farm hand	1	Food preparation in commercial kitchens (takeaways, restaurants, hotels)	9
Manufacturing and processing food in factory (fresh fish, bread, frozen meals, puddings, cheese, poultry)	9	Food sales in takeaway restaurants (serving, delivering, flyering)	7
Cleaning machines in food processing factory	1	Security and cleaning for pubs and clubs	6
Food packing factories (sandwiches, fruit and vegetables, teabags)	5	Builder on new supermarket site	1
Food waste and recycling (disposing of out-of-date milk, recycling bottles)	2	Retail convenience store assistant (shop assistant, cleaner, security)	3

Anderson and Rogaly, 2005; Royle, 2005; Craig et al, 2007; Shelley, 2007; McKay et al, 2009; Wills et al, 2010; Allamby et al, 2011; Scott et al, 2012; Strauss, 2013). The strong presence of the food industry in our interviewees' experiences is partly explained by it employing 3.8 million people or 14 per cent of the labour market in 2012 (Defra, 2012). A related explanation for this prevalence lies with the structuring of the food industry, which has long been 'closely linked to processes of flexibility and the associated growing disempowerment of its low-wage, and increasingly migrant-based, workforce' (Scott et al, 2012, p 16). In common with the Scott et al (2012) study, we found forced labour practices in farms, food processing and packing factories and minority ethnic catering businesses, but our evidence also extends to the consumer end of the supply chain, including the construction of supermarkets, cleaning pubs and in small retail convenience stores.

Indecent work: low wages, long hours

The starkest finding emerging from analysing across the 107 labouring situations was the prevalence of what the ILO has called 'indecent work'. By this we mean work that contravened basic employment standards guaranteeing a minimum wage and maximum working hours. The majority of asylum seekers and refugees we interviewed experienced work situations in which they were either forced to work for 'no pay' or their promised wages were 'partially withheld' – a key indicator of forced labour explored later in this chapter. But even when interviewees were paid in full for their work, they routinely received extremely low wages. We were able to extract meaningful wage and hour data for 74 labouring situations described by our 30 participants, which showed that more than three-quarters (54) were regularly paid less than the National Minimum Wage. The average differential between the legal and actual wage was £2.60 per hour, but as Figure 3.1 illustrates, this masks dramatic variations in the size of the gap between minimum wage and actual wage, from £0.15 to as much as £5.37. In some cases, the actual received wage was even lower than the paid wage due to the presence of third parties who controlled and withheld workers' pay (see further discussions below).

Figure 3.1: Comparing actual wage rates in 71 labouring situations to legal minimum National Minimum Wage

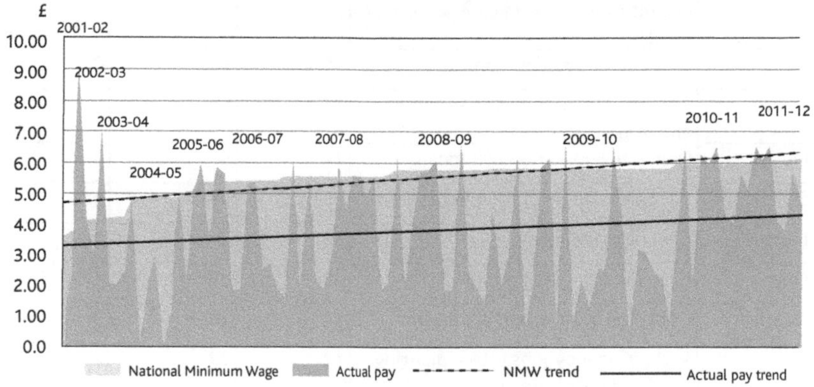

Hourly pay rates are nevertheless deceptive in many of these cases as they conceal very low income levels due to the small number of hours worked. A daily wage of £15, £20 and £30, often for 10–12 hours' work, was consistently reported for informal work in takeaways or cleaning. Even lower rates were mentioned for flyering (delivering takeaway menus) – a flat rate of £10 or £15 for 1,000 flyers. Across the 39 labouring situations for which we could extract data, the average weekly income was £129, with 18 being less than £100 a week – this included weekly pay as low as £30. What is particularly notable in scanning across interviewees' work experience histories is that these extremely low hourly, daily and weekly pay rates are as prevalent in 2012 as they were 10 years earlier.

Additionally, we found evidence of extremely long working hours that contravened UK Working Time Regulations (see Table 3.7). While opt-outs are possible by collective or workforce agreement, there is a General Weekly Limit of 48 hours a week, a Maximum Working Day

Table 3.7: Interviewees' experiences of excessive working hours

Name	Labouring situation	Working hour day (hours)	Working hour week (hours)	Rest days per week
Abigail	Trafficked into domestic servitude	20–24	140	0
Ma'aza	Trafficked into domestic servitude including childcare	20–24	140	0
Pascual	Packing chickens in a factory	18	126	0
Siamak	Security guard and cleaner for pet shop	16	96	1
Parviz	Shop assistant selling electrical goods	15.5	46.5	3
Doreen	Food and clothes factory packing	15	60	2
Mohamed	Kitchen hand in takeaway	15	n/a	n/a
Lydia	Trafficked into third party exploitation – live-in care worker on call	14–24	98	0
Rose	Live-in care worker – on call	14–24	98	0
Happy	Trafficked into domestic servitude and prostitution	14	98	0
Ivy	Domestic worker and childcare	14	98	0
Siamak	Kitchen hand/leafleting in takeaway	13	n/a	n/a
Husseln	Car wash attendant	13	n/a	n/a
Gojo	Care worker – residential	12	35	1
Ada	Domestic worker and child carer	12	60	1
Jay	Various agency jobs – tree planting and food processing	12	72	1
Tino	Domestic worker and child carer – live-in	12	72	1
Muedinto	Kitchen staff and cleaner, hotel	12	72	1
Dedem	Recycling bottles	12	72	1
Jay	Recycling used bricks	12	72	1
Dedem	Security (and cleaning) at convenience store	12	84	0
Pascual	Processing food in a factory – bread	12	84	0
Gojo	Care worker – residential	12	n/a	0
Lydia	Trafficked into third party exploitation – security guard in various business locations	12	n/a	n/a
Assanne	Packing recycled clothes in factory	11	66	1
Angel	Care worker – residential	10	60	1
Shahid	Shop assistant in cosmetics shop	10	70	0
Shahid	Shop assistant in takeaway business	9	63	0

of between 8 to 10 hours with at least one rest of not less than 20 minutes where a worker's daily working time is more than 6 hours. In 27 labouring situations, our interviewees worked more than a 48–hour week, and in 29 situations they worked more than a 10–hour day. In 13 cases, they had no day off during the week.

Forced labour practices

Analysis of our interviewees' testimonies of work revealed that *all 30* had experienced *one or more of the ILO's 11 forced labour indicators* at some point in their working lives in the UK (see Table 3.8). More significantly, these were not one-off episodes but covered the vast majority of migrants' labouring experiences in the UK, with more than half (18 out of 30) experiencing two or more forced labour practices on more than one occasion. A *striking 78 of their 107 work experiences exhibited forced labour practices.* Fifty-nine labouring situations involved two or more indicators, and shockingly, 26 had *at least four indicators*. It is noteworthy that forced labour experiences in formal and informal waged jobs tended to have between two and three indicators, whereas those labour situations of trafficked migrants involved proportionately far more forced labour indicators.

As Figure 3.2 shows, 'abuse of vulnerability', 'withholding or non-payment of wages' and 'deception' were the three most frequently experienced forced labour practices. At least half of interviewees also had an experience of 'excessive overtime', 'abusive working and living conditions' and 'intimidation and threats'. In contrast, and in common with other recent studies on forced labour and migration (Allamby et al, 2011; Kagan et al, 2011; Scott et al, 2012; Geddes et al, 2013; CSJ,

Figure 3.2: ILO forced labour indicators experienced across 78 labouring situations

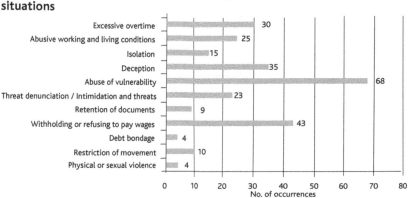

Table 3.8: Interviewees' experiences of forced labour practices

Pseudonym	Number of labouring situations with ILO indicators	Types of labour situation with ILO indicators	Most indicators experienced in any one labouring situation
Abigail	1	Trafficked into domestic servitude	10
Ada	1	Domestic work	3
Alex	3	Takeaway work	1
Angel	4	Care work; restaurant; hotel assistant; domestic work	2
Assanne	2	Factory packing; painting and decorating; nightclub cleaning	8
Dedem	4	Security; recycling bottles; factory packing; manufacturing	3
Doreen	1	Shop assistant	7
Faith	2	Residential care worker	4
Frank	2	Factory packing; machine operator – third party exploiter	4
Gallant	4	Trafficked into criminal activities; manufacturing; takeaway; potato farm hand	8
Gojo	4	Cleaner; residential care worker; administrator	4
Gregory	2	Factory packing; factory cleaning	2
Happy	1	Trafficked into domestic work/ prostitution	11
Hussein	5	Car wash attendant; electrician; takeaway; restaurant waiter; painter and decorator	3
Ivy	1	Domestic worker and childcare	8
Jay	5	Tree planting; food processing and packing; recycling bricks; domestic work and childcare	7
John	3	Cleaner in NHS centres; disposing factory waste; warehouse distribution	3
Lydia	3	Trafficked into third party exploitation in various jobs	11
Ma'aza	1	Trafficked into domestic servitude, including childcare	8
Mehran	3	Various food processing jobs	4
Mohamed	3	Various takeaway jobs	5

Table 3.8: contd

Pseudonym	Number of labouring situations with ILO indicators	Types of labour situation with ILO indicators	Most indicators experienced in any one labouring situation
Muedinto	3	Cleaner; hotel kitchen staff	5
Nanda	1	Factory packing – third party exploiter	7
Parviz	3	Shop assistant; pizza deliverer	3
Pascual	2	Food processing jobs	6
Rose	1	Live-in care worker	6
Sergei	3	Takeaway; factory packing jobs	2
Shahid	3	Takeaway; shop assistant	4
Siamak	3	Car wash; takeaway; security guard	3
Tino	3	Domestic work and childcare; glass collecting in nightclub; construction worker	5

2013), practices of 'physical or sexual violence', 'debt bondage' and the 'retention of documents' were relatively uncommon. We now set out a brief summary of the range of experiences under each indicator.

Abuse of vulnerability

The ILO recognises that employers and other parties may deliberately use a vulnerability to impose more extreme working conditions than would otherwise be possible. Abuse of vulnerability is not a straightforward indicator to detect, however, as millions of workers in the UK are forced to accept indecent work with extremely low pay, long hours and insecurity through a general lack of alternatives. Nevertheless, the ILO (2011, p 16) argues that if it can be proven that the employer is deliberately exploiting this vulnerability 'to impose more extreme working conditions than would otherwise be possible, then this would amount to forced labour'. The abuse of specific and often multiple vulnerabilities was the most widely experienced forced labour indicator among our interviewees, affecting all of them across 68 separate labouring situations (see Figure 3.2). As discussed in Chapter 4, it was usually the vulnerabilities of socio–legal status of asylum seekers and refugees that were exploited by employers and recruiters. Arguably the most prevalent way in which our interviewees' vulnerability was abused was through their employers using the knowledge that they lacked papers – whether the right to work as asylum seekers, or the

right to remain in the UK due to being undocumented or refused –
to impose more extreme working conditions than otherwise legally
possible. At least half of our interviewees experienced this basic tactic
across more than 30 jobs. For example, Alex told us that without
recourse to alternative means of livelihood after his asylum claim had
been refused, he had no choice but to find work in several takeaway
restaurants. Each time his employers knew he was undocumented, and
each time he was paid far below the National Minimum Wage. In one
case, he received 50 per cent less than his fellow workers with papers:

> "... he recognised that I have to work and then when people
> recognise that you have to work and you don't have any
> obligation, they're not going to help you, they're going to
> misuse you."

Others endured this same experience – of undocumented migrants
being paid far less than fellow workers who did have **regularised** status
or papers. This points to a much wider pattern of deliberately employing
migrant workers without permission to work to perform the hardest
tasks under abusive conditions while forcing them to stay long hours
after other workers have left. This finding anticipates discussions in
Chapter 4 where we show in more depth how a migrant's precarious
immigration status and lack of rights to residency, work and welfare
are instrumentally exploited in a variety of ways in the labour process.
But we also found evidence of how constrained socio–legal status is
not only exploited after the fact, but also actively *constructed* by actors
to exact forced labour. Arguably the most powerful ways in which
these manifold vulnerabilities were brought into being was in the
stories of our trafficked migrants. Their existing vulnerabilities were
initially exploited by their traffickers through deception, then actively
expanded by their traffickers rendering them undocumented, and
finally diversified either by the traffickers or their eventual employers
through highly gendered forms of power as well as more familiar
practices of forced labour such as isolation, confinement, threats and
acts of violence and other menaces.

Withholding of wages or refusing to pay the worker at all

The practice of withholding wages or other promised benefits, or
refusing to pay the worker at all, forms one of the most serious and
commonly experienced mechanisms of forced labour. It occurs in
situations where workers are performing labour in the expectation

of payment but the employer either has no intention of paying the individual for the work performed or intends to withhold, unreasonably and without just cause, substantial sums from the worker's wages' (ILO, 2005, p 20). While all our interviewees experienced extremely low levels of pay, 25 experienced having promised or expected wages withheld across 43 separate labouring situations.

One of the most common experiences of withheld pay was non-payment of wages for the first 1 to 2 weeks as *'deductions' for training, trial or deposit*. In his first week of informal shop work, Shahid worked 12 hours a day continuously for seven days on the promise of £310, only to be told afterwards that he would not be paid because it was a trial and training week. Also common was the normalised *partial payment* of wages on a regular basis. After Tino became irregularised and moved in with his partner's family, he agreed to provide paid childcare to her relatives and friends, but their promises of up to £50 a day were consistently broken, blaming 'family problems' for the missing money. Withholding wages was clearly not restricted to the workplace employer – nine interviewees told us about similar situations where their pay had been withheld by *labour market intermediaries* such as temporary employment agencies, labour providers, gangmasters providing casual labour to 'hirers', and other 'third party' actors such as friends and partners who had lent them National Insurance numbers (NINos) or bank accounts to use. Agencies were particularly adept at using a variety of manipulative techniques to cheat workers out of pay, irrespective of whether or not they had the right to work. This included: making deductions for the cost of supplying safety clothing and equipment that were requirements of the job; withholding the first two weeks' wages as a deposit only to then abruptly terminate the employment and retain the money; or asking a group of workers to do special overtime shifts on double time pay only to never be paid.

Perhaps more significant still was evidence of wage withholding by *third party intermediaries*. Newly arrived migrants on short-term visas find it very difficult to open bank accounts, and migrants without leave to remain cannot open a bank account; yet employers or agencies will typically only pay workers through a bank transaction. This leads to migrants – with or without the right to remain – using another person's bank account that makes them vulnerable to losing control over their wages (Burnett and Whyte, 2010). Moreover, undocumented migrants including asylum seekers routinely lack both a NINo and the identity papers such as passports that are required for them to legally access paid work. Subsequently, many undocumented migrants will turn to those who can supply such papers. Nanda's friend gave her a NINo to use and helped her to open a bank account that he then controlled. When Nanda got an agency job in a packing factory, her partner took all her wages, telling her that it would pay for her rent, food and clothes. Doreen's realisation that her new husband had no money pushed her to seek work on her spouse visa. She had found a job in a convenience store, but after having trouble opening a bank account of her own, her wages had to be paid into her husband's account. From the outset he controlled and blocked access to her earnings:

> "… it is hard to open an account when you're new. So he said use mine. So I said fine, because I thought I'm in a genuine relationship … when you go to any agents if you don't have an account and all your documents are true, actually this is for my husband, is it fine, they said no problem. So I used *one* of his accounts. When the money went there he was actually taking it. So in the end I was like working for him. I don't know. Working for him."

At the other extreme were trafficking or domestic abuse cases where workers received no pay or very little pay while working for long periods in highly confined, coercive and abusive situations; these are discussed in more depth under other ILO indicators.

Deception

Deception in a forced labour situation involves 'the failure to deliver what has been promised to the worker, either verbally or in writing' (ILO, 2012a, p 7) in a way that traps them in work they have not freely chosen or cannot escape from. Twenty-two of our interviewees experienced being deceived into either entering or continuing in their jobs or work across 35 separate labouring situations. At one end of the deception spectrum – and in the majority of cases – were false or misleading promises about working conditions (discussed more fully under other indicators). This included *deception about the nature of the work they would be doing or about wage rates and overtime pay*. Abigail was under the impression that she would be a nanny looking after children, but her job turned out to be domestic servitude with no children; Hussein agreed to take a painting and decorating job for £60 a day only for the wage rate to be cut to £45 per day after he turned up for work. There was also *deception about unpaid training and trial weeks*. Pascual, who worked informally via a gangmaster in a chicken packing factory for seven months, was told it was a 'UK convention' not to pay workers for the first week on the job. Moving along the deception spectrum were forms and practices of outright deceit and fraud that were used to entice and entrap people into migrating across borders into labour situations that were very difficult to exit from. Some were lured to the UK by family or acquaintances, with the explicit promise of being given an education only to find themselves confined or isolated in unpaid domestic labour scenarios. For example, Gallant was deceived into leaving his family on the promise of a 'better life' in Europe but on arrival in Greece, he discovered it had been a trap as his family were asked for more money for his safe passage.

Excessive overtime

The ILO (2012a, p 25) defines the forced labour practice of excessive overtime as being 'obliged to work excessive hours or days beyond the limits prescribed by national law or collective agreement'. Workers can be denied breaks and days off, have to take over the shifts and working hours of absent colleagues, or be on call 24 hours a day, seven days a week under some form of threat (for example, of dismissal) or in order to earn at least the minimum wage. Using the UK Working Time Regulations outlined earlier as our measure, we found that 21 interviewees had experience of being forced to work excessive overtime across 30 separate labouring situations. The worst conditions tended to be found in live-in domestic work settings, either in household service or care, where being on call 24 hours and seven days a week without protected breaks or days off was normal (see the discussions under the abusive working and living conditions indicator for further debate). But excessive hours were a feature of many jobs, irrespective of workplace. Muedinto, a refugee with the right to work, had found a job in the kitchens of a well-known hotel chain on £6.20 an hour for a 35-hour week. Bullying was rife, and he was given little choice but to frequently work up to eight hours overtime and a 70-hour working week at short notice. His extra hours were never paid. Pascual routinely worked slaughtering poultry, in freezing conditions, 18 hours a day with just one 15-minute break; he worked seven days a week over seven months for just £80 a week or 63 pence per hour. He described how his body began fall apart but a day off was never allowed by his informal gangmaster:

> "I remember one day I refused completely to come [to work] ... after four months I was feeling the body is finished, the body didn't want to do it. When I tried to wake up I fell

down, I was feeling faint and I didn't have a doctor to treat me, I didn't know where to go ... they rang me ... 'why you not coming to work?' I say 'I'm not feeling well'. 'Oh, we are coming to pick you' ... then they start frightening me to be sacked.... And I didn't even answer them and I just keep quiet because I was very stressed but the next day I went there...."

Another common experience for those we interviewed was being told that they were free to leave as others would readily replace them if they did not agree to extra hours. Being reminded of their expendability was often used at the precise moment when extra hours were being demanded. Mohamed experienced this when he complained to his employer that other workers in the takeaway were allowed to leave when their agreed eight-hour shift was over, but he was being told he had to stay until the kitchen had been cleaned, which could mean a 15-hour day. The coerced performance of excessive hours was typically part of a wider experience of abusive working and living conditions that we now turn to.

Abusive working and living conditions

A frequent experience for our interviewees was being forced to perform difficult, dangerous and degrading work. Such conditions are a key aspect of contemporary forms of precarious labour, and this has been recently acknowledged by the ILO in their expanded 11 indicators of forced labour, which state forced labour is present when 'victims are likely to endure living and working conditions that workers would never freely accept' (ILO, 2012a, p 23). This includes degrading (humiliating or dirty) or hazardous (difficult or dangerous without adequate protective gear) work that is in severe breach of labour law. Forced labourers may also be subjected to substandard living conditions, made to live in overcrowded and unhealthy conditions without any privacy. Nineteen interviewees experienced being forced to endure abusive working or living conditions across 25 labouring situations.

One set of such experiences related to hazardous and dangerous work under duress. Excessive working hours and highly physical work went hand in hand with a disregard for health and safety in many jobs where our interviewees experienced or witnessed a lack of training, inadequate protective gear, injuries and even fatalities. Being forced to stand up all day, perform physically demanding manual labour at high speed without proper breaks and pushed on by an employer telling them to work harder were common experiences. Jay recalled the threat of physical violence in an agency job in which he was forced to carry on planting trees in the rain, his racist boss telling him to "keep on working, you black, you strong, you know" with the threat of violence to back it up. Parviz got an informal job repairing, selling and delivering home appliances which involved a lot of heavy lifting and left him with a serious occupational injury to his back. His employer knew his precarious situation and readily exploited it – on occasions he was forced to work up to 16 hours a day. Whenever workers attempted to draw attention to dangerous conditions, their employer or agent targeted them for retaliation.

Such abusive behaviour often went hand in hand with *verbal abuse and humiliating and degrading treatment*. Labouring situations that involved our interviewees *both working and living with the employer* – whether as a domestic servant, sex slave or carer – were often marked not just by extremely hazardous and dangerous conditions but also the humiliating and degrading treatment they suffered at the hands of their employer. Gallant described how he and fellow labourers were made to live "like animals" outdoors in a tent in freezing conditions, eating only takeaways. Some of our interviewees also experienced domestic abuse and violence at the hands of their partners or relatives with whom they lived and worked for, which combined with the role of precarious socio-legal status (discussed in Chapter 4). This exposes a conceptual weakness of 'forced labour' described later, in Chapter 6. Abusive working and living conditions were frequently connected to intimidation and threats.

Intimidation and threats

According to the ILO (2012a), the forced labour practice of intimidation and threats typically occurs in response to either workers' complaints about their conditions or stated desire to leave their jobs. In addition to violence, other common threats include denunciation to the immigration authorities, loss of wages, further worsening of working conditions or withdrawal of 'privileges'. Constantly insulting and undermining workers also constitutes a form of psychological coercion, designed to increase their sense of vulnerability. In addition, we include threats and acts of violence against fellow workers witnessed by the interviewee where these appeared designed to create, or have the effect of creating, a workplace and labour process ruled by fear of violence against workers. Threats tended to be used on our interviewees by employers as a tool of control in the workplace, to build submissiveness to poor treatment at work, and to discourage individuals from supporting fellow workers who were victims of workplace violence. Fifteen interviewees experienced intimidation and threats across 23 labouring situations. Overlapping with some of the previous indicators, these included the threat of dismissal for taking a day off due to being unfit to work, or asking for missing pay through the Citizens' Advice Bureau, being intimidated for speaking out against contraventions of health and safety, or seeking better conditions. Threatened violence as a mechanism of pre-empting attempts to negotiate or exit exploitation was experienced more starkly in trafficking cases. Gallant's traffickers regularly threatened to kill his family back home unless he complied with their wishes. When Gallant tried to resist working for the gang, the terrifying threats intensified:

> "... I hide myself because he was threatening me through the phone and ... telling me 'I'm going to do this to your dad, I'm going to do this to this' so I was so scared I had to listen to him, because I thought he will definitely kill my dad if I don't listen to him. And he actually phoned my dad once and ... when I spoke to my dad, my dad was like crying. I had to do whatever they wanted me to do or they asked me to do. I had to do. No matter how difficult."

In other cases, the experience of witnessing acts of physical violence towards other workers instilled such fear of similar abuse that it acted as a form of power, self-disciplining workers to work 'harder, faster, better' and obey their employer's wishes, closing down any space for negotiation. Yet noted in the discussion of the withheld wages indicator, an equally potent form of threat and intimidation alongside violence was the instrumental use of irregular immigration status and the threat of denunciation to the UK authorities. No fewer than eight interviewees experienced their vulnerable immigration status being used directly to coerce them into work (discussed further in Chapter 4). Jay was a refused asylum seeker when he started a romantic relationship with a British woman. After several months, he revealed to her that he was a refused asylum seeker legally barred from working and was staying with a friend, at which point she invited him to live with her. But when he moved in he found she had two children with physical disabilities and was immediately expected to take on a role as carer, cleaner and cook, and be on call for sex in return for food and accommodation. When Jay tried to negotiate an improvement in his conditions, he was coerced to work without pay through the threat of denunciation:

"... at first I had a good relationship but she ended up mistreating me, working for her, looking after the kids, she never paid me, she used to tell me sometimes – 'oh you fucking African if you do anything I will call the immigration office and they will send you back to your country'...."

Restriction of movement

One of the more familiar and evocative mechanisms of coercing forced labour is through the physical confinement of workers in the place of work. During the Transatlantic Slave Trade, it was common practice to chain enslaved Africans from capture, through transit, and then in the fields and factories. Although contemporary slavery rarely involves chains, today, the spectre of confinement has resurfaced in the sweatshops of India, Bangladesh and China, where evidence is emerging of workers being locked in factories for up to 19 hours a day (BBC, 2013a). In the ILO's (2012a) framework, the confinement of workers, whether through locking into the workplace or highly restricting their movement, is a very strong indicator of forced labour, designed to prevent contact with outsiders and extract the maximum amount of labour from the individuals. Nine people experienced forms of confinement and enforced immobility in 10 separate labouring situations. Although relatively low in frequency, where confinement did take place, it was both strongly enforced and central to that person's exploitation. As with other indicators, the more extreme experiences of confinement were associated with trafficked cases, domestic work and victims of domestic abuse. Doreen and Happy were physically locked by key in the homes they lived and worked in, while Ivy, Lydia, Abigail, Gallant and Ma'aza were effectively confined through their movements being controlled by their employers. Those working in domestic work, child or adult care in private houses were effectively restricted due to caring responsibilities or the very long hours they were expected to work. We will explore this in more depth in the next section and in Chapter 5.

Retention of identity documents

The ILO (2012a) argues that forced labour may be present where a worker's identity documents or other valuable personal possessions are confiscated by their employer, and the worker feels that they cannot leave the job without risking their loss. In many cases, without identity documents, the worker will not be able to obtain other jobs or access essential services, and may be afraid to ask for help from authorities or NGOs. The issue of document retention involving asylum seekers and refugees is more complex. This is because asylum applicants do not normally have their documents as the Home Office retains them on entry. Those smuggled or trafficked to the UK also do not have their own documents, and if false documents have been used to get them into the UK, they were usually taken from them at the airport by the smuggler.

The retention of documents was nevertheless experienced by seven of our interviewees across nine labouring situations. The majority of these were connected to trafficking or trafficking-related cases in which our interviewees did not have their own documents as they had been given false documents to get them into the country that were then taken at the port entry by the trafficker/smuggler. However, the fact that asylum applicants normally have their documents retained by the Home Office when they apply for asylum can create additional vulnerabilities when later trying to access work. Frank, a refused asylum seeker at the time, was owed a week's wages after leaving his factory packing job due to fears of an immigration raid, but when he rang up to claim his unpaid wages, the agency asked to check his papers and he decided to forgo the money. Gojo, a refused asylum seeker, found a cleaning job with a commercial cleaning company. However, when her first two weeks' wages were due to be paid, papers were demanded and her pay was withheld. She ended up paying her friend £50 to help her procure a fake Home Office letter stating she had the right to work.

The role of the state in creating undocumented and irregular migrants is central to their rendering as hyper-precarious workers, vulnerable to forced labour with little or no protection or alternative. A general sense of being undocumented, unknown, and invisible to wider society furthermore permeated working experiences and had a debilitating effect on workers' sense of being able to challenge unscrupulous employers.

Physical and sexual violence

Another mechanism of coercion experienced by some of our interviewees was the threat and application of physical and/or sexual violence. In the ILO's (2012a) approach, such violence comes within the scope of the criminal offence of assault. The discussion of our interviewees' experiences of threats and intimidation highlighted the extent to which symbolic violence in the form of threats and abuse created an intimidating workplace environment for many interviewees. Actual physical or sexual violence was less common, with three interviewees experiencing such practices across four labouring situations. Nevertheless, as we discuss in Chapters 5 and 6, when physical violence was present, it played a decisive and destructive role in procuring forced labour and preventing exit. Nanda, who had been made destitute after her asylum claim was refused, moved in with a man who had arranged for her to work while withholding her wages. During their relationship, she suffered domestic violence and attempted suicide on several occasions, but was too scared to go to the police:

> "I did suicide attempt. I was in [...] hospital. I got liver failure and everything; they give me blood and everything, my blood level gone down. They said it's like domestic violence they said if you want you can call police. I said, I was scared, I was scared I didn't do nothing."

Isolation

As a forced labour practice, isolation takes many different and simultaneous forms according to the ILO (2012a). It may involve workers being isolated in remote, uninhabited and hard-to-reach locations, or equally being isolated within highly populated areas behind closed doors, or having their mobile phones or other means of communication confiscated. Importantly, isolation can also be connected to the business premises being 'informal and not registered, making it very difficult for law enforcement or other agencies to locate' (ILO, 2012a, p 12). Twelve of our interviewees experienced a range of isolation practices across 15 separate labouring situations. Once again, social and physical isolation was a prominent feature of the working lives of those working in domestic and care work in private homes. Deliberate strategies of isolation took many forms, including conscious attempts to discourage forced labourers from talking about their situation with fellow workers or outsiders, leaving the home or having free time to do what they wanted without supervision. This amounted to isolation from the practical knowledge of unfamiliar social, cultural and physical environments, and closed down the sense that other options or chances existed. Ivy could leave the house in the UK where she worked, but only if accompanied by members of the family she worked for. This isolation contributed to maintaining the deception that she would one day be allowed to go to school:

"In the UK first of all I don't know anywhere to go and secondly I don't know anybody so only this man and his wife and they were, I was looking after the children for them, I would clean the house. But every day they would tell me that they are looking for the school for me and so be patient. Me I was believe them because I don't know that they are lying to me you know. So up to three years."

Only a few interviewees experienced extreme forms of isolation, but all had fragmented and limited social networks in the UK and little contact with support services at the time they were in labour exploitation. Their lack of family or trusted social contacts, and limited knowledge of UK systems, rights and protection, therefore contributed to them feeling they had no choice but to agree to substandard work.

Debt bondage

According to the ILO (2012a, p 21), debt bondage occurs when a person becomes 'a security against a debt or loan [and] ... [t]he individual works partly or exclusively to pay off the debt which has been incurred'. Immediately it should be noted that such debts are often bogus and inflated, and unlawfully presented as contractual, which makes the practice of debt bondage another form of deception. These so-called debts are more commonly associated with trafficking cases and are incurred during the process of recruitment and transportation, and then used as a form of power over the trafficked worker. The practice of debt bondage in the ILO's definition was not widely experienced by our interviewees: only three people – Abigail, Happy and Lydia – told us about four situations in which an accumulated 'debt' was explicitly linked to their enforced and unwaged labour. Abigail was trafficked to the UK while in forced labour through a relationship originally stemming from her being trafficked out of her country to an employer in a Gulf state. Abigail's mother told her that she would be playing with children, but in reality she was a domestic servant, working a punishing 20-hour day, seven days a week. When she tried to leave, her employer told her that she now belonged to her:

"I said 'I'm going to go. I'm going to leave this house', I said to the lady. She said, 'you're what? You're going from the house? I paid a lot of money to have brought you here. You cannot go anywhere. You came only for a two-year contract and you need to finish that."

Here we see how the 'cost' to the employer of employing Abigail in the Kafala system of sponsorship (Esim and Smith, 2004; Mahdavi, 2013; O'Connell Davidson, 2013) was presented to Abigail as a contractually based debt that required two years of service to repay. A similar form of control was placed over Happy. Having been deceived by a woman into accompanying her to the UK on the deceit of getting an education, after one year working as a domestic servant in confinement, Happy was told she would have to pay back £10,000 for bringing her to the UK, which would later be the tool of coercion used to force her into prostitution. In these cases, the debt was presented at a later date as having been incurred in the process of bringing them to the country of work, and was used as a tool of coercion and control over their bodies. All of these debts were bogus and inflated, which also made them a form of deception. Other types of debt also featured where individuals had cast around friends in times of need for cash – particularly to raise funds for legal fees – or had accumulated large debts to their family back home who paid for their transit to Europe, which pushed them into indecent work.

From practices to processes of forced labour

So far we have shown how the 30 asylum seekers and refugees interviewed for this study reported experiences of forced labour practices across the 11 ILO indicators. However, as discussed, the ILO also argues that experiencing any of these forced labour indicators in isolation does not automatically mean that a person has been in forced labour. Rather, the 11 indicators have to be considered against a wider set of processes in which forced labourers experience one or more mechanisms of coercion – threats and violence, confinement, debt bondage, withholding of wages, retention of identity documents, abuse of vulnerability – at one or more of three possible moments of forced labour: unfree recruitment; work and life under duress; or the impossibility of exit.

Based on our application of this, we found that 22 of our 30 interviewees had been trapped in forced labour as defined by the ILO while in the UK, and five of these had been trapped more than once. Of the 29 labouring situations we regarded as ILO forced labour, 16 showed strong evidence of involuntariness or coercion at all three points in the forced labour process. The following three in-depth case studies relate entry routes into the UK and subsequent socio-legal status to emphasise how forced labour is a process, not just a moment, and to illustrate the interface between forced labour and asylum.

Asylum seekers trapped in forced labour: Assanne's experience

Assanne fled to the UK after "troubles in my country", but after his claim for asylum was refused, he became destitute and found temporary accommodation in the house of a friend he had made through the asylum process. Needing to contribute to household costs as well as save up money to pay for the legal costs of a fresh claim, Assanne found an informal manual job in a clothes recycling factory. He took the job on the expectation of being paid £200 for a 55-hour week, working 9am to 8pm with a one-hour unpaid lunch hour five days a week, and the first week considered a training period on half-pay. However, after his training week finished, Assanne would never receive the promised wage in full again, his weekly pay varying from "£20 or £150 or £100" to sometimes nothing. Here we see the process of *unfree recruitment* in action: Assanne was not forced to work for the employer against his will, but he was *deceived* into entering that employment by false promises about the work, meaning he did not freely consent to those conditions:

> "Every Friday there is a new story, there is a new excuse....
> He would say things like 'this week you haven't worked hard
> enough, I've got no money and because you haven't worked
> hard enough I haven't sold anything or I haven't been able
> to do this'. So yes, he did put the blame – so sometimes he
> would say 'the bank hasn't given me any money so I can't
> get any money out the bank'."

This systematic *withholding of wages* was, in turn, a key mechanism by which the employer then imposed extremely *adverse and abusive working conditions under duress*. The 55-hour week would often stretch to 66 hours or longer, with Assanne performing very physically intense, tiring and *hazardous* lifting and machine work:

> "… everybody was just dressed in their normal clothing,
> there were no safety helmets there was no safety overalls....
> There was no machines to carry any of the bundles, the big
> stuff the bundles, it was all done physically, very dangerous.
> They were 55 kilos, it wasn't easy."

Despite such long hours and physical intensity, his employer would clamp down on any breaks, exercising extreme control of every movement while at work:

> "He used to just say 'look if you go to the toilet three times
> that will cost me for three minutes say four times that will
> cost me an hour. And you can't go to the toilet to urinate
> unless it's your break, and if it's a cigarette break I'll take it
> off your money....'"

The employer would also regularly blackmail Assanne and other
workers into working *excessive overtime* by threatening not to pay them
until they had finished:

> "Sometimes we were due to finish, the lorry turns up, oh
> it's got to be packed now, it's got to be filled, it's got to be
> loaded onto this lorry. So an hour goes by, sometimes we'd
> end up, we'd take three hours to load this lorry. So instead
> of finishing when we were meant to finish, the lorry would
> turn up and we'd have to work this extra time ... he would
> say actually if this lorry doesn't go, I won't have any money
> to pay you."

This exploitative labour regime was backed by intimidation and threats
of violence. Assanne describes how violence was a constant feature of
his workplace, particularly on a certain day of the week when arguments
and confrontations caused by the employer withholding promised pay
escalated into the employer physically fighting and chasing his workers
off the premises:

> "Sometimes there were fights. Sometimes people would
> just run off or he would chase people out, or sometimes
> we'd have words then we'd have to make it, other people
> would have to calm the situation down. Every Friday there
> were fights."

The fact that employees never came together against the employer
wasn't simply out of fear of the employer's violence: a key factor here
was the migrant workers' precarious immigration status and fear of the
authorities, which underpinned their reluctance to resist and created a
vulnerability that the employer was able to exploit. Assanne was in no
doubt about how his own vulnerability had been abused.

Faced with such extreme exploitation, one might ask why Assanne
continued to return to the workplace each week for 10 months
before quitting, and why, given his experience, he would later return
to the same job for a further six months. Here we see how Assanne's

---

vulnerable situation was exploited by his employer to *effectively prevent him from leaving*:

> Assanne: "Every day I would say I'm not coming back tomorrow. It was difficult because one the work was hard, he wasn't very nice as a person, the hours were too long, too much, so you know that basically you are working and you know that at the end of the week you've done these hours but you are not going to get paid, so it's hard."
>
> Interviewer: "Why did you not look for another job?"
>
> Assanne: "It wasn't easy. I did look but it wasn't easy find a job in this situation, but I did look."

With no alternative source of income, he was dependent on this employer – something the employer appeared fully aware of – and worked on in the hope that he would eventually receive the £1,000s in unpaid wages. It was only when Assanne's fresh asylum claim was lodged and he accessed Section 4 support that he was able to leave. But once his claim had been refused and he was made destitute again, he had no alternative but to return to the clothes recycling factory for a further six months of exactly the same forced labour practices, only now Assanne had not been unfreely recruited – he went in with eyes wide open. This time, however, it was not Assanne who exited the labouring situation, but the employer. After forcing his workers to perform a 20-hour shift under the deception of settling pay arrears the next day, he disappeared. Assanne was owed in excess of £8,000 in unpaid wages that he would never see again.

Irregularised migrants who become trapped in forced labour: John's experience

John originally came to the UK to visit his brother on a six-month visitor visa while living off savings. During his visit, he had become romantically involved with his brother's housemate who persuaded him to stay longer in the UK and because he wanted to pursue an education. However, John became undocumented when his visa lapsed and his application for a study visa was refused. Needing to contribute to household bills, some friends who were in a similar situation gave him the telephone number of an anonymous woman who ran an agency supplying cleaners that was known to find work for undocumented migrants. When she finally answered his calls, getting a job without papers was fairly straightforward:

"She started taking my details. I gave her my name, then she asked me if I got NI [National Insurance number]. Told her I don't have NI. 'Don't you have a temporary one?' I said no. And she said, 'right normally.... I would give you a temporary NI then you will see from there how it goes like ... [then] she was asking ... 'do you have a work permit or visa?', something like that, but she wasn't able to say that [openly]. And to my surprise, not very surprise because people told me ... she doesn't even ask [for my papers]. You imagine because she knows that most of these people that she's employing maybe they don't have papers... she don't even have an office this lady.... She take those details my name, date of birth, she says the NI she will sort it out, then I have to wait."

Eventually, John received a call from the agent offering him a temporary cleaning job at an NHS health centre, initially for a five-day week, working three hours a day. John gave her his bank account details but a mixture of excitement, pride and fear led him not to ask about the pay rate. At the end of that week of work, the agent texted John that the NHS centre wanted him back for another week and that he would be paid at the end of that second week. However, John did not receive any of the wages promised, and the agent now stopped answering his calls and texts, leaving John momentarily devastated. Here we see the moment of *unfree recruitment* through *deception* and the *withholding of wages* – John had worked on the explicit promise of being paid after the second week only for his wages to be withheld. Nevertheless, his friends told him to keep trying her, that this was how it was for them, that she would eventually give him more work and pay him. Months later, the agent rang John out of the blue to offer him another NHS cleaning job, and recalling what his friends had said, John agreed to work again for her. Reflecting on his decision to go back to the person who had previously not paid him, John reveals how his deeply vulnerable state of mind shaped this decision:

"... the fact that you are moving away from the house, going out to do something, is, is, it's a very big thing to somebody who has got no, no future....You are living in a world where you don't know where you are going, so the hopes were like, OK let me carry on doing this. Probably at the end of the tunnel there, something will come out, you know. That was the belief I was believing. It was a little bit of daft really, coming out of the house in the morning, you think you going to get a job, maybe the little that you had, maybe pocket money, you're using for transport to manoeuvre around for shifts, but nothing really is coming … kind of charity work what you're doing, but you're not registered as a charity worker, that was the only difference. But really at that period, even if it was few months I was still happy….'

This time, John was not unfreely recruited into forced labour and he did eventually get paid, but he was once again severely exploited, paid just £90 in total for three weeks working from 7.30am to 1pm, five days a week – for £1.09 per hour. Although John was not in a position to negotiate or reject these conditions, it is yet another example of how a labour market intermediary – this time an employment agency – knowingly *abused the vulnerability* of an undocumented migrant without the right to work to exact forced labour.

Trafficked into forced labour: Lydia's experience

After being tortured by her own government, Lydia's parents arranged for her to escape to the UK using someone else's passport, to live with her cousin who financially contributed to Lydia's transit. Lydia was very keen to access education but had no real sense of what awaited her in the UK, and thought nothing of her cousin *taking back the passport* she entered on because she had no reason to believe that such papers were necessary. She recalls how her cousin had *isolated* her and *intimidated* her about strangers and repeatedly told her from the moment she arrived what she had to do to get by in the UK:

> "… he warned me not to get involved with talking to other people. So he always made sure that he prevented me talking to other people all I needed to do was listen to him, that was the best way of living in this country."

Lydia spent her first weeks helping with household chores before her cousin told her that she needed to find work, which Lydia consented to "because I needed to get some money for studying". Her cousin introduced her to his friend who ran an employment agency and began to send her to different temporary security jobs, including overnight, which typically lasted for a number of weeks and involved 12-hour shifts. At the point of entry into this labouring situation, and throughout its duration, Lydia had every reason to believe she would be paid with the money going into her cousin's bank account:

> "The guy said that he would be paying money but then, because I didn't have [a bank] account, my cousin suggested that the money would be paid into his account because that's what all the people who come here do."

When she later asked her cousin about her pay, he told her that he would be deducting it from the money he had lent to her parents for her travel. Again, although Lydia had not consented to this arrangement, she accepted it was fair but later reflected on how he never told her how much she had earned, nor how much he was owed. After a month of security jobs, the agent informed her that he had agreed with her cousin – who had gone abroad for a while – that she should start a new job as a live-in carer for a family. Lydia was told nothing about her pay, the hours of work, the job or the family's needs, but did not feel able to say no:

> "... I had just come to the country and then I was being sent to stay with complete strangers and I was going to stay with them all the time and I was so worried because I didn't have a place of my own and I didn't have any money I just had to accept to go."

On the day she started, the agent told her that he had agreed to pay her cousin £700 to £800 a month. It was only when she moved in with the family she discovered that she would be on call 24 hours a day, seven days a week with one day off a month caring for a man with complex medical needs with just one day's training in lifting. She describes being trapped in a permanent state of work:

> "... I am supposed to be on call – if he sleeps I can a little bit sit down and rest but I was expected to get up in the night when he calls me because I had the monitor.... I was very, very tired most of the time. The only sleep I could get was during the day when he goes asleep because he had some carers to give him a wash, they could wash him, put him to bed maybe sleep a little bit and I could doze off myself for a few hours, if he slept but if he couldn't sleep that meant that I could be up."

Working extremely long and *excessive hours* in a physically exhausting job that she would never have freely entered was tempered by the continued hope and expectation that her wages, currently being paid into her cousin's account, would gain her access to a school or college in the future. Lydia's belief was reinforced by her cousin's reassurances and the fact that he was family:

> "He said he was saving all my money ... because education here is very expensive. So I was like 'ok' I think he's trying to help me out somehow...."

Gradually, however, Lydia began to have doubts that grew as the years went by. This increased as the daughter of the family she worked for became suspicious about Lydia's treatment and revealed that they were paying £1,600 a month for her service and wanted to know how much of this Lydia was receiving. After five years, Lydia became increasingly desperate and now confronted her cousin with her knowledge that the family was paying £1,600 for her, which of course amounted to *tens of thousands of pounds in unpaid wages*. At first the cousin attempted to further *deceive* her by telling her that part of these wages was to pay for the cost of having a NINo and a bank account. But as she continued to press for her wages, she began to experience the now familiar unfolding of *threatened violence*. Lydia describes how the cousin had ensured that other family members and the agent knew that she had left her country because of the threat of torture by the government, and they all used this very real threat of violence should she be deported to silence her from telling anyone about her situation:

> "They kept threatening me that if you start making things like this, we see we telling you this is the money we are paying to you, we are paying for your insurance, we are paying for using the bank account, if you are making things worse for you if the police ever find you they will just put you on a plane and send you back home and you would start suffering again...."

In summary, Lydia had been *unfreely recruited* into a long-term forced labour situation by her cousin through the deception that he was rescuing her from persecution, and that by working she was saving up for education. By *confiscating her travel documents*, keeping her under close supervision, and instilling the fear of strangers into her, her cousin *constructed a vulnerability that he then abused*. As she began to challenge

—

and question her situation, the cousin's family began to increase the threats and intimidation, further isolating her and *deterring her from trying to exit from exploitation*. The *withholding of wages* was another tactic by which exit was prevented for so long as Lydia continued to labour in the belief that her cousin would eventually pay her. Lydia did eventually escape, but her relatives tried very hard to threaten and intimidate her from talking to anyone about what had happened, and she never recovered any of her wages. Lydia's case is the strongest example among our interviewees demonstrating a direct link between forced migration – needing to leave to escape torture and persecution – and subsequent entry into forced labour through risky migration strategies that are a product of the very limited possibilities for travel to a safe country created by deterrent immigration policies and border controls. This results in vulnerabilities that can be exploited by traffickers (for a detailed discussion of immigration controls producing trafficking, see O'Connell Davidson, 2010).

Conclusion

This chapter has revealed that forced migrants who arrive in the UK as asylum seekers or as trafficked migrants, or who become irregular after their visas expire, can become trapped in severe labour exploitation and forced labour while living here. Our 30 interviewees had worked in a wide range of sectors in the UK, for periods lasting from days to months or several years, across a spectrum of decent work, severely exploitative labour and forced labour. This work was in a wide range of jobs in catering and hospitality, care, domestic work, food packing or processing, cleaning, manufacturing, retail, construction, security and other sectors. Most of these jobs involved one or more of the ILO's 11 indicators of forced labour. The most common experiences were the abuse of vulnerability of compromised socio-legal status and the withholding of wages. Of three groups we identify – asylum seekers on entry, trafficked migrants and undocumented migrants (explored further in Chapter 4) – we found that those trafficked to the UK were in the most exploitative forms of forced labour including domestic servitude, sexual exploitation and care work. This chapter has also revealed that forced migrants routinely enter labour situations that from the outset feature highly adverse conditions of little or no pay, debt or threats and experiences of violence. Others enter work on the expectation or promise of decent pay and conditions, but find themselves increasingly constrained within deteriorating circumstances that close down avenues for exit (Anderson and Rogaly, 2005). However, while experiencing a forced labour practice might be a sign of unlawful labour exploitation, it does not automatically mean that a person has been or is in forced labour as understood by the ILO. Rather, the 11 indicators have to be considered against a wider set of processes in which forced labourers experience one or more mechanisms of coercion – threats and violence, confinement, debt bondage, withholding of wages, retention of identity documents, abuse of vulnerability – at one or more of three possible moments of forced labour: unfree recruitment; work and life under duress; or the impossibility of exit. We now deepen the analysis of these power relations through an exploration of the role played by asylum seekers and refugees' socio-legal status in their experiences of forced labour.

Note

[1] A supplemental ILO Protocol to Convention No 29 on Forced Labour was adopted in the 103rd session of the International Labour Conference, 28 May–12 June 2014.

The significance of socio-legal status

Introduction

> "I been to appeal, and they refuse ... my support is cut ... my friend just give a place for live, you know – for sleeping, eating. But I thinking better I doing something, I working somewhere.... Because I don't have support this country, I don't have a document for job.... I doing so many job. I working in car wash, in building job, in take away, in pet shop. I doing anything because what can I do? I don't have any support and ... I need the money because if I want to take a solicitor you know they need the money, I don't have the money, and I don't have anyone." (Siamak)

Our entry point to this research was our knowledge from past research that refusal of an asylum claim and subsequent destitution could create the circumstances that leave individuals with no 'real and acceptable alternative' to entering or remaining in severe exploitation (Dwyer and Brown, 2005; Lewis, 2007, 2009). As this opening quote from Siamak illustrates, the removal of asylum support payments and housing when an asylum case is refused triggers destitution – the lack of ability to meet basic needs without turning to someone else for help (Lewis, 2007). Siamak describes his need to raise cash through difficult and dangerous informal employment to contribute to his friend supporting him, and to raise funds for a solicitor to pursue his asylum claim.

Overall, this book asks how and why people who make a claim for asylum in the UK might be susceptible to forced labour. Following the focus on the experiences of labour exploitation in Chapter 3, this chapter concentrates on our second key explanatory framework for understanding the intersection of forced migration and forced labour: the role played by immigration systems. The first part of this chapter outlines a three-part typology that emerged from identifying individuals who had a claim for asylum in the UK and experience of forced labour: asylum seekers on entry, irregular migrants and trafficked migrants.

Although most of our participants had complicated immigration histories, these three groups show three distinct intersections of forced labour and asylum in terms of the ways they entered the UK, and how this related to their entry into work.

The second part then goes on to identify four salient aspects of the role of socio-legal status in producing and moulding (Anderson, 2010) exploitative labour situations. The first two relate to the relationship between irregularity and work. The single most significant factor structuring entry into exploitative work among our interviewees was the destitution created by loss of an asylum claim and lack of rights to welfare or work. This sparked an urgent need for survival and cash that was significant in *entry* into exploitative labour for our interviewees who entered the labour market as refused asylum seekers. Destitution as a central dimension of unfreedom in recruitment was also significant for irregular migrants in our study. The second issue is the instrumental use of socio-legal status as a tool of coercion to impose substandard working conditions of 'work and life under duress' *within* work situations. Fear of deportation and abuse of the vulnerability of those working without authorisation were used by employers to coerce and control, but we identify how deportability and 'illegality' have wider disciplining effects in the lived experiences of workers.

The third aspect nuances the suggestion of an interaction between irregularity and susceptibility to forced labour by examining how even *after* gaining status and having permission to work, some in our study encountered work featuring forced labour practices. This demonstrates that the intersection of forced labour and socio-legal status cannot be simply explained through a straightforward documented/ undocumented status binary. Sustained periods of precarious work and immigration status can be difficult to break out of, creating a lasting precarity track (Goldring and Landolt, 2011). The fourth point unpicks the overarching notion of 'illegality' by drawing on the narratives of our interviewees who were keen to differentiate 'illegal' working from use of constructed documents. We consider the lasting negative effects of criminalisation for the three interviewees charged with using false documents. Overall, this chapter considers how forced labour processes interact with and are facilitated by aspects of socio-legal status.

A typology: entry into the UK and entry into forced labour

Although their backgrounds and journeys varied considerably, our participants had arrived in the UK via three distinct modes of entry – asylum seekers on entry, irregular migrants or trafficked migrants

– exposing three principal intersections of forced labour and asylum. Tables 4.1, 4.2 and 4.3 offer a brief summary of each of the 30 interviewees' journeys into the UK, and how this related to their entry into work before, during, or after claiming asylum.

Seventeen interviewees (4 female, 13 male) were *asylum seekers on entry* who lodged an initial claim soon after entering the UK by various air, sea and overland routes (see Table 4.1). They had experienced personal harassment, imprisonment, and torture, and the death or disappearance of family members in their country of origin. Some used their own passports; others, desperate to escape and with few other options available to them, paid smugglers to arrange their passage and claimed asylum once in the UK. While the UK was a chosen destination for some because other members of their family were already resident, others unexpectedly ended up in the UK when smugglers let them down. On many occasions people simply took any available opportunity to escape persecution without knowing their ultimate destination.

Table 4.1: Asylum seekers on entry

Pseudonym	Sex	Entry to UK and asylum process	Entry into work	Years in UK at time of interview	Age band
Alex	M	Enters UK after overland smuggling and immediately claims asylum. His claim and appeal are refused.	After asylum refused	4	25-30
Assanne	M	Enters UK, claims asylum; is detained and quickly refused; submits an appeal and is dispersed. His claim is refused, he appeals and later makes a fresh claim.	After asylum refused	5	25-30
Dedem	M	Enters UK after a long overland smuggling journey, claims asylum. Is dispersed but quickly leaves dispersal area. Not clear whether appeals made.	Probably during asylum claim	11	40-45
Faith	F	Enters the UK, makes a claim for asylum and stays with relatives. Detained three years later when travelling within the UK. Is later granted refugee status with five years leave to remain.	After granted leave to remain	10	30-35
Frank	M	Enters the UK, claims asylum and is refused. He appeals and goes to a judicial review which fails.	After asylum refused	7	30-35

Table 4.1: contd

Pseudonym	Sex	Entry to UK and asylum process	Entry into work	Years in UK at time of interview	Age band
Gojo	F	Enters the UK and claims asylum at the airport. She is quickly refused asylum and a year later is refused an appeal.	After asylum refused	10	30-35
Gregory	M	Arrives in the UK, probably on a tourist visa, and claims asylum a few days later. He arrived before 2003 and applies for but is refused permission to work. Is refused asylum but not informed until a year later. He appeals and is refused several years later.	After asylum refused	12	35-40
Hussein	M	Arrives by boat and claims asylum. A solicitor helps him apply for permission to work after delays in his case.	During asylum claim	2	20-25
Mehran	M	Enters the UK after a long overland journey and claims asylum on entry. After two years, granted four years' exceptional leave to remain. He then waits two years for the Home Office review his application for indefinite leave to remain, which is granted.	After granted leave to remain	13	40-45
Mohamed	M	Enters the UK after selling his home to raise smuggling fee and claims asylum which is quickly refused. He appeals and is refused.	After asylum refused	4	48-50
Muedinto	M	Enters UK and claims asylum which is granted within a few months. Unable to speak English, he finds work some months later through friends.	After granted leave to remain	5	30-35
Nanda	F	A smuggler arranges travel to the UK and tells her to claim asylum on arrival. Her claim is quickly refused with no appeal rights as her country of origin is considered 'safe'. She later submits a fresh claim and is granted Section 4 support.	After asylum refused	6	40-45

Table 4.1: contd

Pseudonym	Sex	Entry to UK and asylum process	Entry into work	Years in UK at time of interview	Age band
Parviz	M	Enters the UK, claims asylum and is refused. After an appeal and a fresh claim, is granted leave to remain.	After asylum refused	4	55-60
Pascual	M	Arrives in the UK as a minor, but is treated as an adult. He is not dispersed, and his asylum claim is refused. He later discovers a relative in the UK and moves to live with him. He is arrested for working, serves a prison sentence, is then moved to immigration detention, is served with a removal notice and is then released and is later granted indefinite leave to remain.	After asylum refused	13	30-35
Rose	F	Enters the UK, claims asylum and is detained. Her claim is refused two weeks later, she spends some months in detention, is granted an appeal and is dispersed. The appeal is later refused. Several years later she makes a fresh claim and is granted indefinite leave to remain.	After asylum refused	9	30-35
Sergei	M	Enters the UK and claims asylum. Loses support after separating from his wife. Eight years later he is granted indefinite leave to remain after engaging a solicitor and making representations to his MP.	After asylum refused	12	35-40
Siamak	M	Enters the UK, claims asylum and is refused. He appeals and is refused within six months. Three years later he makes a fresh claim and is granted leave to remain.	After asylum refused	5	45-50

Seven interviewees (three female, four male) were *irregular migrants*, sometimes referred to as undocumented or 'illegal' migrants, who entered or remained without legal permission from the state (Valentine, 2010) (see Table 4.2). Lacking any rights to legal residence, work or welfare, these irregular migrants claimed asylum at varying points to attempt to regularise their status and due to fear of persecution if returned to their country of origin. With one exception, the people in this group entered 'legally' on various valid visitor/spouse/student or work visas and subsequently became undocumented and irregular as their visa expired and they 'overstayed' for various reasons. The seventh entered with false papers and remained undocumented for several years.

Table 4.2: Irregular migrants

Pseudonym	Sex	Entry to UK and asylum process	Entry into work	Years in UK at time of interview	Age band
Ada	F	Enters UK on a visitor visa. Overstays and claims asylum. She is initially refused but later granted a short period of leave to remain.	During asylum claim	7	45-50
Angel	F	Enters UK on a student visa but becomes irregular after college is removed from Home Office approved list. She claims asylum after several years and is initially refused.	Before asylum claim	5	30-35
Doreen	F	Enters UK on a spouse visa to live with husband but relationship ends. She enters into a new relationship, which becomes abusive and makes a claim for asylum after escaping. Her claim is initially refused.	Before claiming asylum	4	25-30
Jay	M	Enters UK on a six-month visitor visa, stays a few days with a friend who then refuses to support him and is forced to find work. Claims asylum when the visa expires. Re-enters work when claim refused.	Before asylum claim, and after claim refused	10	40-45
John	M	Enters on a six-month visitor visa to visit family member. Applies for and is refused a student visa. Overstays and later claims asylum when it becomes dangerous for him to return to his country of origin.	Before asylum claim	8	30-35

Table 4.2: contd

Shahid	M	After some years in exile in other countries, enters the UK with false papers. Claims asylum five years later. This is refused; he represents himself to appeal and to judicial review. This was refused and he made a fresh claim.	Before asylum claim, and after refused	11	45-50
Tino	M	Enters the UK on a student visa, completes two higher education courses and enters highly skilled employment with a work permit. The employer fails to update the Home Office and his visa become invalid. After a year he claims asylum, is refused, appeals, and is granted indefinite leave to remain.	Before and during asylum claim	10	30-35

Finally, six interviewees (five female, one male) entered the UK as *trafficked migrants*, meaning they had been brought to the UK by means of threat or deception specifically for the purpose of sexual, criminal or forced labour exploitation, as defined by Article 3 of the UN Trafficking Protocol 3 (UN General Assembly) (see Table 4.3). Four female interviewees were trapped in forced labour situations prior to entering the UK. Two had been in domestic servitude in an Arab country and arrived in the UK with the families they were working for. They had both been encouraged to migrate for work as minors by family members to protect them from ethnic persecution and poverty resulting from the loss of one or both parents. The other two female trafficked migrants in our study were deceptively relocated by unscrupulous agents or extended family members, specifically for forced labour in the UK. They had also experienced either labour or sexual exploitation before entering the UK in their countries of origin, and their hope of escaping these experiences and the poverty of their families was instrumental in their acceptance of offers of education in Europe, which later proved to be bogus as they were coerced into domestic servitude. All females claimed asylum weeks to years after escaping sustained periods of work in domestic settings including domestic work, care and sexual exploitation. The single male was trafficked 'through' the asylum system and subsequently forced into criminal activity. It is significant that five of this group were under the age of 18 on entry to the UK, and it is clear that 'points of vulnerability' prior to arrival in the UK were significant in shaping risky migration strategies often linked to trafficking of children (Hynes, 2011). Poverty is recognised as a significant background factor heightening risk of forced labour in Europe (Andrees, 2008).

Table 4.3: Trafficked migrants

Pseudonym	Sex	Entry to UK and asylum process	Entry into work	Years in UK at time of interview	Age band
Abigail	F	Enters UK in domestic servitude with family she works for in an Arab country. After several weeks she escapes. Her asylum claim is refused but she is granted leave to remain on appeal.	Before claiming asylum	7	20-25
Gallant	M	As a minor is approached by a man who persuades him to go to Europe. After a long overland journey he is told to claim asylum on arrival in the UK. He is detained and age assessed, then released to stay with the man and granted discretionary leave. Later the man takes him away to engage in criminal activities. He returns to the UK and applies for leave to remain after turning 18, refused, and later granted after a fresh claim.	During asylum claim	9	20-25
Happy	F	Travels to the UK with a woman who knows she wants to escape sexual abuse at home and offers her an education. The woman takes her directly from the airport to her house. After one-and-a-half years she escapes, and after several years makes a claim for asylum when escaping from violent domestic abuse.	Before asylum claim	8	25-30
Ivy	F	As a child, she goes to work in a relative's house. Escapes after two years, then, still a minor, is taken by an uncle on a promise of education to the UK. After three years she starts attending college. After nine years working in the house she escapes and makes a claim for asylum, which is refused and she appeals.	Before asylum claim	10	25-30

Table 4.3: contd

Pseudonym	Sex	Entry to UK and asylum process	Entry into work	Years in UK at time of interview	Age band
Lydia	F	Enters the UK through travel arranged by a relative to escape persecution. The relative takes her directly from the airport to his house, and within a few weeks they arrange for her to work. She escapes after some years, and is supported to claim asylum.	Before asylum claim	10	32-35
Ma'aza	F	A relative arranges for her to work in an Arab country as a minor. After nearly two years the family bring her to the UK. She escapes and stays with a woman she meets for one night before claiming asylum.	Before asylum claim	3	23-25

As this chapter argues, these three modes of entry were important in influencing individuals' entry into forced or severely exploitative labour in England as well as constructing barriers to leaving. For the majority of asylum seekers on entry and irregular migrants, their experiences of forced or severely exploitative labour came after their immigration status changed – whether because their asylum claim was refused or their visas expired – and they became destitute. An important factor that differentiates *trafficked* interviewees from those we identified as *asylum seekers on entry* or *irregular migrants* is first, that the coercive relationship began before entry to the UK, and second, their lack of choice or control in relation to entering the UK.

The typology highlights how, for 'asylum seekers on entry', the asylum system can be seen as contributing to their entry into exploitative work, while for irregular and trafficked migrants it offered (at least initially) a possible way out of forced labour. However, as we return to in discussions in Chapter 5, the asylum system can only be seen as offering temporary respite as the problems of destitution and risk of return to exploitation are never far away.

Role of socio-legal status in forced labour processes

In order to better understand the role of socio-legal status in shaping migrant susceptibility to labour exploitation, the second part of this chapter discusses four salient processes: the destitution of refused asylum seekers and irregular migrants; the instrumental use of socio-legal status as a tool of coercion; the ongoing precarity of those receiving leave to remain; and 'illegality' and criminalisation of working.

Unfree recruitment: destitution facilitating entry into forced labour

For the group who applied for asylum at or soon after entry (asylum seekers on entry), destitution resulting from the removal of housing and cash support on refusal of their asylum claim was the principal driver pushing them to seek cash through paid work. These interviewees became enmeshed in forced labour processes produced by the lack of any real and acceptable alternative but to accept exploitative labour due to not having the right to work or welfare, and fearing return to persecution. Their compromised socio-legal status therefore closed down space for negotiation of conditions, and is central to understanding how unfree recruitment into forced labour operated.

Seventeen of our 30 interviewees had their asylum claim refused at least once during the asylum process, and 16 interviewees were refused asylum seekers at the time of interview. As refused asylum seekers, they lacked any substantive rights to residence, work or welfare. Some had periods receiving limited Section 4 support offered under limited circumstances to those unable to travel or complying with arrangements for voluntary return (see Table 2.1, Chapter 2). The voluntary return or enforced removal of refused asylum seekers has long been a cornerstone of UK immigration policy. However, there is a significant 'deportation gap' (Sigona and Hughes, 2012) between those eligible for deportation and numbers actually removed. The official government position is that people refused asylum should leave of their own accord (IAC, 2008). Many refused asylum seekers continue to be monitored through requirements to report to a local immigration or police office. Others stop reporting and live outside the system rather than face the menace of returning to their country of origin. Additionally, the Home Office is unable to return certain refused asylum seekers to their country of origin if foreign governments refuse to provide appropriate travel papers or cooperate with removals (McIntyre and Mogire, 2012). The destitution that refusal triggers has been well documented and remains an ongoing issue that successive UK governments have failed to address (Dwyer and Brown, 2005, 2008; Amnesty International UK, 2006; Lewis, 2007, 2009; British Red Cross, 2010; Bowpitt et al, 2012). A **case resolution** exercise 'concluded' 500,500 cases reviewed in a legacy cohort of asylum applications made before 2007, making 172,000 grants (36 per cent) and 37,500 (8 per cent) removals (Vine, 2012). However, of 268,000 identified as 'Other' (duplicates, errors),

98,000 cases were assigned to a 'controlled archive', meaning these individuals were untraceable and may or may not still be in the UK. It is not possible to make an accurate estimation of the numbers of asylum seekers refused and not removed since 2007, but the overall population of refused asylum seekers in the UK is likely to have dropped from an estimated 450,000 or more in 2007 to somewhere between 50,000 and 150,000 at the end of 2013.

The removal of support and the sudden lack of means to meet basic needs – particularly of food and shelter – presents individuals with highly constrained, stark choices in order to survive. Pascual describes the panic of having support removed, and Frank illustrates the common difficulties of those needing to negotiate a safe place to sleep:

"'We are going to make an arrangement for your deportation....' The stress actually was rising and because they mentioned the letter, you leave the house, from this time I say, oh my god, where am I going? And then the morning that day I didn't have no friend, I went to the train station, I sleep there, I found some homeless people.... It was November, very, very cold and it's snowing and I didn't have no blanket at all. I wanted to commit suicide, yes, I wanted to kill myself because I didn't know what to do. What to do. To return back, I think, war is the worst, it will kill me anyway, even be tortured badly. Better to drink something to die." (Pascual)

"There is a shed [location] where if it rains, you cannot get wet, so I just cornered myself down there.... I had my bag with me, all just pulling it around, just going, until this friend of mine.... Later on he got destitute as well, but he was lucky, he got a place at [homeless hostel] one room.... I told him I'm still struggling to get a place to stay. But he told me, no worries, you can come and stay with me in this little room, but make sure you come late. And make sure you leave early.... I'm coming, around midnight you know just squeeze myself in. 4 or 5-o-clock am I have to move out. Imagine in the cold weather outside at that time.... It went on and on, it was really, really, really harsh." (Frank)

The fear and desperation that refused status and subsequent destitution triggers are clear. Caught 'between a rock and a hard place' (see McIntyre and Mogire, 2012), evidence from our study clearly shows that lacking rights and entitlements to work or welfare makes it necessary for some refused asylum seekers to enter work in order to meet their basic needs, as Sergei, who lost support following a relationship breakdown, and Frank, describe:

> "We just receive the asylum support and we just manage. But when we separated I had to survive so…. NASS very quickly stopped every support….A couple of friends helped me to take a job." (Sergei)

> "I became destitute, no roof over my head, no income to support me, nothing…. I'm just like someone who is thrown into a desert. So at that moment, I felt the pinch and I started thinking, what can I do next?...You know, of trying to get something to do." (Frank)

Interviewees in this position were very clear that their socio–legal status created a requirement for them to work without authorisation, and thus enter the labour market in the weakest position, with no power to negotiate exploitative terms of employment. Parviz expresses this 'choice' powerfully:

> "It was after that [refusal] that I felt myself very desperate to survive…. I had to work to stay alive – to live – and I didn't have an alternative choice….When they were telling me – that I didn't have work permission – I said yes, I didn't have work permission. But I had right to live. Therefore anybody with no work permission, should they die?" (Parviz)

Gallant also expressed his absolute lack of options as a refused asylum seeker after escaping exploitation:

> "I was working in a takeaway for £15 a night…. I was refused asylum seeker. I didn't have no benefit nothing at all, so I had to do it." (Gallant)

Gregory felt he was left in an impossible limbo as someone who had become stateless, was refused asylum and with no welfare support, left with no option for survival but to engage in 'illegal' work:

> "Few times my support was stopped I decide to try and find some illegal work you know….Yes is this time, because is

very hard time for me and was stressful situation because, I living in limbo because my country not accept me back.... Home Office not decide give me anything."

Interviewees typically sustained only very short-term, irregular work as refused asylum seekers, balancing exploitative and very low-paid jobs with precarious unemployment (Clement et al, 2009), transactions or charitable support to eke out a living. After being refused, Rose spent the small amount she had saved while in receipt of asylum support payments on travel to London and to pay a solicitor who pocketed her cash and did nothing. She found herself in the capital with no money, no contacts, and homeless on the streets. Desperate, she began tidying rubbish and clearing outside a pub:

"Because in Africa if you ... want to find a work, you do it and then they will pay you.... He called me in his pub.... I explained to him why I was trying to clear his garden to get a bit of money to eat.... He told me when there is anything to do, cleaning or sweeping I can come and they will give me some money. So he just gave me some money and it paid my ticket. All I wanted was to pay my ticket because I had nowhere to stay. So when he paid me that money I bought a bus ticket for the whole month.... I was just sleeping on the buses.... When the bus goes to one side then say all change please this bus stops here ... then I change and I go to another side and then I go back but that's how at night, I used to spend the night.... I just buy drinks, coca cola or water. And then when I wanted to wash, I used to go to [tube station] and then I washed with the water in the bottle and I bought myself a toothbrush and I would refresh myself and then I go again."

This stark choice between destitution or undertaking unauthorised paid work was a dilemma also faced by irregular migrants, such as Jay, Angel, Tino and Doreen, who overstayed or fell into irregularity due to changes in their personal circumstances that nullified their original visa. However, those refused asylum, for example, Siamak, Frank, Parviz, Alex and Gregory, initially avoided work as they feared that if caught, any illegal activity would damage their ongoing claim and any appeals against asylum refusal decisions. Seeking paid work was always a last resort for refused asylum seekers – a risk only taken when other forms of support were exhausted. If meagre savings or contributions from family members ended, or if friends moved on or could no longer have a house guest, the threat of homelessness in particular, coupled with the need for food and other basics meant finding any form of paid work became a necessity. Some took up work to avoid exhausting their highly limited support networks, and spoke of being ashamed of the burden they placed on friends. Work offered the possibility of being able to contribute towards the households of those who were informally supporting them, as Assanne explains:

> "The Home Office refused me my support, financial support and also my accommodation.... At this stage, I was staying with this friend but there were all these things that needed to be paid – food, electricity, rent, council tax, everything.... I can't stay with someone if he's got all these bills and everything he has to pay so I made a decision that I had to find work to sort of assist with these payments. So I started working."

Others, like Gojo, felt she had to undertake domestic household and childcare duties in return for board, lodging and occasional spending money supplied by a friend. Although it was difficult to find people willing to talk about these situations, perhaps because domestic chores were not seen as a 'job', transactional arrangements did emerge as part of the landscape of survival traversed by several interviewees, and were 'one of the most important social resources' available to those who were destitute (Crawley et al, 2011, p 39). Rose, after experiencing life on the streets following refusal, was similarly grateful when she was taken in by a couple she met through attending a local church:

> "Anything that needed doing in the house, housework, they had a child, sometimes to take the child to school, sometimes to do some cleaning in the house, really any housework that needed doing. I was also doing ... they were feeding me, they were housing me, so I was doing what I could ... they were just Christians helping a fellow Christian."

For destitute refused asylum seekers staying with friends, unpicking where 'exchange' ends and compulsion begins is complex and highly contextual (for a useful discussion, see Crawley et al, 2011). Although support of irregular migrants by other migrants, who themselves may be only marginally better off, can be interpreted as mutually supportive or as the pooling of resources (Cross, 2013b), there is a fine line between house guest and servant (Lewis, 2007). Transactional relationships can be more voluntary, as described by Gojo or Rose, for example, or may become servile and disempowering, as in the case of Jay, whose romantic relationship descended into an abusive, coercive care arrangement (see Chapters 3 and 5). Work performed for shelter or food described by our interviewees mostly did not involve forced labour indicators. Yet the lack of viable alternatives beyond severely exploitative work in the informal labour market on the one hand, and a reliance on charity on the other, is indicative of wider 'varieties of unfreedom' that are an important feature of inequitable labour arrangements in contemporary capitalist societies (O'Neill, 2011). In this way, the production of precarious socio-legal status, and specifically, the intentional destitution of refused asylum seekers (Joint Committee on Human Rights, 2007), makes the UK government complicit in the creation of a hyper-vulnerable workforce (see also de Genova, 2002; Khosravi, 2010; Castles, 2013). In such instances, the absence of basic citizenship rights of refused asylum seekers and irregular migrants creates and sustains a situation of destitute individuals being dependent on the non-negotiable charity of others and thus vulnerable to exploitation, even if the motives underpinning that exploitation may in the first instance be well intentioned. These dimensions of unfreedom are discussed further in Chapter 6.

Instrumental use of socio-legal status as a tool of coercion and control

The role of socio-legal status in facilitating precarious work for vulnerable migrant populations is well established (McDowell et al, 2009; McKay et al, 2009; Anderson, 2010; Dwyer et al, 2011; Fudge, 2013). We found that in situations of forced labour, the instrumental use of precarious socio-legal status by employers was a predominant tool of coercion used to discipline workers who have 'no real and acceptable alternative' to compliance. The narratives of many of our interviewees furthermore revealed how their socio-legal vulnerability was frequently invoked by employers precisely to impose worsening conditions. Linking to the ILO's recognition of processes of deteriorating working conditions in forced labour (2012a), although work conditions that from the outset crossed the line into exploitative work may have been knowingly entered into, it was frequently at the point when employers sought to impose practices that moved along the exploitation continuum towards forced labour that threats related to socio-legal status emerged. In the accounts of our interviewees, threats of denunciation to the authorities, violence, or other forms of intimidation often emerged when workers 'pushed back' (see Chapter 5) against the imposition of excessive working hours, withheld pay or various abusive working and living conditions.

Jay, who claimed asylum after his visitor's visa expired, and worked for an agency as a refused asylum seeker, here describes violence, abuse and employer impunity:

> "A big bloke who used to drive the van, if you complain, you get one slap you know.... I was scared of the immigration and the police.... Most of the time he say to me 'You are a foreigner, there is nothing you can do here.'... What will I say? If I don't work and [earn] money to pay my accommodation I'm going to end up living in the streets."

The view that employers used those who could not legally work to "their advantage" (Jay) was commonly expressed. Those we interviewed were consistently clear that the forced labour processes they were trapped in were directly related to two principle aspects of their compromised socio-legal status: the 'doctrine of illegality' that makes it impossible for those working without authorisation to exercise any employment rights (as Jay and many others were reminded, "there is nothing you can do"); and risk of deportation and broader experiences of 'deportability in everyday life' (de Genova, 2002).

All of those who worked without authorisation either assumed, or knew, that their 'illegal' status left them without the power to challenge their employers, and left them without recourse to legal remedies to secure wages they were owed or better working conditions, described here by Shahid:

> "He knows very well ... [my refused asylum seeker status]. That's why people are in a position to exploit ... this is where the fear is.... If I go to the police and say that I work for him and he do not pay me that money ... will it be helpful for me? Will I get any protection that I was not allowed to work and instead of that I work? [Laughs] No."

This sense of powerlessness disciplined workers not to challenge exploitative practices as they emerged. One of the better-paid jobs held by Dedem during 10 years in the UK as a refused asylum seeker was working as a security guard for a shop for an agreed wage of £210 a week that was routinely docked at £200:

> "I couldn't talk about my rights why you are paying me less money. I am doing the long hours. Twelve hours, seven days, 84 hours I'm working for him and I'm sweeping, mopping, brushing, I'm doing the shelves and the security.... I couldn't ask him about that £10 and I was always afraid that if I said that, 'No more job, that's it go'."

Although our interviewees who negotiated informal work were very much aware of a large population of undocumented workers, the secrecy surrounding irregularity militates against both individual negotiation in the workplace and any opportunity for broader-based solidarity:

> "Most of us, people who have been in the country illegally, you fear to disclose your illegality to even some of the people that you know because you not sure of them.... Because of immigration status. So you are like, you are hiding, you can't, can't come out and you know, fight for your rights." (John)

The instrumental use of status was not solely restricted to corrupt employers. Both Ivy and Lydia detailed how the family members who had trafficked them used the 'illegality' of their entry and continued presence in the UK (with the ever-present threat of deportation) to maintain their ongoing domestic servitude.

The omnipresent fear of disclosure among irregular migrants erodes social relationships (Sigona, 2012). Status is not for discussion, few can be trusted and the potential for supportive personal relationships or the development of wider networks of support are constrained. Although co-workers may share a common precariousness, isolation and a pressing need to protect personal security dominates lives. Both workers with and without permission to work feared dismissal from temporary precarious employment if they did not perform well, and this operated to discipline workers into working hard and not drawing attention to themselves by making mistakes or talking with other employees. However, for those engaged in unauthorised working, this generalised fear and atmosphere of obedience and silence was magnified. Working relationships required negotiation of an assumed identity so as to remain as hidden as possible. For example, Frank managed to access work using the documents of someone with French nationality, and spoke of the necessity of avoiding building relationships with fellow workers:

—

"When you are fearful, you don't perform well, you don't perform well because you don't know anytime anything can happen....You cannot build that relationship, through the fear that they will discover who you are and that they can report you. So you fear, you don't know who to relate to, because of who you are, because you know yourself I am illegal here and if I open my mouth anyhow, then I will get into trouble. If you have a French document, then you are a French citizen, and you maintain that. See, so where are you coming from, I used to say that I come from Lyon, but have I ever been in France? No, so I had to keep [to] that."

Despite those travelling to distant factories sharing long daily journeys with co-workers, silence and secrecy prevented any opportunity for sharing experiences, as Pascual described: "We just kept quiet … nobody mind people's business, everyone quiet for a long time." Immigration status was considered an almost taboo topic at work, as Gojo found in a cleaning job:

"One lady, I've only realised now when I saw her on Facebook, that's how I realised that well – she didn't have a status that time. Yeah but now she's got it. But when we worked together we never got to a point of discussing such things 'cos it was like a sensitive issue that you couldn't."

This tangible sense of powerlessness attached to irregularity means that knowledge about status is a carefully guarded currency. Indeed, this is reinforced when we consider how the secrecy among workers contrasted with the overt use of knowledge of insecure status as a form of power used by employers. Many interviewees described situations in which their employers deliberately took on migrant workers 'without papers' so they could exploit their labour and pay well below the minimum wage in the knowledge that these workers would never report them or seek redress, as the 'doctrine of illegality' denies recourse to securing employment rights. Mohamed was keenly aware of his differentiation in the workplace, and said he was usually referred to by the name "illegal" (in his language).

"They said if you got papers for staying in the UK we can pay you more but if you have got no stay in the UK we cannot give you much money for insurance…. He dishwasher, I dishwasher, same, but for one paper he got

£77 or maybe £80 by tips and for me £20. I said 'please this is not humanity, I'm working £20 he's working £80'. But they said no, 'If you want – £20 – if you don't want, you can go'. They know you are no paper you cannot claim, you cannot go anywhere to claim.... More and more work. Because they know that you have got no paper that you are not allowed to, and if you are not working, you got no money you got nowhere to stay."

This was one of several experiences that point to a pattern of non-payment and excessive hours beyond the personal experiences of our interviewees. Workers seemed well aware of the systematic engagement of unauthorised workers for the worst tasks, who suffered abuse and were forced to stay long hours after other workers left. This apparently deliberate use of unauthorised workers' compromised socio–legal status to impose more extreme working conditions than would otherwise be possible provides clear evidence that precarious immigration status – being irregular, or a refused asylum seeker – was a vulnerability exploited by employers and recruiters to impose a range of coercive and abusive practices.

Yet, as pervasive as the effect of the 'doctrine of illegality' is, for forced migrants the threat of denunciation to authorities and consequent risk of return to persecution in their country of origin is a particularly powerful disciplining force in labour relations. After escaping one situation of prolonged withheld pay in informal childcare work, Tino claimed asylum but was dispersed away from his son. In order to maintain contact, he felt compelled to find cash work to pay for travel to supplement poverty-level asylum support payments (Pettitt, 2013; The Children's Society, 2013a). He again experienced wages being withheld in a glass collecting job which he left to take up what he hoped would be a better paid construction job, accessed via an intermediary he had met through the church. After not being paid for weeks, he approached the site contractor and reported the agent who had employed him. The agent subsequently lost the building contract, and threatened to denounce Tino to the authorities:

"So when he found out that.... I am the one who contact that company then he was now threatening me.... saying he's going to get me, he's going to tell the Home Office that I've been working illegally when I'm not allowed to be working."

The threat of denunciation and deportation operated in both direct and indirect ways as a disciplining device in exploitative working relations. While we did hear of several cases such as Tino's, where an explicit threat was made, as de Genova (2002, p 438) has argued, the disciplinary operation of state apparatus for the 'everyday production of migrant "illegality"' was never simply intended to achieve the putative goal of deportation, as it is 'deportability, and not deportation *per se*, that has historically rendered undocumented migrant labor a distinctly disposable commodity'. We found this assertion to be true in the narratives of those workers who did not mention an explicit threat of denunciation made by an employer, but rather alluded to lives imbued with multi-faceted fear of detection and criminalisation or deportation which served to discipline workers not to challenge severely exploitative labour relations. For a forced migrant, denunciation of 'illegal' working could damage any ongoing asylum claim, and result in return to countries where human rights abuses are commonplace. These individual fears are layered by the threats to wider family members from a loss of income or persecution. Here, we begin to see how the generalised concepts of migrant 'illegality' or 'deportability' need to be nuanced to appreciate the multi-dimensional unfreedoms experienced by forced migrants in forced labour in the UK. The generalised condition of deportability and fear of removal affects all irregular migrants, and, to some extent, other categories of temporary or employer-sponsored visa holders (Fudge, 2013). However, deportability in everyday life constitutes a qualitatively different threat in the lives of forced migrants who fear persecution if returned to their country of origin than other types of irregular migrants (as discussed by Bloch et al, 2011; Bloch, 2013).

Permission to work, refugee status and the precarity track

Discussions so far have largely focused on how the lived experiences of lack of a right to work, welfare or residence produce 'illegality' in unauthorised work, destitution and deportability, leaving refused asylum seekers and other irregular migrants with no real and acceptable alternatives to exploitative and sometimes forced labour in order to secure a livelihood. How, then, do socio-legal status and forced labour feature in the lives of those who had permission to work after gaining leave to remain? While a positive outcome to an individual's asylum claim removes any immediate fears related to residency and removal, it does not bring an immediate resolution to problems related to work and welfare.

One important negative effect of the establishment of a separate system of welfare support for asylum seekers is that positive resolution of asylum claims and any subsequent transition in socio-legal status (for example, to refugee, humanitarian protection, or discretionary leave status) can render individuals susceptible to homelessness and poverty. This is due to a number of intersecting factors including the short 28 day transition period allowed for the move from asylum support into mainstream accommodation, a general shortage of available social housing and poor coordination between the **UK Border Agency** (UKBA) and mainstream housing providers. In addition, research has shown that, at times, social security and employment support agencies are not responsive to the particular needs of refugees (Dwyer and Brown, 2008; Dwyer, 2008; Shutes, 2011). It has also long been recognised that refugees continue to experience high levels of unemployment and disadvantage in the labour market (Bloch, 2004, 2008).

Unable to work to gain skills and experience as asylum seekers, or to present 'illegal' work experience on their CVs as refugees, those who had secured leave to remain faced very limited job opportunities. Despite only working after receiving refugee status, Mehran, who had previously faced violent bullying while at work, spoke of language barriers and illness continuing to limit his work opportunities: "I had no ability to speak to somebody to help me about my job ... the depression make me very down."

Similarly, Gregory, a college graduate granted indefinite leave to remain, outlined the frustrations of being on Jobseeker's Allowance for two years. Unable to get references from previous employers and with an 11-year gap on his CV because of his protracted asylum claim, Gregory was not hopeful about his future work prospects, especially in the current economic climate. Hussein, an asylum seeker who somehow, for reasons that were not easily discernible, had managed to obtain permission to work from the Home Office while his claim was being processed, sought out many different jobs through community networks and proactively approaching numerous businesses. However, he turned his back on multiple employers who, viewing him as an 'asylum seeker' (and therefore a member of what they regarded as a highly exploitable, low-cost and disposable workforce), attempted to get him to work for little or no pay. Faith entered work only after getting refugee status, but explained how welfare-to-work policies for unemployed jobseekers discriminated against those who had secured leave to remain when they attempted to search for work:

"Most employers were refusing to take us. If you're on jobseeker's, then they ask you if you've worked and you'll say, no, you haven't. Then, they'll say you're not experienced. How am I going to get experience when the Home Office won't allow you to work because you're waiting for your status? Then, you try to convince them to take you on a work trial. They'll still refuse. The Job Centre has those work trials, but they never used to give it for us to go for work trials."

Indeed, nearly all our interviewees who had received leave to remain found it extremely hard to find decent work and were thus restricted to working in the highly casualised, insecure and low-paid, low-skilled sectors of the economy. Clearly, obtaining permission to work by being granted refugee status or other leave to remain does not protect against unscrupulous employers continuing to use migrants' vulnerabilities for exploitative purposes.

Before returning to consider gradations of 'illegality', it is also important to note that other aspects of migrants' social status and migration trajectories were important in structuring labour experiences. Wider familial expectations and responsibilities and the necessity to remit money home were important factors in explaining why asylum seekers in receipt of support payments and refugees who were not destitute and were allowed to work felt compelled to accept whatever work they could find, even if it was severely exploitative. For example, refusal of her asylum claim and a period of destitution had prompted Rose's initial entry into severely exploitative labour conditions. However, on being granted leave to remain, she remained in overtly exploitative care work (where she went nearly a year having wages routinely withheld), under pressure to continue to send remittances home and also to save the money required to arrange family reunion for her children: "Whatever I can afford for school fees. I have to send money…. Hundreds of course, I've got three children they all in secondary schools."

Similarly, Gojo, who, as subsequent discussions will show, continues to pay a heavy price for her conviction for unauthorised working, had to seek work when in receipt of Section 4 support to pay her father's medical bills and her children's school fees in her homeland:

"They put me on Section 4. I was getting £35 vouchers every week … from there, when I carried on working, I stopped working when my father died in 2007 and it was just for my daughter's fees which I was struggling to manage with. And then from there, that's when I got caught.... I didn't have an alternative."

Likewise, Ada had managed to get by on approximately £40 per week asylum support until the pressure to support the family she had left behind in her homeland triggered a need to seek work:

"I was receiving ... demands from home to send money for the upkeep of the children ... the stress was much, they need me to send money, they need me to send money. I told them I was trying my best to see what I could do."

The granting of discretionary leave to remain and the associated access to mainstream social security benefits that her change in status prompted did not resolve Ada's financial problems. Living on £67 per week Employment Support Allowance, she continued to send home money from her meagre income whenever she could.

Such pressures to remain in jobs characterised by conditions of forced labour were further intensified in some cases by the material and bureaucratic conditionality of UK family reunification rules. Besides the costs of travel, visas and legal advice for those who wanted to bring their families to visit or live permanently with them in the UK, the rules governing family reunion are onerous for those granted particular types of leave to remain. While those granted refugee status are eligible for support with the legal and travel costs of family reunion, individuals granted humanitarian protection, discretionary leave, or case resolution indefinite leave to remain, must demonstrate they have both sufficient finances through employment to sponsor joining family members and provide adequate accommodation for them. This intense pressure to save thousands of pounds led Rose, Gojo and Muedinto to remain in extremely exploitative job situations where wages were withheld and excessive overtime enforced. Muedinto's part-time cleaning job was not enough to prove he could support his family, so he took a job in a hotel kitchen and regularly worked overtime, for which he was not paid, as outlined in Chapter 3. Despite this treatment, he stayed in the job for months "in order to have some money to bring family here".

Although the insecurities of unauthorised workers are deep and multiple, as outlined above, the ongoing barriers to gaining decent work for those who do secure limited or indefinite leave to remain demonstrate that the facilitation of labour exploitation cannot be understood as a product only of irregularity. This reinforces Goldring and Landolt's (2011) findings based on research on the intersection of precarious immigration and employment status in Canada, that migrants' labour insecurity should be viewed as part of a work–citizenship matrix that includes documented status. Furthermore, it is important to emphasise that both documented and undocumented migrants are susceptible to forced labour (Scullion et al, 2014). The experiences of those interviewees who had success in securing their status supports the view that periods of precarious migrant status have a lasting and negative impact on migrants. At the time of the interview, the only four exceptions were Lydia, Abigail, Frank and Tino, who were in 'decent work' or gaining experience and education through volunteering and further or higher education courses. Lydia had engaged in numerous quality volunteering opportunities and progressed to study an undergraduate degree; Abigail was not in work (including precarious labour) but was studying and engaged in well-structured volunteering; Frank was in professional work; and Tino, who had arrived as a student, was in highly-skilled work related to his UK professional qualifications prior to claiming asylum.

Dilemma of false papers and the legacy of 'illegality'

Given discussions so far, it may be tempting to view asylum seekers and refugees as passive victims of exclusive and uncaring policy. While it is clear that policy that effectively promotes officially sanctioned destitution for some, and minimal rights for others, severely curbs people's ability to support themselves, limited individual agency remains possible even in desperate circumstances (see the discussions about resistance in Chapter 5). Faced with the treatment handed out to those who did not have permission to work, a small number of interviewees decided to acquire false papers to access employment (see also Chapter 3). The substantial expense involved and also fears that using constructed or borrowed documents could have potentially catastrophic consequences on any pending appeal or new asylum claim if an individual was discovered, meant that such decisions were never taken lightly. False papers were, therefore, only acquired as a last resort when all other avenues to accessing work had been exhausted. In many ways, current policy encourages the criminalisation of asylum seekers and refugees, and stimulates an environment in which fraudulent papers, fake identities and shared NINos are used by some in order to access paid work to survive. However, it is particularly interesting that other asylum seekers and irregular migrants actively chose to resist the pressures they faced, and refused to make use of such documents, including John:

> "I'm not a criminal, I'm only an immigration offender, yeah. They have to differentiate this.... They have to know that in Britain there are many people that are out there, there are loads of them. You see them in the streets or wherever, you think things are fine, but they are really in trouble."

Many people like Alex (who had a background in law enforcement in his country of origin) spoke of the shame at needing to work without permission and never previously engaging in unlawful activity in their former lives:

> "What kind of job can I do without the right to work? Nothing. I can pay £150 for forging the National Insurance things and I can go to work, but if somebody find me out, it's going to be trouble. I'm going to go to jail for at least six months. I'm going to go to detention centre for another six months and after they can deport me, they are going to send me out with every week sign, every week I have to have a tag, everything's going to be worse. I'm not going to go to some kind of job like this."

Although fear of the consequences of being discovered using constructed documents was part of their decision to avoid obtaining false papers, those who resisted assuming false identities differentiated between the necessity to undertake clandestine work in the shadows and actively using a fraudulent identity. Shahid described how he viewed a gradation of 'illegality':

> "Being involved in illegal activities that are with documentation, I don't like them. And it also involves a lot of risk as well. For example, if I'm caught working illegally then I'm not supported by Home Office. It's a natural thing that I cannot sleep in the street, I cannot starve, so just to survive I had opted to work, I could justify in a sense. But if I make illegal document, that's a serious crime to me. I don't want to."

Gregory's story provides insight into the kinds of dilemmas individuals had to resolve when deciding whether or not to obtain false papers.

From the outset of his asylum claim, Gregory found reliance on asylum support problematic. He did not get on well with the people he was housed with, feeling he had nothing in common with them. He was also frustrated with having to get by on minimal support, and wanted to be able to work in order to support himself and send money back home to support his disabled mother. However, he had no desire to jeopardise his claim by working, and initially reluctantly accepted his situation. As time went by, becoming increasingly exasperated, he applied for and was repeatedly refused permission to work. After "living in limbo" for seven years, reliant on intermittent Section 4 support, he had had enough. Believing his only options were to steal, work or starve, he was adamant he would not steal as it was morally wrong, nor was he was prepared to starve; he therefore had to work without valid papers, a decision he justified as fair because it was the only remaining viable alternative. Nonetheless, he made a further distinction between working with another person's documents and obtaining false documentation: "I know the work I doing is not legal, because I work … pretending to be another person.… But is only work purposes, not a documental purposes." Eventually he started to do agency work via contacts who were working as informal gangmasters and registering themselves with various agencies, but then sending people like Gregory who did not have permission to work to do shifts in their place for 50 per cent of the available pay. This was possible because the agencies were not cross-checking the individuals who turned up against the documentation they held. Although at the beck and call of his contacts, who would call at short notice and expect him to acquiesce to their demands, this was preferential to Gregory who was adamant he would not be drawn into *obtaining* fake papers for himself.

Some other interviewees 'compelled by necessity' (O'Neill, 2011) took the decision to act differently, sometimes with dire consequences. Dedem describes how acquiring false papers provided only tenuous security:

> "I always wanted to work like legally … like put your head up and say I'm working, I'm a hardworking man, so I need to work. But when you are working – like illegally with illegal paper, you know your back is not safe, you still feeling down, you still have no rights."

Pascual, who spent almost a decade as a refused asylum seeker, was convicted for working using false papers and given a six-month prison sentence. Both Gojo and Dedem were also subject to criminal convictions for using false documents. Their subsequent criminalisation, which came about because they were unable to legally work due to their status, had long-term negative impacts on their immigration and employment security. Gojo's unspent criminal conviction was a barrier to finding any work, even after securing leave to remain:

> "That's when I got caught. That's when they arrested me and then they did a thorough investigation … then I have been to court [place] with this case and then which is a mark that was left in my life as well even though now I've got my status…. I've applied to [lists five mainstream employers] but they wouldn't take me…. I worked illegally before I got my status and now I've got my status and it shows … it's because I've used the false identity to gain the job…. That's what they've said. So this act and the word that they put that fraud, it's something that just says, well we can't take her."

Unspent convictions related to 'illegal' working continued to blight Pascual and Gojo's future as asylum seekers criminalised for immigration offences but who subsequently acquired rights to residence and work. The legacy of highly coercive 'illegal' working arrangements previously entered into out of necessity may continue long after refugee status has been secured (Refugee Action, 2006; Goldring and Landolt, 2011).

Conclusion

The stratified system of socio-legal status that defines and limits the differential entitlements to residence, work and welfare that are variously available to different migrants enmeshed within the UK asylum system renders many vulnerable to highly exploitative working arrangements and/or forced labour. We began the study interested in considering the experiences of three principal migrant groups defined by immigration status: asylum seekers, refused asylum seekers and refugees. By considering the intersection of asylum and forced labour, it quickly became apparent that a different set of three immigration categories were significant, presented in our typology of *asylum seekers on entry, irregular migrants* and *trafficked migrants*. The three charts (Tables 4.1, 4.2 and 4.3) presented in the first part of the chapter show how entry into the UK and subsequent socio-legal status interact with forced labour processes. Those who entered as asylum seekers in our study typically entered exploitative employment after their asylum case was refused because of the destitution they faced without access to welfare or housing. Those who were irregular migrants or trafficked were in forced labour before claiming asylum, and the asylum system offered some respite from the necessity of engaging in exploitative work.

The destitution produced by lacking substantive rights to work and welfare means refused asylum seekers and other irregular migrants are routinely 'compelled by necessity' (O'Neill, 2011) to undertake unauthorised work in order to survive. As Shelley (2007, pp 145-6) notes, 'with opportunities for legal employment closed down and welfare limited to pitiful amounts, little wonder some asylum seekers start unauthorised working.' Accepting even the most exploitative kind of work becomes a non-negotiable need in the face of policies that officially sanction enforced destitution for those who remain in the UK.

Beneath the overall finding of the importance of socio-legal status in structuring labour market entry and experiences in the UK lies a dynamic interaction between restrictive migration regimes and globalised labour market transformations that can produce forced labour. Such liminal workspaces serve to both protect exploiters and evade encounters with immigration or labour regulators. These experiences often remain hidden because of the taboo status that 'work' has in and around the refugee sector due to the government's outlawing of asylum seekers' rights to work. Absence of the three central elements of socio-legal status – rights to work, welfare and residence – shapes the lives of those with constrained status through processes of 'illegality', destitution and deportability in everyday life. However, the overarching concepts of 'illegality' and deportability require nuancing, to appreciate the differences between working without permission and use of false documents, and to recognise the particular risks to refugees facing return to persecution.

We have further considered how a positive outcome to an asylum claim does not immediately resolve ongoing issues of work and welfare, especially in cases where individuals are trying to meet their wider responsibilities and support family members in their countries of origin by sending remittances home or meet the costs associated with family reunion. In such circumstances, serious exploitation by unscrupulous employers and forced labour remain real possibilities (Katungi et al, 2006), even for those who have secured leave to remain and the right to work. Additionally, the legacy of constrained socio-legal status and the criminalisation of those asylum seekers and refugees prosecuted for 'illegal' working continues to blight the lives of many even when rights to residence, work and welfare are ultimately acquired. As Goldring and Landolt (2011, pp 337-8) state, 'intersections of legal status and work establish pathways or tracks that are difficult to jump over or move out of. A shift to more secure legal status may not necessarily be accompanied by a reduction in job precarity'. Socio-legal status provides unscrupulous employers with extra means to threaten and coerce a workforce with a limited or non-existent understanding of acceptable working practices in the UK. Current immigration policy, in restricting access to basic rights to residence, work and welfare at various stages of the asylum process, helps to create the conditions in which severe exploitation in the workforce and forced labour are able and likely to flourish among asylum seekers and refugees. We now proceed to contemplate the different ways in which asylum seekers and refugees in our study struggled to resist and exit their situations.

5

The struggle to exit exploitation

Introduction

Discussions thus far have largely concentrated on *structural* aspects of unfreedom – the practices of coercion, menace of penalty and the abuse of vulnerability related to socio-legal status underpinning entry into and continuation in forced and severely exploitative labour situations for our interviewees. As noted in Chapters 3 and 4, working conditions were difficult and sometimes dangerous, and the preclusion of exit, or the constant threat of dismissal, were routine forms of coercion used to discipline workers to accept exploitative working conditions in almost all of the working situations encountered. Although the closing down of space for negotiation of work conditions was common to all of these situations, in this chapter we turn our attention to the ways that workers *actively resisted* poor treatment within unfree labouring environments, and as such, workers' *agency* is this chapter's central focus.

The previous two chapters detailed structural factors that shape forced migrants' vulnerabilities to various work unfreedoms. The first part of this chapter begins by augmenting these understandings through a presentation of a more psycho-social and agentic picture of forced migrants' lives – that of the 'migrant project', an important framework to appreciate when considering the possibilities and politics of resistance covered in subsequent discussions. It then moves on to consider how resistance has been conceptualised in ways useful to our analysis of resistance within unfreedom. The second part offers an empirically grounded analysis of how workers negotiated, resisted and rejected their exploitation within unfree labour situations, including examples of nascent solidarity in hidden spaces that allowed for usually informal and often fleeting forms of effective organising. In the third part we move on to explore how workers exited from forced/unfree labour situations, drawing a tripartite distinction between those who 'ran away' or escaped from confined-coerced forced labour, workers who 'walked away' or changed jobs, and those who were 'pushed away' through the job ending or dismissal from insecure work. The final section explores the idea of a continuum of unfreedom and its resonance for discussions of hyper-precarity that follows in Chapter 6.

The 'migrant project'

The treatment of labour situations as isolated in ILO approaches and scholarly work it influences routinely fails to account for why migrants may knowingly enter or remain in unfree or forced labour. However, if we place the agency of migrants centrally, it becomes clear that continuation in and resistance to particular unfree labour situations can only be understood as part of wider migration trajectories and long-term transnational social relationships (Bastia and McGrath, 2011; Mai, 2011; O'Connell Davidson, 2013). Drawing on Bolivian migrants' experiences of garment work in Argentina, Bastia and McGrath (2011) usefully draw attention to the need to consider temporality in the migrant project – movement across time, not just space – in understanding engagement in unfree labour as a means to achieve a better future. Similarly in our research, despite knowing they were being exploited, in many cases workers are weighing up much longer, lifelong goals and ambitions. Many of these goals have emerged already in the book so far. We have heard how Lydia stayed in her live-in care job without pay, believing her cousin was retaining her wages for her education. Gojo, Rose and Muedinto remained in jobs where wages were withheld due to their anxiety to keep a job to save money to cover the costs of family reunion. This is why the analytical lens of the 'migrant project' is required to frame discussions of resistance in this chapter.

The idea of 'better futures' must also be understood as linked to migrants' transnational social position, and may not be limited to an individual migrant. Many migrants have compelling reasons to gain work in order to remit back to family members at home, perhaps to pay life-sustaining costs such as medical expenses, or to save up money for costly family reunification. The need to save up money may also be linked to debts that are often incurred in the course of migrating, and are tangible reasons for entering into or remaining in certain types of work. As O'Connell Davidson (2013, p 8) remarks, 'if quitting means being forced to return to the country of origin, the right to quit is meaningless to those who have heavily indebted themselves in order to migrate'. What is particularly vital in understanding the notion of 'exit' from a specific 'forced labour' situation is recognition that workers' perceptions of their own obligations (O'Neill, 2011) to support families or honour debts are 'powerful disciplining mechanisms which can very effectively be harnessed to the cause of exploitation' (Phillips, 2013b, p 8). We revisit this idea in the final section of this chapter.

Conceptualising resistance

Before proceeding to a discussion of the research material, it is important to consider briefly the challenge of recognising workers' agency in resistance to, and negotiation of, severely exploitative labour situations given the emphasis on involuntariness in the conceptualisation of 'forced' labour. How, then, can the idea of resistance sit with a forced labour definition dependent on coercion? Much of the discussion around trafficking and forced labour, both in policy and practice circles and in some academic literature, tends to assume exploitation or coercion as oppositional to 'free' labour or consent. As O'Connell Davidson (2013) discusses, fixing free/slave and forced/voluntary as dualisms has limited value for understanding how and why migrants undertake journeys that may leave them under obligation to debtors requiring them to accept, or leaving them unable to retract from, severely exploitative labour conditions. Indeed, in pursuing viable livelihood strategies, workers may accept exploitative working conditions, and can indeed 'consent' to 'forced' labour, albeit in situations of severely constrained 'choice'. Hence, despite highly constrained circumstances, we can detect resistance not only in exiting from unfree labour but also *within* the unfree labour situations described in this book. We need, then, a more nuanced conceptualisation of resistance as meaning more than 'exit' alone.

Resistance has become a much studied and oft-referred-to concept, and is a notion that encompasses a huge range of modes, scales and targets. However, this breadth results in a definitional ambiguity, as Weitz (2001, p 669) remarks, leading 'some scholars to see it almost everywhere and others almost nowhere'. Resistance, particularly in political science and sociology, has traditionally been seen as something visible, sizeable (such as large-scale protest movements), and arguably out of the reach of 'ordinary' peasant, working-class or proletarian individuals. Yet identifying everyday, prosaic and banal resistance has become commonplace following Scott's (1985) challenge to these early conceptualisations. Scott's assertion that resistance can also be far more subtle and 'everyday' was taken up in attention to 'foot dragging' and other so-called 'ordinary' weapons of relatively powerless groups (see, for example, Willis, 1977; Comaroff, 1985; Ong, 1987). However, more recent work suggests that these perspectives run the risk of romanticising and glorifying resistance. Katz is one such writer who is concerned about the voyeuristic practice of seeing every 'autonomous act to be an instance of resistance' (2004, p 241). She urges caution regarding the slippage between agentic acts and those more transformative types that really *are* capable of changing social relations, for example, of oppression and exploitation. In a similar vein, and particularly focusing on labour geographies, Mitchell argues that there is an emerging tendency to over-valorise the ability of workers to alter damaging contexts, and it might be necessary, on occasions, to 'understand those moments when workers are *all but powerless*' due to surrounding structural violence (2011, p 563; emphasis added).

Cataloguing approaches to resistance, Hollander and Einwohner (2004) illustrate the complex nature of resistance, and emphasise that, even while resisting power, individuals or groups may simultaneously support structures of domination. Such an ambiguity leads Katz (2004) to differentiate three forms of resistance: *resilience*, *reworking* and *resistance*. This differentiation is useful for unpicking the variety of acts of rejection of exploitative work, and for critiquing the extent to which an individual's exit from forced labour might be considered to necessarily resist or undermine dominating power. She suggests that the primary effect of *resilience* is recuperation, survival, and recovering or asserting dignity. Hence workers' acts to cope and continue in severely exploitative labour as a form of livelihood, survival, or to access limited funds to meet remittance obligations can be cast as resilience. Furthermore, forms of exit that involve 'walking away' may offer some relief for the worker, but are unlikely to improve the terms of the job or workplace if the employer knows they can find another, more compliant, employee. Thus, as Katz identifies, acts of resilience may have contradictory outcomes: they may sustain individuals but ultimately support the trajectory of damaging powerful processes.

For Katz, *reworking*, however, involves attempts to alter the conditions of existence to enable more 'viable terrains of practice' (2004, p 247). The negotiations within unfree labour outlined in the second section of this chapter encroach on the space of dominating power where they transform unequal power relations through recouping unpaid wages or attempts to alter conditions. Katz therefore reserves the term *resistance* to describe acts that subvert or disrupt conditions of exploitation and oppression. Importantly for thinking about how we might respond to tackling forced labour among refugees and asylum seekers, Katz suggests that organised opposition movements can create the political space or opportunity for various autonomous initiatives – acts of resilience – that can restore or strengthen acts of resistance. We now move on to empirically explore the emergence of various such acts in our research.

Pushing back: negotiation, resilience and rejecting exploitation

This section focuses on how workers managed and coped in their attempts to alter worsening conditions by 'reworking' (Katz, 2004) exploitative labour situations through negotiating pay, hours or tasks (see below, regarding 'exit'). For those working without authorisation, the sense of powerlessness surrounding 'illegality' and fear of detection routinely operated to discourage workers from pursuing negotiation or redress. There were nevertheless signs of nascent solidarity among workers in some of the labour situations our interviewees experienced, discussed at the end of this section.

The struggle to demand pay was constant for those workers who were routinely underpaid or who had their wages withheld. Workers were continually weighing up their situation and balancing the prospect of pay and the need for cash to survive against leaving and facing a possibly worse situation of worklessness and homelessness. With little by way of political or legal capital, and for those seeking to evade violent confrontation, workers employed under non- or semi-compliant documents resorted to diplomacy, engaging emotional and moral arguments in an attempt to persuade errant employers, agents or 'exploiters' to honour agreed payments. Tino, Gojo and Rose, for example, each revealed their caring responsibilities for children to their employers in an attempt to apply moral pressure to get access to their wages, but this information was turned back on them as a tool of coercion as employers realised their desperation. Delicate negotiations undertaken by workers in casual or bit-job arrangements grappled with the pressure to please employers in a bid to secure ongoing work. John describes how the £90 he was eventually paid for two weeks' cleaning work came as a result of repeated, gentle persuasion to elicit hoped-for empathy:

> "The way I was asking, I didn't say [shouts] 'where is my money?'.... The way to ask her, you know, I'm using transport to come to work, so I'll be late that day.... OK I could walk, but I was doing this in a gentle way, so that maybe she could feel for me."

Others, seeing violence as the only effective remedy, preferred to avoid confrontations that carried a risk of injury or possibly criminal charges. Hussein left a building job and was reluctant to pursue withheld pay:

"I said to him 'give me the rest of the money', he said 'no', I said 'that's it, I'm walking, I'm not coming tomorrow'.... I get stressed. If I call him he'll start talking with me, I'm going to do something to him ... so better I don't need his money, just stay away from me."

Workers also told us about their attempts to negotiate and improve unsafe or deteriorating working conditions. Mohamed, dishwashing in a restaurant kitchen, saw other workers finishing at 12 after an eight-hour shift, but for him "time not finish" as he was only allowed to go when certain tasks, not his agreed shift, were finished. His complaint and attempt to negotiate was immediately met with threat of dismissal. For Mehran working in a food production factory, simply asking for a break from heavy lifting work led to a threat of dismissal:

"I was working one day in the factory, they always put me on somewhere where you have to lift a very, very big trays and working very hard and putting them in the machine. For example, one hour, two hours, three hours, and all of my body is sweating and sweating and then, I have to ask him, please change me for half an hour and he said 'no, if you want to work can you continue, if you don't ... you are not coming again to work'."

We can see how many of these attempts did not succeed in 'reworking' oppression in Katz's terms as workers' negotiations were frequently ignored or deflected by employers through use of threats. Some of these acts are therefore perhaps more akin to Katz's (2004) notions of resilience as 'getting by'. There were, however, a few examples that would perhaps meet Katz's definition of resistance as disrupting conditions of exploitation. As mentioned in Chapter 4, Tino was not paid wages by a man he'd met at church who arranged construction work for him. He went directly to the agency and learned that they were paying the intermediary for his labour. Following a discussion with others at the church, he found out that his case was not isolated, cementing his decision to leave:

"He was employing people from the church. Some people were from the church who didn't have papers, some to do cleaning and everything. So he was not paying, so later on people discovered, I discovered I was not the only one who was not getting paid."

His complaint to the agency led to the intermediary having his subcontract removed, and the sharing of information at church led the whole group to stop working for the intermediary. Dedem was successful in recouping wages, not for himself but for a friend, through direct and collective confrontation with an unscrupulous employer, hinting at the development of solidarity and mutual aid with others:

> "So, five months the guy came from [country name] and working for him, he has no money at all. So, I had to put a knife under his ear, I said 'I'm going to cut your ear'. So this kind of things … then on Saturday we had a meeting, so about, we had five cars and all the people they come with baton … like baseballs and cricket bats and you know."

This demonstration of might secured the worker's wages without resorting to violence.

Organising: nascent solidarity in hidden spaces

Spaces for sharing knowledge or information with other workers were highly constrained across the labour situations of our interviewees. Hence, any spaces for solidarity or snippets of time for talking and sharing among workers were tiny and hidden. Despite these challenges there were some small windows of informal connections that contributed to challenging exploitation through momentary solidarity and sharing of information and knowledge.

The workplaces encountered by our interviewees were characterised by a lack of trade union presence. This was particularly the case for those working within private domestic spaces where organising is notoriously difficult, and which have arguably been neglected by unions (Lutz, 2010). However, the labour spaces of those working in formal jobs (with their own or others' papers) at least provided the prospect of organising through trade union activity. Only one interviewee – Faith – had been actively involved in trying to organise workers to join a union, but this was discouraged in her residential care workplace. Faith, who had leave to remain and was working under a contract, challenged unsafe conditions in her work as a carer in a residential home by withdrawing her labour:

> "I used to stand and fold my hands and say I don't want to be involved because, at the end of the day, by lifting a

person who's not supposed to be lifted, you are not only hurting yourself, but then think of the person."

She described how snatches of time between shift changeovers could be used to share information on conditions and issues in the workplace:

"We just used to sit and chat before it's changeover time. That was when we were talking. Then, when the other staff are doing sleepovers, they'll come and say, 'you're so courageous. We can hear you speak out in the meetings, so why can't we do something?' Then, all those people who tried to get together and do something, they ended up leaving, so nothing really came up anyway because people were like, it's better for me to leave than for me to be treated like this."

However, a colleague who brought in union leaflets, was forced to resign:

"There's a lady who ... brought those pamphlets and then she was encouraging people to join GMB [union] so that they could stand up for us in that workplace.... Someone grassed her and then she was called to the office, so she resigned on her own because they said it's either she leaves or [they sack her]."

Faith herself soon left that job believing that the management might make a spurious accusation of harm to a client to silence her, and that if this happened, it would damage her ability to work with vulnerable adults, shutting off future employment in care work. This shows the considerable challenges of organising in the exploitative workplace where union membership may be actively discouraged – workers motivated to organise may simply reject exploitative work and move on. In such circumstances workers push back or 'rework' exploitative labour relations, but their leaving may not challenge oppressive power as the employer is likely to continue their maltreatment of other workers.

For other workers in the formal sector, awareness of trade unions was peripheral at best. Despite having refugee status, Mehran had only managed to find work in food manufacturing through agencies. He was aware of a union presence, but associated this with permanent workers, and found his low level of English a barrier to engaging with other workers:

"I think the people that was working permanently there was a union, they have cards and every month they have a meeting. But, personally myself, just thinking if you not able to speak English, and understand what the people says, it's really, really — you have a lot of difficulty."

Despite these challenges, Mehran repeatedly confronted the agency about both conditions and level of pay, but saw that those who complained had their days and hours reduced, and was himself moved to working in a 'high-risk' area — in the refrigerated area — after complaining. Nonetheless, brief snatches of connection to other workers allowed him to assist those who spoke no English: "yeah on the line, or ... when they have some problem they gathering and speaking about the work and the agency, then we speak to each other." Gregory similarly spoke with other workers about conditions: "yeah, I talk to people, I find out how much they pay them. They actually pay minimum wage." However, he did not hear about unions in the factories he was working in, and did not seek out such information because he accessed work using others' papers and was told by them to remain hidden.

Language and cultural differences were highlighted as barriers to connecting with other workers. Muedinto worked only after gaining refugee status. Following some part-time and short-term cleaning jobs he secured full-time formal work in a hotel where he shared a language with his manager and some other senior staff, but the other workers were from different countries. The language barrier meant hours worked were not discussed, and he felt there was an unequal power relationship between casual and permanent staff: "it was difficult because they were working with permanent job they have an advantage over me." The issue of language barriers points to how possibilities for resistance and organising are very uneven for those who may come from countries without large populations in the UK (or their particular workplace). Despite sharing long journeys to and from factory workplaces with other workers, Pascual, working as a refused asylum seeker, found the language barrier stood in the way of workers sharing knowledge and information:

"Well, the Kurdish people they can speak.... Some Somalians as well they can communicate ... and they can pray because they pray they are all Muslims. Some of the people they can speak each other. But we, who we can speak with?"

However, this prompted him to learn a new language from a couple who befriended him:

> "I found that two friends I show you [in a photograph] and his wife French speaking.… I start learning to speak French, then I'm good speaking French because of them."

This shows how cosmopolitan competency can bridge cultural and linguistic boundaries within bottom-end labouring spaces (cf Herbert et al, 2006).

Irregular, insecure, multi-national workers: organising the unorganisable?

The final aspect of 'pushing back' we want to emphasise links to discussions of 'illegality' and deportability in Chapter 4. As described, the instrumental use of socio-legal status to impose conditions of control and coercion served as a constant reminder to those working without authorisation of their very insecure position. This insecurity also functioned to effectively discipline workers militating against negotiation within work situations or collective action between workers. Most significantly, the entwining of immigration and employment rights in the UK means that the 'doctrine of illegality' for those working without permission in practice denies formal routes to legal redress.

> "Nothing happen to them.… I have got no anywhere to complain. How would I complain? The first thing [they would say is] I am illegal, why you working?"

Mohamed describes here the feeling conveyed by most of our interviewees who were acutely aware of the disparity of power within the workplace and the immunity of employers because irregular workers were left without complaint mechanisms. Those working without permission made an explicit link between unauthorised working and their lack of bargaining power. Fear of denunciation to authorities and deportation generated mistrust that frequently precluded the formation of solidarity with other workers in the workplace. Frank, as a refused asylum seeker using a friend's papers to access agency factory jobs, described working 'with fear' as precarious work and insecure immigration status combined within the workplace:

> "There was a mix of people, British, Arabs, but people were afraid of each other, you were working but you don't trust your co-worker because you don't know who he is. So you are working, but talking about yourself is a no-go zone. So you kind of work, but you are kind of spying on your colleague."

Frank believed that agencies regularly changed workers in the factory where he worked to deliberately limit knowledge of rights:

> "If you are quite lucky enough you can work up to one week, two week a month something like that....The reason for that was, because the agency, when you kind of know how the system worked there, you start kind of knowing your rights and all stuff, they change you; they bring new people."

There were, however, signs of solidarity among workers in resisting the Home Office, if not employers. Frank was tipped off by other workers about an immigration raid so, as someone working with false papers, he did not return:

> "After two weeks my shift was in the morning, all of those who went to work the night shift, they were arrested and put in detention. So we started receiving calls; they said 'don't go there because some of our friends have been arrested'."

A generalised fear of other people was apparent across our interviewees who were, or had at one time been, refused asylum seekers. For Nanda, this climate of secrecy and mistrust was in stark contrast to the open, mutually supportive context she experienced in asylum initial accommodation:

> "When I came new I was in hostel I used to say hi to everyone, we are altogether in the dining area, [but] those three years [since], it's made people.... I was feeling like I been in the jungle. Everywhere I was scared, really scared. I'm scared with people. I never scared with animals, but now I'm scared with people."

Several interviewees mentioned the belief that co-nationals report others to the Home Office if they have a disagreement, described here by Faith:

> "The Home Office used to pay money to people if they get them people they knew that were not in the system, that were illegal immigrants. People used to use that to report other people, so most people now have lost trust.... They can quarrel for just a small issue and then they will be like 'I'm going to call the Home Office for you'."

This mistrust relating to immigration status in the UK compounds the 'boundless social universe of mistrust' (Hynes, 2003, p 2) generated by experiences of persecution and exile that characterises refugees' social worlds. Faith described how even after gaining leave to remain, she continued to be suspicious, due to the risks of political surveillance from her home country extending into the UK:

> "You need to be careful even here. I know that they are here at times in the country. You need to be careful because sometimes there's a time – even now, I bar withheld numbers from my phone."

Clearly this undermines the possibility for solidarity between irregular workers, particularly those who have fled persecution and who have prior experience of living under heavy surveillance.

Exit: escape, walking way, being pushed away

In this second section, we move on to look at what might be considered as stronger acts of resistance to forced labour: how most of our interviewees eventually did exit from severe labour exploitation. To frame our discussion of how exit operated across the spectrum of labour situations they encountered, we begin by examining the somewhat exceptional case of Happy. In many respects, Happy's experience typifies the kind of situation imagined by what Agustín (2007) has called the trafficking 'rescue industry'. This illustration from one of the strongest experiences of confinement we found provides a useful exemplar to explore how escape from confined–coerced situations might contrast with exit from labour situations where confinement and isolation were less apparent.

Happy was trafficked to the UK by a woman she met in her local market who promised her an education. But instead of going to school as promised, Happy was confined to the house as a domestic servant, rising at 6am every morning to get the children their breakfast and ready for school before cleaning the house and cooking. With no sign of the education promised by her trafficker, Happy queried the situation after a year of unpaid domestic work:

> "Yeah, I am inside their house, and, no more phone, nothing. So I would just be there cleaning the whole house, doing the housework, make their bed, cook before they come back from wherever they go to. So, that's all I was doing ... for one year, and I have to ask her now, that this is not what she said to me, that [she] is gonna to put me into school."

Happy's trafficker told her that she owed her £10,000. To pay off the supposed 'debt', the woman brought men to the house who paid to have non-consensual sex with Happy:

> "They would phone there and the men would come to the house and they were sleeping with me. And I said to her, I don't like what she is doing to me, that, I want to, I want to go. And she said to me that if I, if I go, then she is going to kill me, and all these things that she is doing, if I ever say to everyone that, they will send me back to [country] and I know that her husband's living in [country] ... [and] they would deal with me when I get to [country]."

As part of a three-year regime of dominating power, her exploiter warned Happy not to talk to or trust white people in particular, who were portrayed as a mortal danger outside the house:

> "She started telling me that white people, they are bad, that if I said anything to them they would put me in jail and the police and ... and started telling me a lot of things that I shouldn't say to no one.... She started yelling me, I can't, I can't go out, because if I go out, if they caught me outside they might kill me or they would put me in jail. So I was scared, so I never go out."

Happy is the only person we spoke to who was constantly confined behind a locked door. After three years of being captive in the house, she grasped the first opportunity to escape when unexpectedly sent on an errand to a shop:

> "So she said to me that she is going to open the door for me, that if I go down this road there is this shop, like an off licence, that I should go there and get her bread. That it is not far, it is just the junction of the street. So I said ok, so she give me £2. So I went there. I ready got the bread and I was thinking, this is my opportunity to run. So I was scared, 'cos she already threatened me because I was scared, so I just went to the side of the corner of the shop. So I sat down there, and I started crying because I don't know where to go, I don't even know where I am. Where will I go to? I don't know the number of the buses, I have not seen anyone since I came.... I saw a man – he was a white man.... I am still thinking what she said to me so I was scared."

Although Happy's situation was one that combined all 11 of the ILO forced labour indicators, including threatened violence if she returned to her home country, her escape demonstrates the importance of basic simple practical knowledge to facilitate durable exit. Happy described how she made the decision to leave, but immediately realised the consequences of the total isolation she endured in the UK: "I don't know the number of the buses, I have not seen anyone since I came". Lacking any practical knowledge of life in the UK, she was dependent on the first person she met. Taught by the woman who brought her to the UK to fear white people, and particularly the authorities, she begged the man who found her at the shop not to call the police. Although this (white) man tried to help by taking her to an African church in another city and she did get away from the forced labour situation, it did not result in her being referred to any support service, anti-trafficking organisation or the police. At the church a couple from her country of origin invited her to stay with them. They told her what had happened to her was wrong, and that she had been trafficked. But they too had insecure immigration status and were reluctant to have any contact with service providers or the authorities. Happy thus remained undocumented and began a relationship and moved in with a man who later became abusive. It was only after escaping several times, after she had been beaten, that a friend encouraged her to claim asylum, at least three years after escaping from the forced labour situation. She said this delay in accessing support was used by the Home Office to undermine her credibility in her trafficking case:

"I wish I knew, because when I got out from there I meet some nice people, people is very nice to me, and what she said about white people is not true, they are more helpful to me. So I was thinking I wished she allowed me out one time, I would have got help, things wouldn't have happened to me that way ... or I wish I got family here or anything. Life would have been better for me."

Lack of knowledge of UK systems and of potential help available from service providers are a corollary of the social isolation experienced by many migrant workers. However, the isolation experienced by those trafficked into the UK directly into forced work situations was almost total in comparison to the limited, but the comparatively open, social contact experienced by those who initially entered as asylum seekers or as migrants who became irregular.

It is clear that running away from confinement and isolation of domestic or sexual servitude in the private realm is a very different form of exit to that experienced by workers in the informal or formal labour market, where job insecurity and the threat of dismissal contributed to the impossibility of leaving. To help understand these differences, we argue that exit from exploitative labour and/or livelihood situations can be divided into three broad types: escape, or running away, walking

Table 5.1: Type of exit from 78 labour situations with 1+ forced labour indicator

ILO indicators	1	2	3	4	5	6	7	8	9	10	11	Total
1. Run away												
Escape						1		3	2	1	3	10
2. Walk away												
Walk away	7	6	10	6	2	2		1				34
Of which left because got asylum support	1		1			2						(4)
Indefinite leave to remain	1	1										(2)
Moved jobs	1	3				1						5
3. Pushed away												
Job ended	5	4	1	1		1		1				13
Arrest	1	1				1						3
Dismissal	4	1	2									7
Visa expiry		1										1
No exit												
Ongoing	2	1	1			1						5
Total labour situations												78

away, and being 'pushed away'. Table 5.1 shows the incidence of these exit types in relation to the 11 ILO indicators of forced labour.

1. *Escape: running away.* The first type includes those contexts when exit involved the need to literally 'escape' or 'run away' from highly confined–coerced labour situations. Table 5.1 shows the strong links between the 10 situations where exit was characterised by escape and a high number of ILO indicators. In seven of these situations, escape was from work in the domestic sphere including two situations that also involved intimate partner or domestic violence. In two other cases escape was from violent partners where the work was undertaken in the public sphere, in one case from a trafficker with work outside the domestic sphere. An association between work in the domestic realm and the high incidence of confinement and isolation that necessitates exit in the form of escape is apparent. Below we discuss in detail three important elements for the gradual building of resilience that facilitated eventual exit: tipping points, visibility, and access to practical resources.

2. *Walking away.* In the majority of labour situations encountered by our interviewees, exit came in the form of walking away or moving jobs. This covered 39 labour situations that featured one or more ILO indicator. These work situations tended to involve more subtle, indirect and relational forms of coercion, and typically exhibited a smaller number of ILO indicators covering a range of precarious or insecure labour situations including formal, informal and transactional forms of labour. Indeed, in these labour situations, employers used the threat of dismissal as a disciplining tool in contrast to 'preclusion of exit' (see also Scott et al, 2012). We differentiate this group from those 'pushed away' (see below) to highlight variation between agential exit whereby the worker chose to walk away or move jobs, and situations where workers were pushed out due to circumstances over which they had no control. By suggesting that workers 'walked away', we do not imply an absence of coercion in the work, nor of multiple unfreedoms. It is also important to highlight that getting away from unfree labour was not necessarily about leaving an employer. For those working with others' papers, and exploited by a friend or contact, it was often this relationship they needed to extricate themselves from.

3. *Being pushed away.* In 24 cases the worker did not walk away, but the job ended due to dismissal – because the job was temporary and had come to an end, or because they were pushed out of the workplace after an immigration raid or, in one case, because of visa expiry. The

loss of work through the job ending reinforces the insecurity of these forms of employment. We now look at each of these different types of exit in more detail.

Escape: the build-up of abuse and 'tipping points'

In the most coercive situations, Abigail, Happy, Ivy, Ma'aza and Lydia all seized a single moment of opportunity to 'get out'. Ma'aza took the chance to run away while walking in a street with her Arab employer family on vacation to the UK. Escape was facilitated by her sudden realisation she could slip away unnoticed in the multi-cultural environment of the UK in contrast to previously, in her employer's country, where she was driven around in a car, and where "all people [looked the] same" apart from her. But escape was triggered by a tipping point when she was blocked from buying a new dress with her 'own' money, and the realisation her employer was not looking after her earnings for her:

> "Me, I want to buy something, she's 'no, for you very expensive'. Why she say like this? I am working, I have money with her, you know, she must give me my money."

For workers in more confined circumstances, events that created a tipping point of physical or emotional exhaustion altered and strengthened their resolve to escape. In situations featuring the 'impossibility of leaving' due to threat or penalty, confronting exit could take a long time. Reflecting on coercion over a period of years, Gallant emphasises how securing pay was far from his mind as a trafficked young person:

> "Well, I was a child I never think about anything, I never thought about money. I just did what they asked me because I just wanted to satisfy them so that they don't do anything to my family."

Gallant nevertheless made several attempts to leave the illegal activities he was coercively directed to engage in, but each time he was threatened into returning to criminal activity. One attempt involved him moving across European borders aged about 15, only to be arrested in another European country where he served part of a 12-month sentence in an adult prison due to holding false (adult) papers. Gradually, his resolve to extract himself from this exploitative relationship strengthened:

"… and afterwards they were asking me other things and I
didn't do it. I didn't do it. Once he was asking me to bring
cigarettes from London and take it to these cities and there
to there, I said no. He said I'll give you good money and
I'll buy you a car, I said no."

His traffickers would spend spells in prison during which time their
control over Gallant lessened, but on release they continued to attempt
to draw him back, and were doing so up to the point when the research
interview took place, some six years after he stopped directly working
for them. But Gallant rejected their approaches:

"'Cos I had enough. I got enough. I mean enough is
enough. And then this guy was released from prison, then
his cousin…. He left me now and he can phone me ten
times a day, I don't care."

He was now able to say 'no' due to the gradual establishment of relative
security constituted by gaining indefinite leave to remain, supportive
social contacts, renewed faith and a religious/moral rejection of
his former life, work experience in regularly paid jobs, and college
attendance.

For those confined to the workplace, just as invisibility formed a key
feature of the practices of coercion and menace of penalty they were
subject to, moments of visibility – of being seen or seeing others –
and coming to see their situation in a different way formed important
moments to furnish resistance and move towards escape. Ma'aza, Abigail,
Ivy and Happy were all in domestic work for prolonged periods (from
one to nine years). The hidden and isolated characteristics of domestic
work in the private sphere are recognised as contributing to making it
one of the most risky sectors for labour exploitation (Anderson, 2007;
Clark and Kumarappan, 2011; Dwyer et al, 2011; Lalani, 2011). For
workers hidden from the 'public' in private spaces, social isolation and
psychological control are central to the subtle forms of menace that
operate as tools of coercion for workers behind unlocked doors. Such
workplaces routinely avoid state regulation, particularly in the UK,
where the domestic realm is unregulated and exempt from numerous
basic employment law provisions, including the National Minimum
Wage (Clark and Kumarappan, 2011).

Abigail was made to go out shopping with the mother of the
family who employed her, and was repeatedly shouted at and sworn
at in public. Part of her degradation as a domestic worker was also

being made to wear invisible, dull clothes: "it must be like brown or something. It doesn't sparkle. She doesn't like that." After arrival in the UK, the contrast of her situation with other people around her who were talking and moving freely, and not wearing headscarves, triggered her to reflect on her situation:

> "Yeah, I'm thinking that everybody's staring at me. I'm thinking that I don't have a life and I don't feel like I am human because of the things I can't do. Because I don't have money, I don't have the power to do anything."

Her lack of knowledge of the UK and sense of obligation to the employer initially stifled her sense of opportunity for escape, but these reflections were clearly vital for her to build the resolve required to escape, allowing her to take advantage of a single moment of opportunity:

> "I feel ashamed. What can I do?... There's nowhere to go. Only I know her. For me, it's thinking the only safe place is her."

On the last day of her employer's visit to the UK, the employer's daughter urged the family to go out for lunch (without their staff). Abigail excused herself from the other staff to go to the bathroom and made her escape through a back door not manned by security. She found her way on to the street where she hailed a taxi. It is significant that a visitor had given each staff member a gift of money that she had managed to conceal from the head of staff who otherwise confiscated cash gifts, allowing her to pay for a taxi. Wandering the streets for hours, she later approached some police officers who took her to a police station where Abigail enjoyed her first full night's sleep in two years. The solicitor she saw the next day advised her to claim asylum.

Equally important to being seen was the sometimes gradual process of workers coming to view their own situation differently, pushing them to begin to resist the curbing of expectations inherent to disciplinary power in confined-coerced situations. In all cases, our interviewees who were trafficked were not only escaping from forced labour, but also from situations their family members had a direct role in setting up. Disbelief at the betrayal and abuse of trust implicit in family networks was a central feature of both the continuation of these situations and workers' growing resistance and eventual exit from them. After three years in domestic servitude, a visit by a plumber who reported Ivy's situation to social services led to her attending college – although this simply meant she had to get the housework done in less time. Nevertheless, going to college allowed her to see the freedoms available to others and to build her resilience to reject the situation arranged by her family and envisage a different future:

> "I started to think differently, I started to realise that this is not the life, even one you are supposed to live. Suppose I had the freedom like the others people, so that I can walking in my future, be what I want to be in life. I felt, realised all those stuff."

Jay, deceived into a servitude-like situation of full-time care through a romantic relationship, described how he incrementally absorbed the abuses of his partner: "no it was just too much, you know like, looking after the kids and the way she treat me, I mean everything, you see I end up hating it." Yet, feeling that he had 'had enough' did not spark his exit; this only occurred after he re-established contact with a trusted friend who offered him an alternative means of support:

> "I just say one day that's it I'm going to move. And luckily I met this guy in [nearby city] who know me back home and he said 'oh, man, come live with me'.… I just said 'oh, I'm going for a walk' and I jump on a bus to [city].… I just leave everything because I was too, very upset."

Jay's experience again highlights an important issue for those escaping from confined-coerced situations: the importance of some sort of alternative, some practical knowledge of outside support and most particularly, somewhere to stay, somewhere to sleep. Jay had made a previous attempt to escape, using the small change he saved from running shopping errands to take a bus to a major city where he knew there was a key refugee service provider. His main concern was to find accommodation – he did not disclose the situation he was being subjected to. He was told that as a refused asylum seeker and a single male that he could not access immediate accommodation. He then visited a homeless shelter but was sent away as ineligible as a third country national (TCN) with no recourse to public funds for housing or shelter. Faced with sleeping rough, he went back the same day to the situation of domestic servitude, childcare, and racial and emotional abuse he was trying to exit from. Jay's experience reinforces the points made above in relation to Happy – that access to basic practical information and relatively small resources (such as an overnight bed or knowledge of public transport) can facilitate exit from even the most severe cases of forced labour which feature multiple, overlapping ILO indicators. More broadly, workers whose housing and sleeping arrangements are tied to employment have been identified as particularly vulnerable to severe labour exploitation (Craig et al, 2007; Wilkinson et al, 2009).

Walking away

While forced labour might be depicted or imagined as a situation that necessitates escape or running away, we can see that in half of the labour situations experienced by our interviewees, workers did just walk away. There were numerous examples of people walking away from 'opportunities' that were identified as likely to be excessively exploitative from the outset, or when conditions quickly deteriorated. Such tactics, in some cases, constituted resisting entering situations featuring forced labour practices in the first instance. Avoiding the risk of denunciation to authorities, and abandoning unpaid jobs, were two prevalent reasons why those not prevented from exiting left a work situation, sometimes in the early hours or days of a job. The threat of being reported to the Home Office triggered exit in several cases where interviewees did not have permission to work, as Tino describes:

> "I just walked away from the situation because he was now threatening me saying that if I keep on badgering him about the money he's going to go to the Home Office."

In many cases, it was a progression of worsening exploitation that triggered exit. Workers' attempts to negotiate in the face of deteriorating conditions by refusing to take on additional tasks, stay excessively long hours or generally submit to extensions of agreed work under threat of dismissal often meant leaving without pay. Hussein had permission to work as an asylum seeker,[1] but despite this, found that employers did not recognise this type of work authorisation document, and he was pushed into informal labour. He travelled around in search of work to support himself rather than rely on asylum support payments, and repeatedly walked out of jobs in the early days, or even hours, of overtly exploitative employment. After a month in one city seeking work, he finally saw a vacancy sign in a restaurant for kitchen staff, and an employee told him the pay was £6 per hour. However, when he spoke to the owner who spoke the same language as Hussein, he was told it was £3 per hour. After six hours clearing tables, ashtrays, and cleaning, the owner then told him to clean the kitchen. It was 11.30pm; Hussein knew this would take a couple of hours, but that he was only being paid to 12pm:

> "… that area is not my job … the chef they can do it but because the chef is his cousin that's why he said, that's alright, I give it to the new guy he will clean it. But I'm not going to clean it. *I'm not going to sell myself like that – cheap.*"

Rather than argue (and because he was concerned that violent confrontation would make matters worse), he walked out with no pay, feeling that negotiation was futile in the face of being blatantly 'ripped off', or his labour being 'sold cheap'.

Several women had to reject dubious offers of help from men. A particularly stark offer was made to Angel, reinforcing the instrumental use of insecure socio-legal status highlighted in Chapter 4:

> "I ask him 'can you do work permit for me? You got lot of business please give me work permit', he said 'oh, come here live in hotel with me, live in 10 years, illegal, nobody knows where you are or where you working. You understand?' I said 'I'm sorry, I don't want to be a, I don't want to be illegal in this country, I don't want.'"

Risks of sexual abuse, and avoiding street homelessness which might increase such risks, were a feature of the 'lack of any real or acceptable alternative' particularly experienced by women, a concern strongly echoed by many of the practitioners we interviewed.

Tipping points were also key to the exit of some workers who sustained months in work where pay was intermittent, or withheld by a third party (such as a person lending documents). Workers in insecure jobs that did not feature confinement to the workplace tended to see from the outset that their labour situation was exploitative, but when the only other alternative was destitution, any work or the promise of pay was welcome (see also Chapter 4). Nevertheless, at certain points, several factors would collide and push people into a moment of awakening to reject the labour situation. For example, after months of working with irregular or no pay, as outlined in the case study at the end of Chapter 3, Assanne 'exploded' and left:

> "Basically that week, I had worked all week and then on the Friday I had worked till three in the morning, 3am and I

went to get my money the next day and there was no money and I just exploded and I thought, I can't! That's why I left."

Frank describes how several things came together in his mind so that he no longer felt that the risk of working with false papers was worth it:

> "I'm working you know, tirelessly myself to get something and then at the end because I couldn't open any account in my name ... so all money was going via him and eating that money.... I'm working for nothing and that pressure pushed me also to think that it may happen the day that they come to inspect the job, the place and if the police come they will just ask me to put a finger on the machine ... and they find a different identity, then I'm gone. *So I started thinking, putting all of those stuff together.* And I realised, it was time for me to back off.... So I told him, thank you very much and that was it. So these are your documents, I went to work and I told them that I'm sick and I want to have some time off, and that was it."

For Frank, leaving the job and employer was a matter of asking for time off and not going back; at the time he was receiving Section 4 asylum support of limited voucher payments so could support himself (and had been working for remittances to support his family). However, it was harder to extricate himself from his relationship from his 'friend' who lent him papers. The friend had become reliant on the income Frank's work brought in, and tried several times to persuade him to go back:

> "I was pissed off really.... Because he said we can talk around it, because he felt that the money he was getting, was quite, you know significant compared to how he used to live. So when I told him that I have to stop, he wanted to know why, but I told him that the pressure that I'm receiving from him was too much, for too little."

Frank's feelings – of being both grateful and thanking his friend, but also being 'pissed off' and recognising how his friend was exploiting him – are an important illustration of the ambiguity experienced by workers who did not always necessarily seek exit despite knowing labour situations were overtly exploitative. We return to this conundrum in our discussion of wider migration trajectories in Chapter 6.

Being pushed away

In other cases, it was not that the worker rejected the work so much as they were forced out or pushed away. Mehran explained how agency workers were the first to go when the factory he worked for needed to reduce shifts due to the economic downturn:

> "I was working in the night shift and the factory was closed later and they reduced the worker.... Of course some people was working permanently they still they not going to give me any more work."

The competition between low-paid, insecure workers and the struggle to secure work is illustrated by Mehran's description of the patronage displayed by other workers who gave gifts to agency staff, he believed, in order to try to secure regular shifts (and regular pay):

> "I saw many people every day come with a flower ... maybe the person who is calling people for work is dealing with differently with the people ... this is a kind of abusing it.... I understood that these flower is not for birthday or not for something.... Maybe somebody give for money to take his mind or his heart to say there is a five days' work or six days' work for you."

The three interviewees who left work due to arrest were not the only workers who told us their workplace had been 'raided' by immigration enforcement officers. In other cases a raid did not lead to the removal of the worker from the workplace. This could have been because the enforcement officers were seeking a particular worker, so others remained undetected. In at least two cases mentioned to us, workers had their details checked and were questioned, but they denied they were working, and were told not to return to the workplace. Removal may not be pursued if the immigration enforcement officers can see when checking an undocumented workers' details that they are not a high priority for removal or likely to be deemed 'undeportable'.[2]

As noted in the discussion of 'pushing back', dismissal was sometimes tied to workers' rejection of exploitation when individuals were dismissed if they complained about or rejected poor working conditions. Parviz, a delivery driver, described how his refusal to take on additional cleaning tasks led to his dismissal without pay:

"I remember we didn't have many deliveries on that particular day so the owner came and asked me to broom outside the shop. I told them that I was your driver not a cleaner and we agreed that I would do whatever you asked me for but not the cleaning. That's why I told them I gave them notice that I wouldn't be working with them the following week. But then they said you should have told us earlier – it's too late and eventually they didn't pay me £120 that they owed me."

Having explored our interviewees' acts against exploitation that can be interpreted as Katz's *reworking*, or even *resistance* in some instances, we now move on to explore persistent experiences of unfree work. At best these may illustrate the opening up of spaces that facilitate Katz's notion of *resilience*; at worst they represent smothering tunnels of entrapment that close down any potential arenas for such resilience.

From exit to re-entry: movement along the unfreedom continuum

This last section tempers the accounts of exit and different types of resistance by interrogating the extent to which movement out of a coercive labour situation can ever be seen as exit, arguing instead, that exit may often constitute merely a movement along the continuum of unfreedom (see the further discussion in Chapter 6). For each of the three groups in our entry into the UK/entry into forced labour typology of *asylum seekers on entry*, *irregular* and *trafficked* migrants, entering the asylum system and receiving asylum support could offer respite from the necessity of engaging in severely exploitative work, but always with the risk of a return to destitution and re-entry into exploitative labour if refused and support removed. As previously noted, even for those receiving leave to remain and permission to work, long periods outside the labour market or in exploitative informal labour makes a shift away from the 'track' of continuing job precarity (Goldring and Landolt, 2011) extremely difficult.

In the majority of work situations encountered by our interviewees, continuation in a severely exploitative labour situation related directly to the lack of any real and acceptable alternative but to submit to the abuse involved due to a layering of multiple unfreedoms. The wish to avoid homelessness and destitution, multiple barriers to decent work, and the additional pressure of earning for remittances or family reunification were pressures experienced by workers both with and without permission to work. Thus, exiting from any one single exploitative work situation did not necessarily significantly improve their situation unless at least one of these important elements was addressed.

For *asylum seekers on entry* cycles of entering and re-entering exploitative work emerged particularly in the work biographies of asylum seekers who were refused and destitute for periods of years. Transition to asylum support by lodging a fresh claim and becoming eligible for Section 4 support or gaining leave to remain provided a positive reason for exit from exploitative work in a few cases (see Table 5.1). For those negotiating fragile and stretched support from friends and acquaintances to avoid destitution and street homelessness, even very small or short-term forms of destitution support (food parcels, emergency housing or Section 4 support) provided an initial chance to exit labour exploitation. As the case study in Chapter 4 outlined, when Assanne was refused asylum, he found work sorting recycled clothes. He stayed in the job for nine months while his employer paid wages only intermittently (£20–£150 for a promised weekly pay of £200). After leaving, he managed to launch a fresh asylum claim and access Section 4 support. However, after some months, he was again refused and his support removed. After a month staying with friends, facing homelessness and destitution, and lacking any viable alternative, he returned to the same employer despite knowing how appalling conditions were: "at this stage I'm really only working to get some bread basically", he said.

Desire to continue in work that might be considered severely exploitative and in spite of little or almost no pay must therefore be understood in the wider perspective of pure survival through seeking a livelihood. Staying in work under threat of dismissal becomes a daily challenge in insecure and short-term jobs, a challenge magnified for those workers without the required documentation. The fear of losing work and the associated risks of homelessness, destitution or inability to remit or support family members routinely operate as an effective barrier to exiting unfree labouring situations. Here we can understand how these wider pressures constitute a 'lack of a real or acceptable alternative' and operate as a coercive force, in entering or continuing in a job despite poor working conditions, and whether or not an employer makes direct threats. In many cases, workers in our study did not seek to leave situations of forced labour; indeed, because of the need to survive, they worked hard to access work and were terrified of losing their job.

Even for those who did not work until being granted leave to remain, including Faith, Mehran and Muedinto, barriers to accessing decent jobs pushed them into exploitative labour. Mehran had only accessed insecure, short-term and temporary agency factory work over eight years in the job market. Ultimately, long periods out of work in receipt of Jobseeker's Allowance, depression, lack of English and an absence of detailed knowledge of UK recruitment processes continued to create barriers to him getting a decent, permanent job:

> "To be honest with myself, the problem is because one is my social contact, my social position is really, really weak."

He believed the context of recession had closed down access to unskilled jobs for those without good English:

> "Yeah I can see many English people and they have skill any good thing and they can't find a job.... Many, many factories closed and the people who have no skills they can't find job and ... the employer, before because of the shortage of the employees, they just not looking; he is strong, he is young, he is reliable to work. But now they just ... choosing the good one."

Mehran eventually passed his taxi licence on a fifth attempt, and was planning to try to become a self-employed taxi driver. Although we earlier highlighted lack of knowledge of UK systems as a risk for re-entering exploitation, many interviewees had learned a great deal from their experience of severe labour exploitation. Those who went on to receive leave to remain could use this knowledge to safeguard against future employment breaches. Muedinto described how he was ignored when his manager adjusted time sheets to underpay overtime: "I was complaining, but no one was really listening to me." This experience taught him to write down his shifts and hours worked in order to avoid being in compromised situations in the future.

For the three interviewees caught working with false papers, their experience of working without permission had resulted in the lasting legacy of a criminal record, as outlined in Chapter 4. Gojo described her criminal record as the feeling of carrying a load she could not put down:

> "Walking a long distance with a baggage and then instead of getting to the destination you take it off your head it's like you just sit down with your baggage.... It was something it was always there, something worrying me all the time."

Due to the struggles she had securing work – applying and being rejected by five mainstream employers – when she found an employer willing to take her knowing of her criminal record, she stayed in the job despite not being paid the correct amount for hours worked: "… because I didn't have an alternative. Yeah if I had the choice to go and apply for another job and get it straight away I was going to do so, move on, yeah. But I had to stay because I didn't have a choice."

Those 'escaping' from confined-coerced situations, isolated from access to knowledge of UK systems or sources of help, were at particular risk of rapidly re-entering exploitative situations to survive. This included all of the *trafficked migrants* in our study. Immediately after running away from the family she worked for, Ma'aza refused an offer of £200 to go home with a man who found her crying in the bus station. Luckily, she came across a woman with whom she shared a language who took her home for one night to stay in her house, and who then told her to claim asylum. Gallant's long journey out of exploitation by traffickers involved a period spent destitute and being supported by a friend – happily someone he described as "good":

> "He says you cannot go anywhere you have to come and live with me. I will give you job, I will take you to work and you have to come with me. He knew I am homeless jobless, paperless, friendless, I have nothing. He knew that. I said ok, when I went to his house he had one room, he rented the room, smaller than here. He is sleeping there I was sleeping there like this. And then, he took me to work a few days, like maybe two days a week – £100. It was good for me because I didn't have anything . And then, slowly, slowly, you know I found my way.… I worked in the car wash for a couple of months. Slowly, slowly, you know, I got my licence, I got a job, and then I got my papers and now I've got my council flat as well. So – here I am!"

Eventually he accessed Section 4 support, and after a couple of years was finally granted leave to remain. Although the journey away from his trafficked situation involved exploitative work, "slowly, slowly" he began as a young adult to find a more durable livelihood and access college seven years after being trafficked to the UK.

Although the *trafficked and irregular migrants* in our study accessed the asylum system as a route away from forced labour, the asylum system may generate susceptibility to forced labour. The circularity of asylum systems can mean exit from forced labour into an asylum claim may lead to only temporary respite from the necessity of engaging in exploitative labour. Of most concern are those who escaped forced labour and accessed the National Referral Mechanism (NRM) for identifying victims of trafficking. Although claiming asylum offers some limited safety and support with basic needs, applicants in the NRM are statistically likely to lose their asylum claim (Stepnitz, 2012), so the asylum system is often cold comfort for those escaping from trafficked situations. While the asylum system is potentially helpful initially as a form of support and respite for the group of trafficked migrants who claim asylum after exiting from forced labour, if refused, they face substantial risks of re-entering exploitation as refused asylum seekers. Thus, any suggestion of the asylum system as helpful needs to be balanced by recognition that current UK asylum and trafficking support systems often fail to effectively protect those exiting forced labour (ATMG, 2012).

Conclusion

This chapter has examined the mechanisms of 'exit' and the rejection of exploitation by workers through attempts to negotiate conditions and, ultimately, the refusal of severely exploitative work. In some cases the rejection of exploitation by walking away from jobs when conditions deteriorated did protect workers from slipping across a line between severe labour exploitation and forced labour. Despite the limitations for organising workers and achieving broader-based resistance to unfree labour, some examples of nascent solidarity existed in the limited and hidden spaces where some workers formed moments of mutual support within the exploitative workplace. However, the reality is that for many of our interviewees, 'exit' often amounted to movement away from one instance of severe exploitation into other exploitative or precarious survival situations within a continuum of unfreedom. The factors that contribute to this movement – persistent immigration and employment precarity – result not only from the socio-legal structuring of constrained rights and entitlements, as discussed in Chapter 4, but also from migrants' wider trajectories across time and space as part of their personal 'migrant projects'.

Three contexts shaped the possibilities for, and success of, acts of resistance to exploitation: the insecure workplace; irregularity at work; and limitations on workers' organising or negotiating. The first dimension relates to coping and negotiating within insecure workplaces including agency or short-term work under fear of dismissal. This raises issues relevant for any precarious worker, irrespective of citizenship status. The limitations on negotiation of conditions within the insecure workplace affects all workers in such work, and constitutes a further layer of unfreedom for those who are in situations that involve forced labour practices. The second dimension of the active need to manage irregularity while at work affects those interviewees in our sample who worked without authorisation. We argue that this group can be viewed as embodying resilience through the very *act of working itself* within an oppressive politico-economic context that denies the right to work and enshrines state-enforced poverty and destitution. Nanda described making this point directly to the Home Office:

> "Because they found out you have bank card, you did work. In that interview I said, I did, I didn't lie to them. I did, because I don't have money, I didn't take any benefit. I can't sleep in road.... I did say that – do you want to kill me? You can kill me now. I was angry, I did, but I didn't take any benefit. If you giving me benefit, why am I going to work?"

The fear of detection of 'illegality' in employment relations significantly compounds the pressures of the first dimension of working under pressures of job insecurity. Nevertheless, our interviewees who were engaged in work involving indicators of forced labour as refugees with permission to work demonstrate that having legal status is not a panacea. Those working in the formal labour market in 'official', 'documented' jobs with requisite permissions, all had their attempts to negotiate conditions or recoup unpaid wages closed down by employers through manipulation into worsening labour conditions and threats of dismissal or false accusations of malpractice. Their experiences demonstrate the third context: the extreme difficulties precarious workers face when trying to organise to improve labour conditions or recoup unpaid wages. These situations are being continuously compounded in the UK by decreasing labour regulation and erosion of labour rights that enhance the impunity of employers (for example, through attacks on legal aid, and increasingly high requirements to qualify for employment tribunals; see Chapter 7). Linking with broader issues that affect all workers and workplaces in the context of austerity, this makes it difficult or impossible for negotiation or acts of resistance to be successful at achieving broader-based change beyond an individual worker safeguarding themselves against forced labour. Discussions in Chapter 6 develop this point to ask how we might best be able to conceptualise the root causes of the unfreedoms underpinning our interviewees' labour and life experiences. We next expand on our concept of '*hyper*-precarity' in pursuit of this discussion.

Notes

[1] Hussein had successfully managed to apply for the right to work as an asylum seeker due to delays in his asylum claim.

[2] A significant portion of the refused asylum seeker population in the UK come from countries to which it is difficult or impossible for the UK government to arrange removal due to problems with diplomatic relations between the UK and those states, difficulties in arranging travel documents or because of conflict and unrest in those countries (Lewis, 2007, 2009; Smart and Fullegar, 2008). It might be considered paradoxical for someone to be refused asylum and not be returned due to risks to safety facing deportees. Indeed, the quality of asylum decision making has become one of the most important agendas of the campaign against the destitution of refused asylum seekers (Williams and Kaye, 2010), and it has recently been claimed that the Home Office operates with a 60 per cent refusal target, significantly undermining the claim that each case is decided on its own merit (Taylor, 2013).

6

Conceptualising hyper-precarious migrant lives: from forced labour to unfreedom

Introduction

So far in this book we have deployed both global and national lenses to ask why vulnerable migrant workers routinely experience labour exploitation, and we have linked this in the UK to the neoliberal labour market regime that has combined with a damaging asylum and immigration policy to render particular international migrant groups hyper-precarious and deeply susceptible to forced labour exploitation (see Chapters 1 and 2). We then moved on to analyse the scale and reach of ILO-defined forced labour in their work experiences (Chapter 3), explored the role of immigration-related socio-legal status in rendering them vulnerable to such exploitation (Chapter 4), and contemplated the different ways in which they struggled to resist and exit their situations (Chapter 5). In this chapter, we now reflectively stand back from these 30 human stories to critically interrogate the very meaning and relevance of 'forced labour' for the precarious migrant labour experience as the conceptual basis for tackling such exploitation. As Phillips and Mieres (2010, p 2) have noted, across the panoply of UN, EU, national government, corporate social responsibility initiatives, trade union and consumer-based activism, it is ILO approaches to forced labour that dictate the parameters of the issue and the terms on which it is engaged. How the ILO defines the concept of forced labour, where it establishes the boundaries of the problem, and in particular, how it understands the forces driving its emergence and persistence are thus definitive of global policy responses in general.

As a result, 'forced labour' has come to be understood as embodying an 'essential' set of practices and relationships (O'Connell Davidson, 2010) that can be differentiated from other non-forced experiences of labour exploitation in the formal and informal economy (Lerche, 2007; Phillips and Mieres, 2010; Kagan et al, 2011). In this chapter we argue for an alternative understanding of forced labour through the theoretical concepts of 'unfreedom' and 'hyper-precarity'. A first section discusses how the rigid binaries of ILO forced labour – such as free/forced, coercion/consent, involuntariness/freedom, employer/employee – both fail to capture the complex and multi-dimensional (McGrath, 2012) processes that specifically render forced migrants vulnerable to coercive and unfree labour, and exclude alternative meanings and interpretations of coercion and control. We highlight the role of state policy, third party networks and intermediaries in non-trafficking situations, gendered domestic abuse settings and transactional work not adequately considered in forced labour debates. A second section develops this analysis by presenting a continuum approach built around the concept of 'unfreedom' as the best way to capture the diversity of migrants' coercive labour experiences, reflecting the impossibility of drawing a line between unfree and forced labour. This links to a final section where we introduce our idea of the 'hyper-precarity trap' – an analytical device to show how neoliberal labour markets and highly restrictive immigration regimes intersect (see Chapter 2) to produce multi-dimensional insecurities that underpin the 'demand' and 'supply' of forced labour subjects (see also Lewis et al, 2014: forthcoming).

Going beyond forced labour

Throughout this book, we have been using the term 'forced labour' to refer principally to the specific forms of 'forced' work practices and employment relations as defined by the ILO. Since its establishment in 1919, the ILO has dedicated a core part of its mission to eliminating 'forced labour', and its legal definitions and instruments largely underpin current policy and the legislative approaches of international bodies, national governments, and the campaigns of trade unions and NGOs (Hodkinson, 2005), as well as the analytical frameworks of much academic research. The result has been the creation of a dominant international norm about what 'forced labour' is, outlined in the ILO's Forced Labour Convention, as:

> … all work or service which is exacted from any person under the menace of any penalty and for which the said person has not offered himself [sic] voluntarily. (ILO, 1930)

It is important to remember that the ILO's forced labour mission emerged during the early 20th century's inter-war period of imperialist competition when new forms of slavery were emerging in European colonies on a massive scale to fuel economic exploitation by the 'mother country' (Lerche, 2007; Maul, 2007; Standing, 2011). This was a time of unfettered national state capital (and even trade union; see Thomson and Larson, 1978) collusion, in which governments and their colonial administrations used various extra-economic constraints to *forcibly compel* large parts of the 'native population' to perform labour, paid and unpaid, for the benefit of the colonial economy:

> The increased need for manpower during the economic expansion of the 1920s was at no point met by the free local labour markets.... The result was pre-programmed social and political stagnation, and the often unscrupulous temporary extraction of manpower from the indigenous communities. (Maul, 2007, p 479)

The 1930 Forced Labour Convention may have committed its signatories to immediately abolish forced labour in all its forms, but in reality, the list of clauses and loopholes ensured that the issue of colonial forced labour was fudged. This reflected the imperial interests of the ILO's tripartite membership dominated by Western colonial powers and their racist attitude to colonised populations: 'both opponents and advocates of forced labour accepted that there was a basic difference between "normal" and "colonial labour"' (Maul, 2007, p 481). As we argue later in this chapter, this dichotomy between those regarded as citizens with full rights and those deemed outside (migrants) is a persistent feature of the contemporary neo-colonial order. During the post-1945 era, the problem of forced labour became deeply politicised – first, as part of the Cold War, with Western capitalism clashing with Soviet communism over the use of forced labour for political and economic advantage. The resulting 1957 Abolition of Forced Labour Convention broadened the different contexts in which forced labour was outlawed but continued to permit or ignore coercion for economic development under certain conditions, a compromise that has continued to cause controversy and division to this day. Since the 1960s, the question of forced labour and workers' rights more broadly has led to confrontation between 'developed' and 'developing countries' over the implementation of basic human rights versus the needs of development. The point here is that the ILO's universalist rhetoric of forced labour norms has always masked a far more conditional and selective application in practice (Maul, 2007).

As briefly explained in Chapter 3, during the past decade the ILO has significantly developed the concept of forced labour through establishing clearer guidelines, indicators and evaluative frameworks on both forced labour and trafficking for the purpose of law enforcement and legislative action. A key driver of this work has been the break-up of the Soviet Union and other socialist blocs, opening up new territories and political space to implement ILO standards. Another factor has been the changing nature of forced labour in terms of the growth of human trafficking into forced sexual exploitation and domestic servitude in particular – areas not covered by the forced labour conventions – as consequences of the 'dark side' of globalisation (Maul, 2007). This conceptual development began with the publication in 2005 of the ILO's six indicators of forced labour (ILO, 2005), and in 2011 these were expanded to 11 indicators set within a framework for identifying when a person could be legitimately said to have experienced forced labour exacted through a combination of involuntariness and penalty (ILO, 2011, pp 14–15).

A second limitation of the ILO approach concerns the imagined employment relationship at the heart of the forced labour. While the ILO forced labour approach has historically assumed an employer–employee relationship, it has started to evolve its definition to take into account other more hidden employment relations and types of employer. For example, it recognises that 'recruiters and employers increasingly oblige workers to adopt the legal status of "self-employed"', disguising the underlying employment relationship and thus associated form of coercion to enable the 'employer' or 'contractor' to avoid responsibility for paying social benefits and minimum wages or for observing regulations on hours of work or leave entitlements (ILO, 2011). However, the ILO expressly excludes economic compulsion, the absence of alternative employment opportunities, and staying in a job because of poverty or a family's need for an income as forms of involuntariness. In our view, the role of other hidden employment relationships through labour market intermediaries – including third parties – and the coercive nature of economic contexts are both vital for understanding why workers may engage in forced labour (Lerche, 2007). These important questions about the value judgements underpinning the indicators and the limited understandings of the social relations of forced labour are central to our arguments in this chapter.

The Abolition of Forced Labour Convention (No 105) (ILO, 1957) built on the 1930 Convention by committing ILO member states to suppress and not make use of any form of forced labour for the purpose of economic development or labour discipline, as a means of political coercion, education or punishment for expressing political views or participating in strikes, or for any means of discrimination (ILO, 1957). The legal definition of forced labour is closely aligned with the UN's definition of trafficking in persons (UN General Assembly

2000). This creation of an 'operational definition' of forced labour has been welcomed by many due to the challenges of detection and enforcement. As Geddes et al (2013, p 35) argue, 'forced labour "in the private economy" is frequently hidden, or difficult to detect, because workers are scared or are being deceived.' This evolution in the forced labour framework has undoubtedly broadened and sensitised – up to a point – the meaning of forced labour to reflect the highly differentiated and geographically uneven contours of contemporary global labouring and, in particular, the ever-growing role of precarious migrants in this context. It has also proven useful to efforts by academics, think tanks, and campaigning NGOs to highlight the growing scale and reach of forced labour in the UK (Anderson and Rogaly, 2005; Craig et al, 2007; EHRC, 2010; Skřivánková, 2010; Allamby et al, 2011; Dwyer et al, 2011; Kagan et al, 2011; Balch, 2012; Lalani and Metcalf, 2012; Scott et al, 2012; Dugan, 2013; Geddes et al, 2013). These and other studies and research reports have raised the profile of forced labour in the UK in both public and political realms, and partly inspired and assisted us in our own study of forced labour experiences of asylum seekers and refugees.

By using the ILO's six core indicators of forced labour during the fieldwork, we – and our eventual interviewees – were able to identify particular experiences of labour exploitation under coercive and menaced conditions. These indicators evoked for our interviewees very clear experiences, practices, social relations, feelings and emotions, demonstrating their usefulness for identifying possible forced labour cases as the first step to achieving possible redress and protection (see Chapter 7 for limits of this, however). As Chapters 3, 4 and 5 have shown, the ILO's 11 indicators have clear resonance when considering the highly constrained choices available to the asylum seekers and refugees in our study and not just those trafficked. Of particular relevance are threats and intimidation involving *denunciation to the authorities, debt bondage linked to cross-border smuggling or trafficking, the retention of identity documents* and *the abuse of vulnerability*, that is, having 'no real and acceptable alternative' (ILO, 2005, p 21) – that is often inherent to shutting down the options of asylum seekers, refugees and irregular migrants with compromised socio-legal status. This makes entering, enduring and not being able to exit severely exploitative working arrangements in the informal economy not simply a coerced and involuntary experience, but in some cases, the only way to meet their basic needs.

This notion, however, that some of our interviewees may have been *physically able* to refuse or exit exploitation but either *felt* unable to or *chose* not to, fundamentally clashes with the ILO forced labour framework and its application in national policy, legal and practitioner contexts. In short, being an irregular migrant or a refused asylum seeker might represent extreme vulnerability, but the occasions on which the lack of an acceptable alternative are regarded as a possible forced labour situation – and thus open to prosecution of perpetrators and protection or redress for workers – are extremely truncated and conditional on the ILO's forced labour definition. This is not least because of the ILO's exclusion of economic compulsion as a recognised form of coercion in forced labour. In our view, this makes the very concept of forced labour, and the resulting policy frameworks around it, deeply problematic and in many respects counter-productive. We are not alone in holding this perspective (see Lerche, 2007; O'Connell Davidson, 2010, 2013; Phillips and Mieres, 2010; Kagan et al, 2011). In what follows, existing critiques are identified and substantiated further with our own evidence.

ILO forced labour: a critique

A first problem is that, despite the ILO's development of forced labour guidelines, the current operational definitions, indicators and guidance for regulatory and legal enforcement are neither adequate nor universally understood, leading to major gaps and inconsistencies in knowledge, detection, prosecution and legal judgements (see Allamby et al, 2011; Balch, 2012; Geddes et al, 2013). The problem of definitional interpretation of forced labour indicators for legal prosecution has recently been evidenced by a UN report on the trafficking in persons protocol in relation to a single indicator – abuse of the position of vulnerability (UNODC, 2013). Despite widespread conceptual understanding of vulnerability and its importance to trafficking, the report found major barriers within nation states to legal enforcement, including a lack of clarity and consistency around the definition of trafficking generally, as well as wide variations in how the general concept was applied to specific cases or circumstances. Similarly, a recent landmark judgment (*CN v UK*) by the European Court of Human Rights (2012) found the UK government in breach of their positive obligations under Article 4 of the European Convention on Human Rights to have in place criminal laws penalising forced labour and servitude. Police officers were adjudged not to have properly investigated allegations of domestic servitude, partly because they were only trained in trafficking law. Criminal laws have subsequently been strengthened under Section 71 of the Coroners and Justice Act

2009 that introduced a new offence of 'slavery, servitude and forced or compulsory labour'. Despite this, the Court heard representations from the UK's Equality and Human Rights Commission that it did not consider the new law to be of assistance because it did not explain how Article 4 should be interpreted in today's conditions: 'there was therefore a risk that the new statute would not result either in clear deterrence or effective prosecutions, and would not improve the failures in investigation' (European Court of Human Rights, 2012, para 63).

The legal barriers to prosecuting forced labour move us to a second critique focused on the very assumptions, norms and purposes of the ILO's forced labour concept. As Phillips and Mieres (2010, p 9) argue, the only reason for constructing a discrete category of 'forced' labour isolated from other kinds of labour relations is to enable 'the criminalisation of perpetrators'. Yet criminalisation narrows down, simplifies and reduces the forced labour concept to such an extent that it becomes disconnected from the actual complexities of exploitation experienced and from their multi-dimensional and contradictory causality. Fundamental to this reductionism is the ILO's binary framing of what constitutes coercion (as opposed to consent) and involuntariness (as opposed to freedom), and its directive that both must be *simultaneously* present and imposed *by the employer/*third party *on to the worker* without their free consent or possibility to exit (O'Connell Davidson, 2010; O'Neill, 2011).

In other words, the ILO expressly excludes *economic compulsion or coercion*, whether through the absence of any alternative or acceptable income opportunities, or the need to stay in a highly exploitative job because of poverty or a family's need for an income, as forms of involuntariness and menace. More complex forms of bonded labour, such as seasonal debt bondage of 'jobbers' in India, are also not regarded as 'forced labour' by the ILO, although they clearly generate economic forms of coercion and the kind of conditions associated with forced labour (Lerche, 2007). Our research clearly shows that wider economic and social contexts are vital for understanding why workers become trapped in forced and severely exploitative labour. The highly constrained choices of asylum seekers and refugees caused by their stratified rights at different points within the asylum process (including limited rights to work and welfare), and even when regularised, severely limit their options and generate inescapable compulsions on them.

Pascual's story exemplifies this harsh reality. A child soldier and torture survivor who escaped to claim asylum in the UK as an unaccompanied minor, Pascual was wrongly treated as an adult and refused asylum. Thrown out onto the streets, he slept rough in a train station until he met a couple who helped him find a room to rent, and told him where a van picked up casual workers at 5am. With no money, clothes, food or place to live, no knowledge of the UK, no means or right to apply for work at the job centre, and unable to speak English, he was faced with a very urgent economic compulsion to find any form of work, no matter how low paid or how harsh the conditions. Nearly *every day* for the next seven months, he would work an 18-hour shift with just one 15-minute break killing and packing chickens in a freezing factory, for just £80 a week. As described in Chapter 3, his gangmaster would not allow even one day off a week, and when physical exhaustion meant he failed to make it to the van one morning, he was threatened with the sack unless he returned to work the next day, which he did. When we asked him why he had worked under such inhumane conditions for so long, his absolute lack of choice was stark:

> "… because I need to pay the rent first thing, second I needed to buy food for me, the third, I need to live, to be alive. If I don't do that, I cannot eat and I cannot drink there is no one who can help me for that situation I was. So indeed I have to force the body to do it."

Pascual's labour experience contravened UK labour laws and was littered with ILO forced labour indicators – his first and last week's wages were withheld, he was forced to work excessive overtime, he was threatened with dismissal for taking sick leave, he worked in highly abusive, degrading and unhealthy conditions, and his vulnerability as an undocumented migrant without rights to work, residency or welfare was abused. And yet, according to the ILO definition, at no point was Pascual in forced labour because at no point did any employer or third party deceptively recruit or force him to work under any physical coercion, confinement, threats, or intimidation to stop him from leaving. Rather, it was Pascual who exercised his own (limited) agency to be exploited; it was, in his own words, *he* who had to "force his body" to work. This reinforces Allamby et al's (2011, p 54) argument that workers are often making a decision, however constrained and narrowed, to remain in these exploitative relationships until they can get out or can no longer take it. However, here we see the absurdity of a conception of forced labour in which the clear abuse of vulnerability is not admissible because it has not been used by the employer/third party recruiter as a tool of coercion or menace of penalty. As Geddes et al (2013, p 96) argue, this challenges 'the application of a legalistic "perpetrator-victim" framing' so central to the ILO approach.

Just as economic compulsion is not considered to be a legitimate form of coercion, penalty or unfreedom within forced labour, neither are gendered compulsions, such as domestic abuse or the fear of sexual violence. Several women spoke of predatory men seeking to take advantage of their insecurity by offering shelter – but at a price. Managing the advances of men who want to use the predicament of women with insecure socio-legal status for sex is a clear indication of how gender violence has a discernible impact on the lives and survival strategies of marginalised female migrants. Women who lack other accommodation and support options are often susceptible to highly coercive domestic and sexual exploitation in return for basic shelter (Lewis, 2007; Taylor, 2009). And the risk of this was a key reason why women might engage in transactional domestic arrangements to avoid street homelessness.

This question of agency connects to a third weakness of the ILO forced labour imaginary, namely, its limited understanding of the parties and relationships involved in labour exploitation. In the ILO world, forced labour in the private economy is a coercive and involuntary process usually involving two parties – the employer (or third party recruiter or provider) and the worker. The ILO recognises that the formal identities of these two parties is frequently hidden through workers being obliged to adopt the legal status of 'self-employed' so as to disguise the underlying employment relationship and enable the 'employer' or 'contractor' to evade legal obligations to pay social benefits and minimum wages or observe Working Time Regulations (ILO, 2011). Nevertheless, coercive exploitation for the ILO and national policy is a *bilateral* affair, between *individual* perpetrators and victims.

Our evidence demonstrates that this conceptualisation is deeply flawed for three principal reasons. First, it does not reflect the widespread proliferation of very long and globalised subcontracting chains where formal and informal work and actors coalesce, creating 'serious ambiguities in the employment relationship' that obfuscate 'who is the real employer and where responsibility lies' for working conditions (Anderson and Rogaly, 2005, p 32). Second, it fails to acknowledge forced labour practices often hidden in complex triangular employment relationships (Geddes et al, 2013, p 96) involving labour market intermediaries – including friends, partners and family members – taking advantage of the precarious situations of undocumented migrants, as highlighted in Chapter 3. Finally, and most importantly, it offers impunity to the distant corporate impresarios of global production and service networks (Anderson and Rogaly, 2005;

Barrientos, 2008) as well as the state policies that facilitate capital mobility while undermining migrant workers' rights.

This latter point is critical to a more expanded understanding of how vulnerability to exploitation is both produced and abused. In the ILO approach, states can be criticised when directly involved in using forced labour, but state policies can never be held responsible for creating the economic compulsion pushing migrants to seek and remain in working conditions that amount to forced labour in the private economy. This underlines the most fundamental conceptual weakness of ILO forced labour as a form of exploitation that can be separated off from the wider political economic system. As Lerche (2007, p 427) argues, this 'cocooning of the forced labour issue' rests on a deliberate ideological decision to de-link forced labour both from labour exploitation *per se* and from 'present-day capitalist development' so that these 'worst forms of "un-decent labour"' ... can be dealt with in isolation, without challenging the overall system that created the conditions for their occurrence in the first place' (Lerche, 2007, pp 430-1). The desire not to challenge capitalism is structurally embedded within an institution forged as a tripartite social democratic platform between (capitalist) employers, trade unions and states. We can thus better understand it, as Phillips and Mieres (2010, p 13) do, as a 'political strategy' of ILO member states to commit themselves to eradicating the worst symptoms of the current neoliberal global capitalist orthodoxy while the 'sanctity of highly flexible labour markets in a large swathe of contemporary economic strategies can remain undisturbed'. In doing so, the ILO – and adherents of its forced labour definition – not only let state immigration policy off the hook, but tolerate forced labour among irregular migrants today in exactly the same way they tolerated colonial labour of the early 20th century.

What these critiques and complexities show is not only the sheer impossibility of defining 'forced labour' against other forms of exploitation, but that doing so deflects us from the contemporary global reality of 'a collection of forms and manifestations of labour exploitation, which form part of a long and complex continuum' (Phillips and Mieres, 2010, p 12). This notion of a 'continuum of exploitation' (see Skřivánková, 2010), encompassing different instances and situations of labour exploitation, represents an important conceptual way forward out of the binary world of ILO forced labour. The continuum of exploitation recognises that some enter labour situations that from the outset feature highly adverse conditions of little or no pay, debt or threats. Others enter work on the expectation or promise of decent pay and conditions, but find themselves in increasingly constrained and deteriorating circumstances that close down avenues for exit (Anderson and Rogaly, 2005). It is thus difficult to draw a line between exploitation in the form of substandard working conditions or the abuse of workers' rights and forced labour. The continuum approach additionally highlights the relationship between more general exploitation in the labour market and the existence of forced labour. As Steinfeld (2009, p 2) argues:

> ... rather than view compulsion in labor relations in terms of a binary opposition divided by type of pressure, it seems more plausible to think in terms of a combined scale of pressures, legal, physical, economic, social, psychological all running along a continuum from severe to mild, rather than falling into a binary opposition. This would not only help us to understand that the various types of pressure employed in eliciting labor are commensurable, [and] operate in surprisingly similar ways at bottom, but also to see that the real focus of inquiry should be upon the choice sets with which individuals are confronted as they make their decisions about conducting their lives, and the ways in which these choice sets may be altered by changing legal arrangements.

We believe that a theoretical way forward in understanding this continuum of exploitation lies in the concepts of 'unfree labour' and 'hyper-precarity'. We discuss hyper-precarity in the final section of this chapter, but in the next section we look briefly at the historical context of unfree labour and its persistence in the contemporary, globalised world.

Introducing the continuum of unfreedom

Following our critique of the ILO framing of forced labour, we suggest that the types of labour experiences explored in this book are best conceptualised as *unfree labour*. The concept of unfree labour was central to the writings of Marx (1976 [1867]). He contrasted the 'free labour' of capitalism to the historical experiences of serfdom and slavery. Commodified labour power of the proletariat was now 'free' in that it was no longer bonded to the landlord, but it did not end toil and exploitation – this required the working class to further emancipate itself from 'free labour' through overthrowing the capitalist mode of production (Marx and Engels, 1848). There has subsequently been extensive debate over whether unfree labour is a hangover of socio-economic relations prior to capitalism, or whether it can develop alongside or within capitalist relations (Lerche, 2007).

O'Connell Davidson (2010) notes that the roots of liberal thought posit that modern society is formed on a social contract that guarantees people both political and economic freedom, locating slavery firmly in the traditional, pre-non-capitalist world. Yet in opposition to the common assumption that unfree or forced labour is a vestige of the past, only existing in pre-capitalist pockets outside prevailing modern capitalist conditions, there is a growing awareness and understanding of contemporary forms of unfree labour (Munck, 2010). Many further contend (Miles, 1987; Brass, 1999; Rao, 1999; Banaji, 2003) that *particular* forms of capitalism (itself inherently unequal), such as neoliberalism, may be *more* exploitative than others, based on the balance of power. Such forms of rampant capitalism can be seen to create conditions for unfree or forced labour. Morgan and Olsen (2009) hold that unfree labour 'is a product of the norms of capitalism because unfreedom can be profitable' (p 14), and that 'freedom is shadowed by unfreedom' (p 10). In this sense, wealth and poverty are central to capitalism and (un)freedom – wealth makes some freer, but its absence makes others less free. This is linked to Phillips' argument (2013b) that unfree labour should be considered in terms of 'adverse incorporation', where poverty results not only from conditions of 'exclusion', as the orthodoxy maintains, but also from the adverse terms on which vast numbers of workers are incorporated.

When considering the (dis)continuities between historical and modern-day unfreedoms, Phillips (2013b) argues that contemporary unfreedom in the global economy differs from traditional forms of unfreedom – slavery, indenture and bondage – in four ways. First, modern forms take a 'contractual' form, are usually short term in duration and are often sealed by indebtedness (see also Breman, 2007, 2010, on 'neo-bondage', or Bales et al, 2009 on 'contract-slavery'). Second, unfreedom is often related to the preclusion of exit – as opposed to a coerced point of entry (see also Mohapatra, 2007) – through indebtedness and/or the withholding of wages, and also because of workers' own perceptions of their responsibilities, obligations or debts which are, in turn, used as disciplining mechanisms by employers. Third, in contrast to traditional unfree labour, contemporary forms frequently involve an exchange of labour for money. Lastly, unfreedoms not only exist at the point of exit, but also characterise the work itself through harsh, degrading, dangerous conditions of work and violations of workers' labour and human rights.

We argue that the concept of unfreedom is helpful in understanding the highly constrained choices and lack of alternatives that lead many asylum seekers and refugees to engage in severely exploitative work. Some of our interviewees' experiences would escape the legislative eye of demonstrable forced labour, yet remain quite patently 'unfree' in manifold ways. We need a conceptual tool that allows us to move beyond unhelpful binaries and instead emphasises the importance of complexities, variations, processes, relations and contexts in understanding labour experiences. In line with several other authors (O'Connell Davidson, 2010; Strauss, 2012a; Barrientos et al, 2013) we are attracted to the idea of a *continuum of unfreedom* as a more dynamic tool to capture unfree *processes*. This idea allows the consideration of the different sites and stages that occur in journeys into and out of severely exploitative and unfree labour. As Barrientos et al (2013) suggest, a continuum evades the unfree/free binary trap and allows the recognition of varied forms and dimensions of unfreedom.

At the heart of understanding unfreedom is an expanded and multi-dimensional understanding of coercion and involuntariness beyond the ILO forced labour framework. O'Neill (2011) is useful in this regard, as he interrogates the UN protocol on trafficking (UN General Assembly, 2000) and the reference to positions of vulnerability emanating from a lack of a 'real or acceptable alternative'. He develops the idea of 'compulsion by necessity' by suggesting that certain acts are involuntary not because there is no choice, but because there is 'no real and acceptable alternative' but to choose that act. It is this realm of coercion that is vital to understanding unfree labour. Even if the point of entry into unfree labour may be seen by some commentators as involving an element of choice, this can rarely be simply construed as a voluntary act, as many asylum seekers and refugees are likely to have entered into the condition through a lack of reasonable alternatives. They may have been compelled further by 'necessities of obligation' (O'Neill, 2011) – necessities that are not just immediate but also driven by familial and kin obligation. Additionally, any potential exit from unfree work is denied or severely restricted due to the absence of protective labour and citizenship rights that may offer viable alternatives to continuation in situations of unfreedom.

A more nuanced notion of coercion and involuntariness within the concept of unfreedom is, therefore, a useful analytical tool for understanding the lives of asylum seekers and refugees and their experiences in the workplace. We define unfreedom as a situation where a person has, or feels they have, no real or acceptable alternative than to work in these conditions and/or for someone or body. Such consideration serves to highlight the blurred boundaries between workers' consent and coercion that some argue delineate forced labour *per se* from wider exploitation in the labour market. It shows how unfreedom can exist in work situations not defined as forced labour through the lens of the ILO.

To help unpack this argument, we suggest here four *dimensions* of unfreedom illustrated through empirical examples from our interviewees.

No real or acceptable alternative to entering and continuing in exploitative labour

The lack of any alternative is of foundational importance to understanding unfreedom. Many interviewees in our study felt when undocumented that they had *no real or acceptable alternative* but to seek and accept highly exploitative work as the basis of survival due to destitution, or other urgent needs linked to socio-legal status that created an urgent need for cash. The 'tunnel of entrapment' (Morgan and Olsen, 2009) in unfree labour is compounded by the insecurity and limbo of deportability in everyday life (de Genova, 2002). Gender dynamics are also notable in this context. Among our interviewees it was exclusively women who were trapped in situations of domestic servitude, controlled by a combination of sexual, physical and psychological violence that often left them genuinely in fear for their lives. The threat of denunciation to the immigration authorities was repeatedly used by men to control and abuse partners with insecure immigration status. Additionally, the gendered, cultural norms that prevailed in their countries of origin added to a pervasive feeling of judgmental abandonment in several women:

> "My family, first of all won't accept me, unless I'm with him. And this child if it's born it … must be his name." (Doreen)

> "If they send me back, it's going to be hell for me. Because in [country] if you give birth when you don't have your husband, it's like a crime. They mock you, and they will tell to you that you are a prostitute, that's the language they are going to use for you. So now, I am just here with a baby [*crying as she is talking*]." (Happy)

> "Here in UK you live with one guy – that is not in our culture. If in my culture people they know that, they will

> think I am just like a street girl…. [UK] government they pushed me in this choice – it's them responsibility. They knows I'm one lady, one girl … don't have any support, they have to protect me, but they no did it…. I'm sorry to say that the system's made fuck my life – my whole life." (Nanda)

Abused by violent men, stuck in an uncaring asylum system in the UK and fearful of having their children removed by their ex-partners' families should they be deported, socio-legal status, gendered violence and cultural norms combine to structure a state of particular 'hyper-precarity' in the lives certain female asylum seekers and refugees. Although the two men in our sample who became enmeshed in enforced childcare as personal relationships deteriorated were also subject to psychological abuse from partners and shared common fears of denunciation and destitution with women living in domestic servitude, theirs was a qualitatively different experience, in that they did not routinely live in fear of domestic violence.

Withholding of a minimum, living or social wage

This dimension encapsulates our understanding of unfree wage relations. It captures instances where workers are suffering from slave-like wages not otherwise considered by the ILO forced labour apparatus. As outlined in Chapter 3, denial of even the statutory National Minimum Wage was common among our 30 interviewees (see Figure 3.1), with a major factor being the informal employment setting combined with the explicit or assumed understanding of the worker having no right to work. While evading minimum wage rates is unlawful, it is only considered to be 'forced labour' when workers are coerced into working excessive overtime to earn a minimum wage. Yet this ignores the reality for undocumented migrants that their irregular and vulnerable status allows employers and third parties to by-pass minimum wage and other labour laws on the basis that such workers are unable to enforce their non-existent rights; moreover, it is their very precarious and thus exploitable status that incentivises employers to employ them. In such 'unfree' contexts, workers find their take-home pay can be further reduced by excessive hours and/or cost of travelling to and from work, having to pay for their own tools or protective work clothes, and being unable to command enough hours to generate a sufficient income to live on. For 'regularised' workers or for asylum seekers receiving NASS or Section 4 support, such low pay can at least be supplemented by in-work benefits and the 'social wage' of free public services. Irregular workers, by contrast, are not able to do this – even where many are paying tax and NI – because they do not have the right to work and thus to claim benefits or claim back any tax and NI deductions from their pay. Furthermore, fear of deportation generally means they avoid public services that their tax and NI contributions help support.

Existence of a web or chain of fixers, agents and beneficiaries that extract value from unfree labour

This dimension captures situations where a web of immediate actors orchestrates the unfreedom of the worker (see also Skeldon, 2011). For example, the worker is working for more than one person – from a simple employment agency and a boss to a series of intermediaries (friends, fixers, agencies and employers). This is not the same as debt bondage, but debt bondage may feature as an element. This is an indicator of unfreedom because the worker may be formally paid the minimum wage, but in reality, their pay goes to someone else first and they receive only a portion of it, or they get paid in full but their labour is rewarding multiple parties in a semi-conspired web. Frank's story exemplifies this well. Although he accessed work as a refused asylum seeker, he was not destitute at the time, receiving Section 4 support. His decision to seek work was sparked by an urgent need for cash to remit to his family in Africa so they could get emergency medical treatment. A friend took pity on Frank and allowed him to use his own passport, NINo and bank account details so that Frank could get an agency job in a clothes distribution warehouse to send money home. The job itself, while physically demanding, tiring and monotonous, was paid at the minimum wage for a 40-hour week with appropriate breaks, amounting to £200 a week. However, his forced labour experience was at the hands of his friend as a third party labour intermediary. When Frank entered into this relationship, he did so in the expectation that his friend would pass on the wages he earned. After a few months, however, the friend told Frank he would be keeping half of his wages as he was no longer receiving Jobseeker's Allowance as a result of supposedly 'working'. At the time Frank had felt *deceived*, and this can be seen as a form of *unfree recruitment* in which he could not freely consent to subsequently imposed conditions that transformed his friend's apparent act of solidarity into a financially dependent relationship; moreover, this unfreedom was buttressed by Frank having no choice but to accept these conditions due to his extremely *vulnerable situation* that his friend was intimately aware of and had *abused*:

"... I was like the instrument for him to get money. So he couldn't go to work but he know that he can sleep nights very well, knowing that there is someone out there, who is working for him and he gets money at the end of the week. And I used to do that because I have a family to support, I cannot stop because otherwise ... he must have thought that this is the prey, this is the prey that I can use to, you know to generate some bit of income."

Having accepted this new arrangement of effectively renting his friend's identity in return for 50 per cent of his wages, Frank very quickly began to experience a further degradation in the relationship as his friend, periodically and without warning, withheld even more money. As his friend began to deduct more money from Frank's weekly wage as the price of using his papers, their relationship became more acrimonious, and the friend would threaten to withdraw the papers or "go to the company and say that I stole his documents and that I used them to find work". Linking this back to the first indicator of unfreedom, what stopped Frank being able to exit this exploitative relationship was his vulnerable situation as a refused asylum seeker unable to legally work with a family in urgent need of financial support. As well as *threats of denunciation* to the employer, Frank was trapped by having no acceptable alternative.

Wider existential feelings of coercion, menace and involuntariness in relation to social reproduction and social life

This dimension captures aspects of the ILO's forced labour indicators that take place at a distance from a bilateral employment relationship or setting that would not be considered forced labour but are clearly experiences of unfreedom. They are informed by the many occasions when our interviewees talked about their experiences of unfreedom in a wider sense: not just in being coerced into work, and unfree during that work, but unfree in their lives. For example, interviewees spoke of feeling desperation in having no real or acceptable alternative to the housing, education, health, food, social life and so on that they had. Such wider unfreedoms include:

- *Illegalisation:* this can be reinterpreted as not having one's own legitimate and legalised identity. Papers may have not been formally retained, but undocumented migrants in particular have been derecognised through the state's denial of citizenship rights, and thus they are 'unfree'.

- *Indebtedness as compulsion:* a worker might not be strictly *forced* to pay back a debt to the employer, but they might have to pay off a migration-related debt by working, for example, paying back the smugglers, the friend, the family, and thus they may feel a 'necessity of obligation' to submit to unfree working conditions.
- *Social isolation:* the worker might not be physically isolated in a workplace, but might feel isolated, alone, unable to speak to co-workers, the police, or indeed any member of the public for fear of the consequences.
- *Degrading treatment:* not having control over fundamental daily necessities such as food, clothing and toiletries was a significant aspect of the imbalance of power experienced by interviewees in daily life, most particularly for those working in the domestic sphere. Significantly, the use of the term 'illegal' or social position of being irregular emerged as a commonplace device of prejudice and abuse from other workers, managers or exploiters, serving to remind interviewees of the powerlessness associated with their socio-legal status.

In summary, the concept of 'the continuum of unfreedom' implies a relationship between more general exploitation in the labour market and the existence of unfreedom. This now links to the final section of this chapter where we introduce our idea of the 'hyper-precarity trap' – an analytical device to show how racialised and gendered migration, work and welfare regimes, and neoliberalism combine to create the 'demand and supply' of migrant forced labourers who are subject to multi-dimensional insecurity and exploitation.

Migrants caught in the hyper-precarity trap

How should we conceptualise the root causes of the unfreedoms underpinning our interviewees' labour and life experiences? What our empirical research on the working lives of asylum seekers and refugees in the UK suggests more generally – irrespective of national context – is that migrants journeying through and around various immigration and socio-legal statuses while under serious livelihood pressures are at risk of entering the labour market at the lowest possible point in their effort to secure work. These constraints on migrants can combine with 'unfreedoms' in labour market processes to create situations of '*hyper-precarity*'. The factors and processes that make individuals susceptible to forced labour incorporate overlapping pathways to precarity. These pathways mean that for any one individual, aspects of socio–legal status, migration context and gender relations compound to create multi-dimensional insecurities that contribute to their necessity to engage in, and close down exit from, severely exploitative and in some cases, unfree, labour.

As introduced in Chapter 1, precarity as a condition is variously perceived as resulting specifically from neoliberal working experiences or as emerging from a much more generalised societal malaise replete with oppressive governmentality and fear. We suggested earlier that we find the concept of precarity illuminating, both as a term through which to explore labour conditions, and also to acknowledge the profoundly destabilising effects of precarious work on broader lifeworlds. That said, we also argue that the concept of work-derived precarity as it has been used by many writers (see, for example, Dorre et al, 2006; Fantone, 2007) is not subtle enough to differentiate the experiences of exploited/ unfree migrants from those workers who are argued to be part of the precariat (Standing, 2011), yet are able to achieve some degree of self-pursued 'flexicurity' from their working lives. We argue that the viscerally lived unfreedoms within some migrants' working lives are better understood as hyper-precarious rather than 'merely' precarious.[1] This section draws through the discussed concepts of precarity and unfreedom into an analysis of what we know about migrant labour experiences in insecure labouring environments, and a discussion of what contributes to the creation of these situations.

The political economy context of migrant workers that shapes their vulnerabilities and structures their hyper-precarious lives was outlined in Chapters 1 and 2. In brief, neoliberalism is having the effect of destroying livelihoods for some in the Global South, impelling migration to the Global North, and creating the conditions for exploitation to flourish in the low-paid labour markets that poor migrants find themselves within in richer countries. The connections between global economic change and related transformations in the world of work are therefore one of the key explanatory frameworks for workplace exploitation. Others have made related points; for example, Cross (2013a) discusses how modern 'economic dispossession' underpins unfree labour mobility; Rogaly (2008, p 1433) urges recognising the importance of 'states' accommodations with large-scale capital in producing degrees of unfreedom and exploitation, including worsening employment conditions'; and Phillips and Mieres (2013, p 4) argue that forced labour 'can result from the terms of *inclusion* in global economic activity, rather than merely from exclusion or marginalization from it'. It is such attentiveness to capital–state relationships that we are urging here in considering the political economy context of refugees and asylum seekers as working migrants. We now move on to the more micro-level socio-cultural processes and characteristics that also have the potential to contribute to the hyper-precarity trap.

Chapters 3, 4 and 5 detailed that 'forced' migrants can experience a range of what might be loosely termed 'pre-migration, journeying and destination country' experiences that erode individuals' abilities to enter and negotiate decent work. It is important to note that these spheres are not separate; exploitation for a migrant can begin in a sending country context and then seamlessly continue through a journey and into a destination country labour market. Such an approach echoes that of Zimmermann and Zetter (2011) who urge attentiveness to the micro-level experiences of refugees in source countries as this underlies, frames and conditions many aspects of ongoing lives in exile. Similarly, Hynes (2010, p 966) argues in her analysis of the trafficking of children that multiple, clustering 'points of vulnerability' must be understood as global processes by recognising factors both prior to arrival (former experiences of exploitation, loss of parents and so on) and after arrival in the UK, including: 'negotiating the immigration and asylum systems, the overarching environment of deterrence of new arrivals into the UK, accessing services, mistrust and disbelief of accounts provided.' We now explore these vulnerability points in turn.

Migrants who move from their countries of origin and end up labouring in the low-paid sectors of Northern economies come frequently from poverty-ravaged regions. Such environments may be disadvantaged in multiple ways, thus producing migrants who are poorly or non-educated, and this may combine with a more general racial/ethnic low social position and lack of knowledge about modes of travel, destination countries' labour markets, rights and so on. 'Migration industry' actors (Castles and Miller, 2009), particularly at the more nefarious end of this spectrum, are known to exploit less informed and vulnerable rural and minority ethnic populations in source countries (Beeks and Amir, 2006). This exploitation may range from promises and lures (for example, assurances of employment, travel to exotic destinations, even opportunities for romance) to outright fraud and deception (for example, coercion into different work, spiralling costs of travel/work recruitment, provision of and transit under false papers/travel documents), and it finds traction among the less informed and vulnerable populations of the Global South. The role of labour market intermediaries can be key here in the multi-placed exploitation of migrants (see, for example, Mahdavi, 2013). As Geddes

(2011) states, these intermediaries could be kith or kin who enable/facilitate migration at the start, who themselves may be linked to (or be one and the same as) smugglers or traffickers, and labour recruitment agents or gangmasters in destination countries that recruit low-skilled temporary labour. At each point of the chain, there is the potential for migrants to be forced, coerced or otherwise presented with an absence of acceptable alternatives but to submit to an exploitative situation.

Overlaying many of these features of exploitation are the multiple dependencies migrants often have on employers and/or recruiters and/or smugglers/traffickers. The glue that holds this web together may frequently be indebtedness. At the extreme end of the indebtedness spectrum lies trafficking and debt slavery. Much trafficking literature is dominated by portrayals of the human rights crisis for those trafficked, and the presumption that the migrant–trafficker relationship (revolving around some kind of control and exploitation) typically continues subsequent to migrant movement. This portrayal is often set up in contradistinction to a smuggler–migrant relationship where migrants are considered less tied to the smuggler after delivery across the border (see, for example, Jeffreys, 2002). Yet smuggling costs are often very high, and can result in a patchwork of debts being owed to various third parties and thus ongoing relationships with each after border crossing (Triandafyllidou and Maroukis, 2012). O'Connell Davidson (2013) therefore disputes the suggestion of 'trafficking = unfree/smuggling = free', and rightly also points to smuggled migrants' fear of deportation once over the border, which leaves them with enhanced susceptibility to 'accept' extremely poor working conditions.[2]

Chapter 3 revealed that formal ILO 'debt bondage' (when a person is held as security against a debt and must work to pay off the debt) was experienced by only a minority of our trafficked interviewees, yet debt featured more ubiquitously among many interviewees' experiences in the sense that it acted as a vulnerabilising force in their lives. Debt may be an aspect not only of non-trafficked irregular migration (as with smuggling), but also of perfectly legal migration. Some of this can be from debt incurred to finance migrants' journeys, some from money borrowed in order to augment remittances to families back home and/or finance family reunification, and some from paying high fees for arranging legal movement and organising employment. In this way, states' immigration policies *themselves* produce migrant indebtedness. Several of the participants in our research who were asylum seekers on entry, as well as those who became irregular then later claimed asylum, encountered the pressure of debt repayment in their lives.

An over-arching, and controversial, point of relevance here is made by O'Connell Davidson (2013, p 1) when she acknowledges that debt has the potential to lock migrants into dependency for many years, yet she says it is also 'a means by which many seek to extend and secure their future freedoms'. This links to ideas around the 'migrant project' and migrant trajectories discussed in Chapter 5. We suggest multi-layered, transnational pressures through time and across different spaces, coupled with the particular fear of deportation experienced by refugees fleeing persecution, discussed below, combine into forms of multi-dimensional hyper-precarity for certain migrants, moving beyond a conceptualisation limited to migrants' labour market position alone (Woolfson and Likic-Brboric, 2008). This perspective fundamentally distances from the employer–employee relationship which forms, and limits, the ILO formulation of forced labour, and is vital for understanding not only why migrants might continue in situations of unfree labour, but also signals the need to critique the notion of 'exit' from unfree labour. In many cases, workers in our study did not seek to leave situations of forced labour; indeed, they worked hard to access work and were terrified of losing their job.

These situations are in turn compounded by host states denying many non-citizen migrants access to basic social rights and protections (both international and domestic protections). The stratified rights associated with socio-legal status for migrants were discussed in Chapters 2 and 4, and the resulting structured exclusions are seen as inherent within many Northern countries' immigration policies. Aside from the direct outcomes of these curtailed rights to welfare, residence and work, many migrants lack full knowledge of their civil and social rights, particularly of their rights within employment (for example, minimum wage, workplace mistreatment). These situations are particularly acute among asylum seekers and undocumented migrants. Access to information about rights and broader access to support and protection are further curtailed for these groups by social isolation, and/or an unwillingness to engage in the public sphere for fear of disclosure to the authorities. There are often few social or economic spaces to meet people from different ethnic enclaves, and hence the acquisition of receiving country language skills (known to be important in forming social networks, employment opportunities and broader protection/rights issues) are limited (Ahmad, 2008).

The concept of 'liminality' has been used to understand lifeworlds in limbo, and the term is broadly taken to mean a transitional stage at, or on both sides of, a boundary or threshold (Turner, 1969). Thus an asylum seeker is waiting for status resolution, and an undocumented migrant might be waiting for some kind of regularised status. Hynes (2011) has suggested that UK asylum seekers are particularly prone to experiencing this limbo as they are subjectified through an asylum system that actively denies normal routines due to policy-imposed liminality. Sigona (2012, p 62) describes the lives of undocumented migrants in the UK (some of whom are refused asylum seekers), and similarly discusses tactics to maintain 'invisibility' and to keep to the margins in order to maintain 'the fragile fabric of everyday life'. Such tactics revolve around a shrinking of spaces of comfort to only those that are inhabited by trusted people, and limited interaction – and a concealment of truth – in all other spaces.

As revealed through various experiences discussed in Chapters 3–5, liminality can be seen as a form of governmentality. As we have discussed, another powerful disciplinary device is deportability – fear of detection and forced removal – which serves to increase unfreedom. We have argued, with others (Bloch et al, 2011; Bloch, 2013; Sigona, 2012), that the useful notion of deportability to encompass the extensions of immigration controls from the border into negotiation of everyday life (de Genova, 2002; Bosniak, 2008) must be nuanced to recognise the heightened material risks of human rights abuses faced by forced migrants if they are returned, in addition to the fears shared by all migrants of losing face, failure of the 'migrant project' and loss of potential earnings to support family livelihoods. The effect is to silence workers who might otherwise organise or take action against breaches of employment and safety conditions. Furthermore, because state enforcement of 'illegal working' is known to target certain types of businesses (such as high profile/high street ethnic eateries), undocumented workers are pushed into even more invisible labour spaces. The hyper-precarity inherent within such insecure jobs, when working with unresolved immigration status (and risk of deportation), is further magnified when these jobs are also dangerous and involve greater probability of bodily injury or death. Risk of injury is not only higher in sectors such as construction, agriculture, catering and cleaning, but in some migrant workplaces there may be little attention to health and safety protection for workers, and those with uncertain immigration statuses are often reticent to access health services with a work-related injury for fear of detection by the authorities (Burnett and Whyte, 2010).

In summary, we have argued that pre-migration, journeying and destination country experiences reduce migrants' ability to experience 'decent' work. Thus poverty and debt, pressures to support family, low expectations of treatment at work, lack of or low levels of education, low social position, mode of recruitment into employment and mode of entry into the destination country may render certain individuals more susceptible to unfree labour relations at particular times. These factors are then compounded in the destination country by compromised socio-legal status, lack of knowledge of rights, lack of access to information, isolation from society, multiple dependencies on the employer, loss of or changes in employment, and debt accrued in migration, contributing to continuums and processes of unfreedom. These situations arise from the ongoing interplay of increasingly deregulated labour markets, characterised by employers' demands for low-cost 'flexible' labour, and highly restrictive immigration and asylum policies that variously structure, compromise and/or remove basic rights to residence, work and welfare for all but the most prosperous of migrants. The confluence of employment, immigration and ontological insecurity for asylum seekers and refugees is an especially toxic experience in their daily lives. This underpins our argument that such situations should be considered as multi-dimensional hyper-precarity that accounts for migrants' transnational lives. These situations routinely have a 'sticky web' character (Goldring and Landolt, 2011, p 330) that leaves the imagery of a hyper-precarity *trap* for unfree migrant workers an accurate and shameful scar on the face of contemporary Britain.

Conclusion

Overall, and in keeping with other recent studies (see, for example, O'Connell Davidson, 2010; Skřivánková, 2010; Scott et al, 2012), we want to emphasise that to try to separate 'slavery', 'trafficking' or 'forced labour' as an exceptional event undermines an understanding of how exploitation is tied up with social, political and legal status, migration, gender and economic systems. Refugees and asylum seekers are part of a much larger group of vulnerable workers in the UK. The problem with the ILO definition is that coercion is assumed to take place between an employer and an employee or similar – it is a highly individualised vision of forced labour where an unscrupulous person or firm forces someone else to work in unacceptable ways or conditions. But in many of the cases we have encountered, the exploitation of labour is not straightforwardly organised by a single employer, and the coercion is not straightforwardly direct, involuntary and slave-like. There is often more than one economic actor extracting value from the forced labourer, such as an employment agency, a gangmaster or an intermediary, and those actors are not always, if indeed ever, engaging in a conspiratorial web. This produces a situation where the worker is experiencing aspects of

ILO forced labour and indecent work as an overall labour experience, but it is not being 'done to' them by one party – they are, in effect, rendered slave-like by a culmination of unfreedoms and social relations that do not fit into the ILO's legal definitions.

Nor do ILO indicators take into account the worker's own agency – exploitation is done to them and is experienced by them, and is defined technically and legally. But we have found that exploitation is sometimes knowingly entered into and is tolerated because these people have no alternative. This is not considered to be forced labour by the ILO because the worker can physically walk away or not turn up the next day. The fact that the worker cannot leave because of wider (structural) social, political, economic factors is not considered to be a situation of forced labour. Our approach is that this is a form of forced labour, but to distinguish from the ILO, we use the term 'unfree labour', and understand that, just as there are many ILO indicators of forced labour, with multiple indicators usually meaning a greater degree of coercion, there is a continuum of unfreedom. Unfreedom structures forced labour. Tackling labour abuses requires attention to building universal workers' rights, and regulation that targets employers and workplaces not workers, alongside support for those with severe exploitation experiences to seek justice and find sustainable livelihood options. It is to these areas that we now turn, in Chapter 7.

Notes

[1] In this way, we are differentiating our use of hyper-precarity from the way Lopes de Souza (2009) explains his preference for the term 'hyperprecariat' over 'lumpenproletariat'. As such, he is aligning his hyperprecariat description with a counter-revolutionary potential, or as a portion of the working class acting as an impediment to the realisation of a classless society. Using examples from Brazil, Argentina and South Africa, he suggests the urban 'hyperprecariat' are subject to cities replete with 'phobopolis' – high degrees of fear due to endemic levels of violence. His focus on criminality and social conflict can be seen in distinction to our understanding of everyday, banale hyper-precarity derived from multi-dimensional insecurities in migrants' lives.

[2] Indeed, the European Commission's Experts Group on Trafficking (2004) suggests that all migrants who end up in forced labour and slavery-like conditions should be considered 'trafficked' no matter how migrants arrive into such situations.

Tackling the hyper-precarity trap

Introduction

> "I hope it should be helpful for people, or somebody to continue to search to these things happen to people like me, or somebody else. Or you can help many, many people who are working like slave here without any money." (Mehran)

Mehran's words express the broader resilience and commitment to challenging labour exploitation demonstrated by the 30 migrants who agreed to take part in the research for this book. Indeed, several made it clear that they were only willing to share the difficult and often humiliating details of their severely exploitative work experiences in the hope that their testimonies would contribute to tackling forced labour. We believe that the existence of this book is a small but important step forwards in this respect because it provides evidence for the first time of how severe and forced labour exploitation among asylum seekers and refugees is an entrenched part of the daily lives of many forced migrants living in the UK. It also shows that asylum – both in terms of understanding forced migrants' trajectories and exile from persecution, and in terms of the subsequent structuring of their livelihoods in the asylum system – is a new dimension for understanding forced labour in countries of the Global North.

In this concluding chapter we summarise our core argument about how and why refugees and asylum seekers are engaged in severely exploitative work in the UK, before setting out how we can tackle it. We first revisit the multi-dimensional nature of migrant hyper-precarity and unfreedom, drawing out how neoliberal labour market regimes interact with both ever-tightening and exclusionary immigration rules and migrants' journeys and lives to structure entry into, continuation in, and barriers to exit from, severe labour exploitation. We highlight forced migrants' experiences of voluntary and statutory sector support, and the ongoing effects of the global financial and economic crisis for hyper-precarious migrants, speculating that workplace conditions are worsening. A second section identifies the relevance of our research for current policy debates in the UK context, arguing that the government's draft Modern Slavery Bill continues to focus on tackling the symptoms while its new assault on workers' rights and its desire in the Immigration Act 2014 to create a 'hostile environment' for irregular migrants will only exacerbate the adverse conditions in which forced and severe labour exploitation can flourish. We argue instead for the reinstatement of the right to work for asylum seekers and an unconditional regularisation of all undocumented migrants, including refused asylum seekers, within a wider strengthening of universal workers' rights and rigorous regulation of employers and workplaces if forced labour among migrants is to be successfully tackled. In the final section, we suggest that achieving even modest change in the current anti-immigrant climate will require a grassroots movement in which migrant self-organising plays a central role in the development of social movement unionism.

Hyper-precarious lives: forced migration, asylum and labour exploitation

This book's starting point is the reality that many people who make a claim for asylum in the UK – and who are therefore (largely) not granted permission to work – nevertheless find it necessary to engage in employment at certain points during their asylum journey. In Chapter 3 we showed that asylum seekers and refugees, including those with permission to work, are regularly employed in the undocumented and unregulated lower echelons of the paid labour market where payment below the National Minimum Wage is a normalised reality. In particular, we found that three broad groups in the UK who make a claim for asylum are susceptible to severe and forced labour exploitation: *asylum seekers on entry, irregular migrants* and *trafficked migrants*. Our key finding was that all of the 30 interviewees had experienced forced labour practices in nearly three-quarters of the 107 labouring situations they told us about. The most commonly experienced forced labour practices were the 'abuse of vulnerability' stemming from compromised socio-legal status and the 'withholding of wages'. This forced labour is linked to sectors of the workforce where insecure, flexible and casualised jobs have become the norm (Anderson and Rogaly, 2005; Clark, 2013) in catering and hospitality, care, domestic work, food packing or processing, cleaning, manufacturing, retail, construction, security and other sectors. But the experiences of our 30 interviewees also point to widespread workplace abuses as part of a broader environment of precarious labour that makes movement along a continuum of exploitation (Skřivánková, 2010) towards forced labour more likely.

So why is this happening? We argued in Chapter 2 that an important backdrop to migrant labour exploitation in general is the historical transformations wrought by neoliberal globalisation since the 1970s. In this context, the concept of 'precarity' has emerged to describe the chronic and deepening insecurity of social reproduction, both in the flexibilisation of labour markets and the dismantling of post-war welfare systems. It is a concept that enables exploration of labour conditions alongside an acknowledgment of the profoundly destabilising effects of precarious work on wider society. However, work-focused notions of precarity (see, for example, Dorre et al, 2006; Fantone, 2007) are not subtle enough to differentiate the experiences of exploited/unfree migrants from those workers more generally identified as part of the wider precariat (Standing, 2011). The viscerally lived unfreedoms within our interviewees' lives are better conceptualised as hyper-precarious rather than 'merely' precarious. This is because for each individual asylum seeker/refugee, the context of their migratory move(s), socio-legal status and gender relations intersect in particular ways to create multi-dimensional insecurities that contribute to the necessity to engage in, and close down exit from, severely exploitative or forced labour.

Such factors are further compounded by ever more restrictive migration regimes and the heightened economic insecurities created by the recent recession. The operation of contemporary asylum systems thus needs to be recognised as an important factor for understanding forced labour in the Global North. States are proclaiming that their very survival and integrity are contingent on the close control and monitoring of migration flows and migrants themselves. Sparke (2006) notes that this control has taken a particular bio-political hue that he names 'carceral cosmopolitanism'. The Janus face of many richer countries' immigration regimes, or the dual dynamic, is that they simultaneously reach out to highly-skilled migrants yet attempt to close the door to the rest of the world, or at the very least, heavily determine the position of such 'other' migrants (Bauder, 2011). The devil in the detail of such managed migration policies for most Global South migrants is that stratified entry and emergent socio-legal status (as discussed in Chapters 2 and 4) delimits welfare and employment entitlements, and therefore exacerbates vulnerabilities in unregulated and low-paid labour markets. Most EU countries have followed a narrow focus on higher-skilled migration, leaving migrants seeking lower-skilled employment at risk of being forced into the shadows of the informal or illegal economy, or being exposed to exploitation and coercion in the formal economy.

Border regimes have clearly created informal, illicit and 'illegal' forms of migration which serve the global political economy (by creating ever cheaper and more controllable labour), and consolidate yet another axis of differentiation between different groups of migrant workers (Friman, 2011). As Cross (2013b, p 1) asserts, 'the tensions between international agendas of labour mobility and mechanisms of control produce an arbitrary outcome for migrants.' Countries like the UK are increasingly closing down routes for claiming asylum and expanding regimes of deterrence while simultaneously restricting and structuring the entry of skilled migrants and shutting down legal routes for unskilled migrant workers. Yet such is their determination, resourcefulness and need, labour migrants still come (Wills et al, 2010). The asylum system is underpinned by a deliberately restrictive and exclusive system of socio-legal entitlement that compounds the corrosive effects of the neoliberal capitalist de-regulated labour market to generate 'hyper-precarity' among forced migrants who claim asylum in the UK. As argued in Chapter 4, the role of immigration-related socio-legal status was central to rendering our interviewees vulnerable to such exploitation. The majority of our interviewees sought work only after their asylum case was refused because their asylum support was removed, and when they had exhausted all other, limited, resources. However, the risk of homelessness and destitution for refused asylum seekers 'compelled by necessity' (O'Neill, 2011) to seek out unauthorised employment is only part of the picture. Some are pulled into severe labour exploitation while in receipt of asylum support, a situation that arises from the poverty of life in the asylum support system, where payments for a single adult have dropped to 54 per cent of Income Support levels (Pettitt, 2013; The Children's Society, 2013), combined with migrants' needs to meet their wider familial responsibilities through sending remittances home.

Service provision journeys: voluntary and statutory sector responses

For those at risk should they return to their country of origin, the UK asylum system could be a source of support, offering a route out of forced labour for those who are trafficked to the UK. However, if such claims are refused, individuals subsequently face the possibility of destitution and the associated risks of severe labour exploitation. Although the UK has established the NRM for identifying victims of trafficking as part of its implementation of the 2005 European Convention on Action against Trafficking in Human Beings, trafficked migrants continue to face formidable institutionalised barriers when claiming asylum, and success is far from guaranteed. A particular concern is the use of evidence from separate trafficking and asylum interviews to undermine individual migrants' credibility, leaving highly vulnerable individuals at ongoing risk of exploitation without appropriate support (Stepnitz, 2012). Policy solutions that focus on the prosecution of traffickers, aside from being too narrow to address wider practices of forced labour, have a number of disadvantages. They may not actually help trafficked migrants, as there are multiple reasons why someone may not be willing or able to pursue a legal prosecution. For trafficked migrants, escape from forced labour often carries the threat of harm to family members at 'home'. The concern to preserve long-term relations in a wider, transnational community is also a major barrier to disclosure and pursuit of legal remedies for such individuals.

Compounding the hidden nature of the problem is the deep fear experienced by individuals who have been warned and even threatened not to reveal their situation to any organisation, as well as service providers themselves often actively avoiding discussion of work experiences due to legality/prosecution concerns over undocumented working – making detection even more unlikely. There are a growing number of important initiatives to raise awareness of and to tackle trafficking and forced labour (ATMG, 2010, 2012; Migration Yorkshire, 2013b; Stronger Together, 2014; Platform on Forced Labour and Asylum, 2014). But even within this specialist focus, in such documents and among the burgeoning number of projects seeking to support people who have been trafficked, there is still little understanding of forced labour that occurs *without* trafficking, and almost no recognition that refugees and asylum seekers are susceptible to forced labour. Migrants in our research experiencing forced labour did come into contact with 'the system', but most quickly lost trust in the capacity of agencies to effectively protect them. Some forced labourers had tried to access services, but because they did not feel able or willing to talk about their experiences, or because the language they used to describe their situation was not understood as forced labour, they were not recognised as needing protection. Identifying forced labour is extremely difficult, as identified by this migrant advocacy worker we interviewed:

> "When someone is fixated on just one of these things, like for instance, 'they talked to me like I wasn't human', if they go and say that to a police officer that's not going to trigger a police officer to think 'it sounds like this is … forced labour'."

In a number of cases, workers described leaving highly exploitative situations to seek help – but this did not lead to adequate support or exit from the forced labour situation. It is understandable that frontline providers working in limited contexts have to focus on particular questions relating to available provision or referrals. But this can mean that important details are easily missed, allowing abuse to continue. Jay, for example, was most concerned about being made homeless if he exited his situation. As discussed in Chapter 5 in relation to the importance of simple practical solutions for facilitating exit, he saved up pennies of change from money he was given for household shopping, left one day on a bus to visit a refugee service provider, but was told he was not eligible for support with accommodation. He then went to a homeless shelter, where he was told that as a non-EU migrant he was not eligible, so he returned to his situation of domestic servitude, and living in the garage. It is undoubtedly significant that only two of our interviewees had pursued criminal charges in relation to their forced labour situation at the time of writing, and even more so that both had been told there was insufficient evidence to pursue a case against their employer/trafficker. Several interviewees felt that attempting to press charges in relation to their forced labour was futile. They were concerned that if the 'perpetrator' was given a short prison sentence, this would simply increase the risk to them once they were released, or that pursuing a case against someone from their own 'community' would do more to damage their own reputation and transnational social networks.

This problem of pursuing criminal cases of forced labour against individual employers, traffickers or third parties highlights a much broader issue addressed in our critique of the ILO formulation of forced labour in Chapter 6. This focus is relevant because the ILO's definitions and instruments underpin UK and many other national legal frameworks for identifying and prosecuting forced labour. Yet current operational definitions, guidance and indicators for regulatory and legal enforcement are neither adequate nor universally understood, leading to gaps in detection and prosecution. Moreover, the exclusion of economic compulsion or coercion ignores the very real economic and social pressures which our research shows are clearly fundamental to understanding why workers become trapped in forced and severely exploitative labour. Arguably most problematic of all in the ILO framework is that it fixes coercion as a bilateral affair between employers and employees, and therefore does not account for long, globalised subcontracting chains, the impunity of distant corporate global production and service networks, and the role of complex triangular employment relationships (Geddes et al, 2013, p 96) involving labour market intermediaries. Yet our research demonstrated that the web of coercion could include friends, partners and family members.

These shortcomings of the ILO forced labour concept lead us to suggest that the types of labour experiences described in this book are best conceptualised as unfree labour. The concept of unfreedom is helpful in understanding the highly constrained choices and lack of alternatives that lead refugees and asylum seekers to engage in severely exploitative work, and, importantly, can incorporate the very real pressure of migrants' obligation to support family members, which is vital for understanding why migrants may not seek to exit even severely exploitative labour situations. Thus multi-dimensional insecurities of welfare, work, race, rights, journeys, the economy and neoliberalism intersect for certain migrants and at particular times to produce a 'hyper-precarity trap'. This provides an explanatory framework for understanding the creation of the 'demand' and 'supply' of forced labour subjects resulting from the intersection of socio-legal status, neoliberal globalisation, global poverty and the social reproduction strategies of migrants. Importantly, forced labour must be understood as a process, linked to both a tunnel of entrapment and to a continuum of exploitation, recognising that in reality it is difficult to draw a line between exploitation and forced labour, and highlighting a causal relationship between more general exploitation and the existence of forced labour. As argued later in the chapter, the reluctance of forced labourers to pursue official mechanisms of redress for employment or criminal law breaches, and the difficulties of accessing civil or criminal justice (likely to become worse due to the legal aid cuts outlined below) make action to bolster universal workers' rights and to target employers, not workers, crucial.

Deepening hyper-precarity in the global financial and economic crisis?

The ongoing global, financial and economic crisis continues to have negative consequences for vulnerable workers, particularly migrant workers, who are commonly the first to lose their jobs in the current downturn, or who may remain in work facing worsening conditions and reductions in pay (IOM, 2009). In comparison to national workers, migrants typically have reduced access to safety nets and other support mechanisms and are, therefore, 'frequently compelled to take any work offered, generally at more substandard pay and abusive conditions than before. This represents a particularly urgent driver for *precarisation* of work and working conditions' (Taran, 2011, p 4; emphasis added). One response to this deterioration of conditions for migrants is to return to countries of origin, an option that does not exist for those whose migration was initially motivated by the need to flee persecution. Many of our interviewees remained in the UK working in exploitative labour because they feared persecution if they returned to their country of origin. This hyper-precarity distinguishes the experience of refugees and asylum seekers in forced labour from those of other groups considered susceptible to forced labour.

Within the Global North crisis conditions have led to a new fiscal orthodoxy of massive government borrowing to refinance domestic markets, accompanied by wide-ranging aggressive public expenditure cuts. One consequence of this in many countries has been the reduction of already minimal social provision. The subtext here is of governments' dismantling of the concept and practice of state responsibility for universal welfare of people on its territory – sold to electorates as 'justifiable' wider welfare reform. Migrants are therefore finding themselves increasingly excluded from social protection, social support and welfare programmes (Cook, 2011). In the UK, asylum seekers and refugees continue to face entrenched poverty, but their needs remain consistently under-prioritised (Crossley, 2013; Pettitt, 2013). There is no reason to think that refugees' need to seek protection will decline, especially in a world where 'conflict and economic wellbeing (among other variables) are inextricably linked in the migration process' (Zetter, 2009, p 4). Recessions in the nations of the Global North and an associated decline in development assistance budgets also increases the likelihood of impoverishment in the Global South which, in turn, may contribute to pressures to migrate. Once an individual has been forced to migrate, the reception they receive in destination countries is likely to have hardened since the onset of the crisis. Many nations of the Global North are currently witness to a toxic mix of racist rhetoric about the scale of economic migration from poorer countries and the purported abuse of asylum-seeking migration channels. The trend towards increasing immigration restrictionism in many richer countries (see Chapters 1 and 2) looks set to continue through times of austerity, as governments seek to prioritise protection of their own 'indigenous' workers from unemployment. Although the stated targets of such protectionist policies are usually irregular migrants, many states' willingness to recognise and accept refugees may decline in response to partisan political efforts to reduce immigrant numbers, and the desire to limit asylum-related welfare expenditure. It is highly likely that,

> ... [t]hose seeking asylum will find it harder to lodge their claims as bona fide refugees; more people will be consigned to "temporary protection" categories; the appeal machinery will be circumscribed; destitution will be covertly engineered; and we can expect a significant increase in the numbers of "failed asylum seekers" being repatriated, probably forcibly. (Zetter, 2009, p 3)

Consequently, more asylum seekers will be driven into the fringes of the economy, where the spectre of workplace exploitation and unfreedom looms large. The direction of policy travel means this situation is likely to be exacerbated in the future. In spite of the well documented, increasing need over the coming decades for migrant labour to fill gaps in the labour market in an ageing Europe (Ruhs and Anderson, 2010), most European governments, including the UK (see May, 2013), prefer to maintain a hard-line stance on immigration. Such hostile political discourse swirls in the public arena alongside more generalised expressions of anti-foreigner sentiment and calls for the exclusion of migrants from accessing labour markets and emergency social protection benefits (Taran, 2009). At present, migration regime restrictionism and labour market de-regulation produces labour exploitation and directly undermines efforts to assert and protect migrant worker rights, as succinctly summarised here:

> Migration governance regimes based on control and restriction measures thwart a deliberate, regulated response to growing needs for labour and skills mobility. When labour does move as it must, it is – perhaps not accidentally – subject to abuse, exploitation and draconian repressive measures. Those who suffer most are the many persons simply obeying – often with little choice – the laws of supply and demand of the globalized capitalist market economy. In this situation, the basic dignity and rights of migrants as workers and human beings are undermined, especially for those in irregular situations. (Taran, 2011, p 25)

Even in the throes of the crisis and forecasting uncertainties, it is erroneous to think that migrants will 'serve as a sort of safety valve for developed economies, by providing labour in times of expansion and going away in times of recession' (Castles, 2013, p 3). As a relative 'constant' in richer economies, concern regarding the well-being of hyper-precarious migrant workers remains as pressing as ever.

Responding to forced and severe labour exploitation of migrants: regularisation, not criminalisation

So what is to be done about forced and severe labour exploitation of asylum seekers, refugees and irregular migrants in the UK? As introduced in Chapter 1, the writing of this book has coincided with a highly significant political development in the shape of a Draft Modern Slavery Bill published in December 2013 that is currently making its way through Parliament, and is expected to receive Royal Assent within the term of the current Coalition government. It represents the UK government's approach to tackling forced labour, and optimistically claims it will establish the most effective regime in the world for tackling modern slavery. Proposals within the Bill include the creation of a 'modern slavery commissioner' with responsibilities for monitoring the work of government and law enforcement agencies, a company commitment in which employers pledge not to use slave labour, and measures to ban people convicted of trafficking offences from holding a gangmasters licence. The Draft Bill, however, has been met with sizeable criticism and disappointment from organisations supporting migrants and refugees as well as academics.

One key criticism is that the first Draft Bill yet again focuses principally on trafficking, and more specifically, trafficking for sexual exploitation. This continues a policy focus on trafficking that, inadvertently or otherwise, deflects both resources and attention away from the broader issue of labour exploitation practices across formal, informal and transactional labour spaces (Flynn, 2007; van den Anker, 2009). This singular trafficking approach to policy-making, while important in itself, marginalises non-trafficked migrants' susceptibility to forced labour. The result is that those in situations of exploitation where a trafficking link does not exist or cannot be proven are currently left without access to the identification, support, reflection, legal compensation and immigration status remedies that have been latterly recognised in the UK as vital for tackling trafficking. A broader criticism of the Bill is that it is focused firmly on tackling the specific symptoms rather than the wider causes of forced labour. Phillips (2013a) has stated that any proposed legislation must go beyond requiring companies to engage in 'corporate self-regulation' and include public regulation of supply chains and company strategies.

The Draft Bill, therefore, does not adequately respond to the contention of many commentators (Geddes et al, 2013) that widespread severely exploitative labour relations, often without any link to trafficking, continue to occur as part of 'the "normal functioning" of global production networks and labour markets' (Phillips and Mieres, 2010, p 23). The Joint Committee report on the Bill urged the government, law enforcement agencies and businesses to do more to fight slavery and protect its victims, and warns that the draft Bill will do little to address the difficulties in securing convictions against traffickers and slave masters as it is barely more than a 'cut and paste' of existing laws. The report places emphasis on prevention, protection and effective partnerships – not just prosecution. Interestingly, an alternative Bill proposed in the report argues for the need for a 'general exploitation' offence precisely to account for offences committed without force, coercion, threat or deception. However, the majority of recommendations, including those on supply chains, the need for an Anti-Slavery Commissioner to be independent, extension of the Gangmasters Licensing Authority remit and, especially, those cross-cutting immigration controls (such as the right for Overseas Domestic Workers to move employer) were rejected by the government.

We share the critical analysis, but would go further. In reality, the UK government is currently pursuing two completely *divergent* policy tracks (Strauss, 2012b) by publicly posturing against forced labour, and in particular, trafficking, while simultaneously overseeing both the further deregulation of the UK labour market and an intensification of the exclusionary asylum and immigration policies that underpin the exploitation of asylum seekers, refugees and irregular migrants more generally. In the sphere of labour regulation, recent policy and sector changes have undermined effective regulation and enforcement of decent working conditions in low-paid areas of the economy. The Health and Safety Executive have been subject to a 35 per cent reduction in its funding (TUC, 2010), and both the Employment Agency Standards Inspectorate and the Gangmasters Licensing Authority have seen their budgets cut extensively in recent years. The UK Coalition government has also been rolling out a series of employment law reforms that change the policy and legal framework for seeking justice through the employment tribunal system. Employment tribunals, set up to provide an impartial forum for the resolution of disputes between employees and employers, are no longer free to access. This, combined with other changes, such as a doubling of the qualifying times for unfair dismissal claims and an increase in associated fees, 'will make it extremely difficult for workers to receive compensation and support if they are treated unfairly by their employer' (Renton and Macey, 2013, p 12).

The recent cuts and restrictions to legal aid will have an impact on vulnerable forced migrants in particular. Legal aid will no longer be accessible for migrants who fail a 'residence test', thus barring people from making legitimate fresh asylum claims, and it will also be cut for bringing a judicial review. This will further limit access to justice for the most vulnerable people in the UK, such as victims of trafficking and destitute children asking for refugee protection. The necessity of raising high fees for those who do wish to pursue fresh claims may further act as a 'driver', pushing desperate refused asylum seekers deeper into exploitative work (Asylum Aid, 2013). As a group that is unlikely to be represented by trade unions, or to have access to lawyers (Busby et al, 2013), these changes signal a real threat to the already precarious rights of vulnerable migrant workers.

Broader rights-based support that vulnerable migrants have previously accessed through voluntary sector organisations is further becoming more insecure as the UK public expenditure cuts bite. Agencies providing temporary shelter and basic necessities for destitute migrants, for example, are being forced to reduce their services as local authority funding is cut or even withdrawn. Many agencies within the statutory, voluntary and community sector are not adequately equipped to respond appropriately to forced labour among refugees and asylum seekers, and there is a need for improved awareness of forced labour indicators, similar to that which has been successful in identifying 'potential victims of trafficking', across the sector.[1] Services to support refugees into work play a critical role in directing refugees into decent work, but have also faced significant cuts.

Finally, one policy measure at the intersection between labour market and immigration that is having a detrimental effect on migrant workers' employment situations is the 'civil penalty regime'. Introduced in 2008 as part of the UK's immigration compliance measures, it is designed to increase employers' responsibilities for monitoring the immigration status of their workforce. However, this penalty regime has been advantageous to exploitative employers (for example, through the withholding of back pay), and has simultaneously pushed undocumented migrants into more clandestine employment where they are likely to be exposed to greater exploitation. Additionally, employers have become increasingly wary of continuing to employ migrants who are legally entitled to work, such as refugees (MRN, 2008). The doubling, in March 2013, of the maximum civil penalty (from £10,000 to £20,000) payable by errant employers is likely to intensify many companies' reluctance to hire migrant workers and push undocumented migrants further into exploitation at the hands of unscrupulous employers. Requirements introduced in the Immigration Act 2014 for landlords, banks and primary health care workers (doctors and nurses) to check immigration status before offering services will have deeply troubling ramifications for the proliferation of everyday abuse and discrimination towards all migrants, and will undoubtedly further facilitate the exploitation of irregular migrants. These changes will also serve to continue to inflame a politically toxic immigration debate in Europe that works against the promotion of equal employment rights for all, including migrant workers, that we identify below as vital for tackling forced labour.

Regularisation, rights and re-regulation

The previous section has shown that government policy is going in completely the opposite direction to what the evidence and analysis presented in this book suggests it should be. In our view, tackling severe and forced labour exploitation among asylum seekers, refugees and the wider precarious irregular migrant workforce in the UK must address the root causes, not the symptoms. As Rogaly (2008, p 1444) argues, 'It lies within the means of the state to provide some protection for [migrant] workers from the vulnerability associated with undocumented status, poverty and workplace abuse.' While we acknowledge that the root causes and solutions have a global reach, the following discussion focuses on the national scale. However politically unpalatable and even unrealistic our proposals might be in the current hostile climate towards immigration, we feel morally impelled to make them and to argue for them.

There are a number of reforms required to the UK asylum and immigration system in the short and medium term that would reduce some of the vulnerabilities to exploitation of forced migrants. First, the deliberate policy of enforcing the destitution of refused asylum seekers that lies at the heart of the current asylum system (Joint Committee on Human Rights, 2007) must be recognised as inhumane and ended. Removing rights to residence, work and asylum support irrespective of whether applicants are willing, or able, to leave the UK creates an exploitable pool of labour for unscrupulous employers. The core remedy is to give the right to work to both asylum seekers *and* refused asylum seekers who cannot be returned to their country of origin so that they can legally meet their basic needs and enjoy the legal protections and rights afforded to workers and employees. Allowing asylum seekers to work would bring greater social inclusion, reduce the negative stereotyping and the dangers such attitudes bring, and provide much needed additional inward investment in economically disadvantaged areas. This must go hand in hand with the state providing 'end-to-end' asylum support until point of return, ensuring access to legal aid and provision of legal representation throughout asylum claims, and improving the quality of asylum decision making, as these are all central to ending asylum seeker destitution (for a fuller discussion of these remedies, see JRCT, 2007; Williams and Kaye, 2010; Crawley et al, 2011; Gillespie, 2012).

Second, the UK must repeal the retrograde step of granting only five-year leave to remain to asylum applicants granted refugee status, and reinstate grants of indefinite leave to remain. A five-year stay cannot be seen to meet UK obligations to offer a 'durable solution' or protect against the *non-refoulement* of refugees, and generates insecurity and temporariness that erode pathways to decent work, again promoting the risk of exploitation. Indeed, migrant support workers we interviewed told us that when refugees have to send off their documents to apply for indefinite leave to remain at the end of the five-year period, they can lose their job despite technically still having rights to work and to access welfare. This administrative formality takes months and pushes refugees just beginning to rebuild their lives following significant upheaval into informal labour, with all the attendant risks of exploitation outlined in detail in this book. Equally, the routine 12-month leave to remain granted to victims of trafficking recognised through the NRM process is insufficient, and makes it almost impossible to secure decent work. Combined with difficulties in accessing benefits due to stricter rules on proving six-month (habitual) residency, those exiting trafficking situations are left highly susceptible to re-entering the same or similar forced labour situations they escaped from.

Third, the reinstatement of the right to work for asylum seekers and granting indefinite leave to remain to refugees should be part of a wider and permanent *regularisation* of all undocumented or irregular migrants living in the UK. By regularisation we mean granting all irregular migrants indefinite leave to remain with full legal rights to reside, work and claim benefits. We also mean wiping clean any criminal records for working illegally or for other needs-based crimes such as stealing food or squatting while destitute and homeless. As shown in Chapter 4, such criminalisation acts as a major barrier to decent work, and can empower unscrupulous employers to exploit those who subsequently receive leave to remain in the knowledge that they have a serious lack of employment and livelihood options. Indeed, one very good argument for such regularisation is that it would stop the criminalisation and prosecution of destitute individuals caught working with false papers for using a false instrument. Another strong argument in favour of regularisation is that the government simply cannot deport the irregular migrant population, last estimated in 2009 at between 417,000 and 863,000 (Gordon et al, 2009). It is also a relatively straightforward policy to implement as regularisations have been rolled out on a frequent basis in other European and North American countries (Apap et al, 2000). For example, Italy and Spain have shared 11 major one-off regularisations since the mid-1980s, regularising nearly 2 million irregular migrants in total (Levinson, 2005).

Nevertheless, regularisation is undoubtedly a complex issue, and existing international evidence on the actual experiences of regularisations suggests they are almost always accompanied by harsher measures for newcomers (Levinson, 2005; Longhi, 2013). There is a very real danger that this would also happen in the UK, as evidenced by the 2007 Strangers into Citizens campaign. Set up by London Citizens, a broad-based alliance of local civic and faith groups inspired by Saul Alinsky's (1971) community organising model, the campaign called on the government to implement a one-off 'earned amnesty' for all irregular migrants resident in the UK for four or more years with no criminal record (Citizens Organising Foundation, 2007). The campaign was, in many respects, an important contribution to challenging the reactionary discourse on immigration as well as 'mobilising newer immigrants in pursuit of their political rights' (Wills et al, 2010, p 185). However, its proposals made politically damaging concessions to the government's hard-line immigration system, as exemplified by the suggestion that irregular migrants with criminal records would be excluded from the amnesty. Not only would this leave a group of irregular migrants still vulnerable to forced labour, as shown in Chapter 4, it would also mean a double injustice denying regularisation and rights to refused asylum seekers who, due to destitution, are criminalised by the state for working illegally.

Inevitably, the restoration of formal rights will not solve the problems of economic exclusion overnight, as an anti-trafficking adviser told us:

> "… even if asylum seekers instantly have the right to work, I think it's fair to say that based on the kind of, shall we say, contemporary social attitude towards asylum seekers, they aren't going to be top of the shortlist for jobs in the mainstream economy anyway. No amount of legislation changes that, that's social. Then they end up sidelined already, so you're already in the margins of the legitimate economy. I think that would definitely lead to exploitation."

What this demonstrates is that regularisation, while an important step forward, is no panacea for solving the problems experienced by asylum seekers and refugees, but has to be supplemented by actions and interventions across many areas. For starters, the government must bring back refugee integration and employment programmes. The levy on migrant visa applications that the previous Labour administration distributed regionally through a Migrant Impact Fund should be reinstated. The examples of those individuals in our study who did manage to escape their hyper-precarity trap point to the importance of funding and support for quality volunteering opportunities (see Wilson and Lewis, 2006), access to educational opportunities, including higher education, which would require much wider support by institutions for asylum seekers to be charged local, not international, fees.

Restoring rights and targeting support for refugee employment, however, is not going to have much effect if the UK economy continues down the path of deregulation, where existing rights and employment standards are being whittled away, and those that do exist on paper are never enforced in practice. This calls for a strengthening of universal workers' rights in the UK, and for the focus of enforcement against forced and severe labour exploitation to shift away from the immigration status of workers and back to the actual working conditions and observance of universal worker in workplaces. Core labour rights – to the National Minimum Wage, to UK Working Time Regulations, and to health and safety regulations – should be applied to all workplaces. These regulations would have to be enforced through a dedicated national workplace inspectorate, with power of entry and real enforcement powers.

Fourth, there is a need to improve awareness among staff, at all levels, working with migrants in diverse statutory organisations and NGOs, that forced labour is a criminal offence. Access to basic employment and immigration advice should be adequately advertised and made more widely available. Health professionals are often a vital avenue for accessing support, reinforcing the importance of universal access to primary health care. Despite doubting the motives of men offering to 'help' her, we saw in Chapter 4 how Nanda became involved in an abusive and exploitative relationship with a man who kept her wages. It was only when she was put into contact with services after a suicide attempt that she discovered the risks attached to working with another person's NINo. Indeed, one feature to emerge from the interaction our interviewees had with service providers is the very valuable role played by those organisations that do offer more holistic approaches to support. If clients are allowed and encouraged to talk about their lives in their own words, and a wide range of factors affecting the individual are taken into account, the kinds of experiences discussed in this book are more likely to be identified.

In short, we believe that the above measures would go a long way to tackling some of the root causes of severe and forced labour exploitation of migrants in the UK. However, the stark reality is that unless the political climate in the UK shifts dramatically towards a more progressive agenda, none of these ideas will feature in any manifesto of the main political parties in the coming years. Changing direction requires building a grassroots movement, a challenge we now briefly turn to.

Resistance, organising and action

The discussions contained in this book have highlighted a pressing need to challenge both the particular risks of severe labour exploitation for those in the UK asylum system alongside a wider need to address precarious and exploitative work practices more broadly. Precarity is a concept that not only describes working and social lives characterised and structured by the uncertainties and instabilities created by global, neoliberal labour markets, but also carries with it with the hope of a progressive politics through collective action by which the precariat might challenge exploitative labour processes and wider insecurities (Standing, 2014). Precarity has been politicised and identified as a potential platform for collective action to challenge both exploitative labour processes and wider insecurity (Foti, 2005; Waite, 2009; Standing, 2014). This interpretation of precarity as a possible point of mobilisation links to how the word has gained prominence in social movement struggles and seeped into the language of those envisioning alternatives to capitalist existence (for example, groups allied to the Euro May Day actions). Although advocates suggest the concept of precarity has the potential to be a powerful new brand of labour activism, others caution against the 'celebratory' imagining of migrants that has featured in the writing of some (Hardt and Negri, 2004). The experience of unionisation in labour sectors where migrants are common shows there are significant challenges around attempting to organise migrant workers in traditional ways within low-paid sectors marked by high turnover, subcontracting and employment agencies (Wills, 2005; Cook et al, 2008; Holgate, 2011). It is even more difficult when these migrants are refused asylum seekers or undocumented workers living with 'illegality' and deportability, making them desperate to 'keep in' with their employers and not to attract the attention of the authorities for fear of arrest and detention.

Nevertheless, our research did unearth evidence of solidarity and resistance among asylum seekers and irregular migrants experiencing labour exploitation, despite the limitations of their highly constrained circumstances, that provides some basis for hope. This was illustrated in Chapter 4, for example, by those migrants who willingly shared basic accommodation and food with others who had become homeless and destitute. Discussions in Chapter 5 further detailed individual acts of resistance, such as 'walking away' from the worst employers and practices, and warning other migrants of recent raids by immigration officials. That said, it needs to be acknowledged that broader-based collectivised resistance among our interviewees was rendered almost impossible by the necessity for those engaged in undocumented work to remain as invisible as possible from the attention of both employers and the government in order to be able to continue working to earn enough to meet their basic needs. Workers resisted these extreme forms of exploitation in their struggles to manage within, and to refuse, reject and exit from forced labour, as discussed in Chapter 5. Most of our interviewees had managed to get away from single or serial forced labour situations by running away, walking away or being pushed away. However, the narrative of 'victim rescue' that privileges the imaginary of a unilinear movement away from severe exploitation is troubled by our evidence that 'exit' in many cases constituted movement merely within an *unfreedom continuum*. In many cases, the moment of exit opened workers up to fresh risks of exploitation. Temporary re-entry into asylum support or limited charitable destitution provision offers vital support, but often constitutes only a respite from the necessity to engage in exploitative work, including for those migrants who were trafficked, if their asylum claim was later refused. Even for those granted leave to remain, multiple barriers to decent work can continue to leave refugees susceptible to labour exploitation, demonstrating that the right to work would be an important equaliser, but would not prevent forced labour in isolation from wider protections of workers' rights.

Clearly for those asylum seekers and refugees trapped in situations of severe labour exploitation or forced labour, the conditions of hyper-precarity they experience regularly precludes opportunities for systematic organised resistance. This said, the example of the Justice for Domestic Workers (J4DW) organisation, based in London, shows that collective self-organisation of precarious migrants is both possible and effective. Established in 2009, J4DW was set up by migrant domestic workers as a self-help group aimed at publicly campaigning about the appalling working and living conditions being experienced by many at the hands of their employers behind closed doors. Going public was incredibly courageous due to the power that their employers had to undermine these workers' immigration status due to visa regulations. We interviewed a member of the campaign who told us how they had built the organisation on mutual aid, with those in work contributing some of their wages to support those migrant workers who had run away from their abusive employers and who had nothing:

> "At the beginning we just want a campaign organisation, okay, but from the very beginning already we see the problem of domestic workers who just appear at our door without clothes, without anything – just the clothes they are wearing, that's all. Some of them are barefooted. We couldn't really ask them to campaign without helping and supporting them with their basic needs. They need to survive – we started to give £1 whenever we need to, [when] necessary, we have so many runaways. The £1 salary is for them to have £1 a month for them – for the travelling allowance so they can find another job."

J4DW also realised the importance to their organising drive of providing basic literacy and language education through which they could also raise awareness of domestic migrant workers' rights and build a community in collective struggle:

> "… I think the most important in organising is educating them…. In that we have ICT, we have ESOL [English for Speakers of Other Languages] classes, we have arts classes but what we put in the curriculum is about their rights. So raising awareness to them they know their rights, what they can fight for. What they need to be aware of the changes in immigration and they learn English. They learn about the UK. We have the life in the UK as well. They learn about all that while improving their English as well while making them – you know that they are now on Facebook, they have the Facebook and that also helps the isolation."

But J4DW remains an exception. In such circumstances, it is therefore vital for other more powerful actors to highlight and challenge the vulnerabilities and coercion endured by migrant workers. Despite the contemporary weakness of organised labour in the UK due in no small part to the neoliberal policies unleashed over the past 35 years, trade unions still have a key role to play here, but only if they change. As Wills et al (2010) have argued, although broadly pro-immigration, unions have a weaker record of achievement in defending and improving the pay and conditions of marginalised workers at the very bottom end of the labour market in recent decades. Moreover, the traditional trade union organisation is a very difficult model to successfully implement with precarious migrant workers due to language, cultural and socio-legal status barriers. This has led to calls for the union movement to become more proactively engaged in campaigning for 'labour standards for all', including migrant workers, to build solidarity between migrant and non-migrant workers at the bottom of the labour market (Wills et al, 2010). Initiatives such as the Institute for Human Rights and Business establishment of the 'Dhaka Principles for Migration and Dignity' offer a central reference point for the treatment of workers in responsible business intended to enhance respect for the rights of migrant workers.[2]

These relationships are starting to form, as witnessed by the developing ties between J4DW and the Unite union. J4DW members have joined a branch of Unite and have set up a trade union working group to act as a communication bridge to the union. In turn, Unite has responded by creating a more flexible union membership system that recognises the fact that many migrant domestic workers do not have bank accounts, as well as supporting them with training on union rights through the TUC. At the same time, Unite recognises J4DW's autonomy and respects its political mission (interview with J4DW). This shows the potential for a new kind of trade unionism, rooted in what has been called 'social movement unionism' (Waterman, 2001). As this hopefully develops at the national scale, the emergence of a politicised transnational activism in defence of migrants' rights (Piper, 2008) will also play a critical role. Again, with declining trade union power and the rising importance of transnational links, a broad range of organisations, including faith-based organisations, worker NGOs, feminist and anti-racist groups and human rights organisations, have become involved in debates around working rights as human rights and in campaigning against migrant worker exploitation (Piper, 2008; Wills et al, 2010). The increase in international mobility, the development of information technology and the enhanced global communication networks that are central aspects of the ongoing processes of globalisation (see Tambini, 2001) may further enhance the potential of such social movements and campaigns in tackling forced labour.

Conclusion

Policies that variously attempt to define and address 'slavery', 'trafficking' or 'forced labour' are both necessary and important. However, in keeping with a number of recent studies (see, for example, O'Connell Davidson, 2010; Scott et al, 2012), we strongly assert that solutions which narrowly focus on tackling 'slavery', 'trafficking' or 'forced labour' as exceptional events within the labouring lives of migrants are flawed. Any understanding of migrants' vulnerability to severe labour exploitation and forced labour must take into account both its routine occurrence, and the fact that this emerges from the complex interactions of wider labour law and restrictive migration and welfare policies. Refugees and asylum seekers are part of a much larger group of vulnerable workers in the UK whose commonplace exploitation within labour markets is mediated and structured by the interplay of broader political, economic, social and gendered processes. Any attempt to tackle the labour abuses and wider precarity of asylum seekers and refugees highlighted in our research would be best served by a strategy that prioritises building and enhancing universal rights for *all* workers, and that additionally guarantees that adequate systems of support and legal redress are available for migrants who experience severe exploitation, while simultaneously establishing adequate systems for the regulation of employers and workplaces to ensure workers can enjoy sustainable livelihoods in the future. Governments must continue to recognise their human rights responsibilities to those on their soil and, especially in light of the ongoing global, financial and economic crisis, make sure that they 'sustain a regulatory role, provide a social protection floor and ensure minimal well-being for all' (Taran, 2011, p 1). However, at this current juncture, it is self-evident that the political will does not exist within governments to ensure that such protections are instigated. The challenge for us all is to make them do it.

Notes

[1] A Precarious Lives follow-up project, funded by ESRC Knowledge Exchange Opportunities to build a Platform on Forced Labour and Asylum, aims to begin a process of developing strategies to tackle forced labour among this vulnerable group (see http://forcedlabourasylum.wordpress.com).

[2] The 'Dhaka Principles' are a set of human rights-based principles to enhance respect of the rights of migrant workers from the moment of recruitment, during overseas employment and through to further employment or safe return to home countries (see http://dhakaprinciples.org).

References

Agustín, L.M. (2007) *Sex at the margins: migration, labour markets and the rescue industry*, London and New York: Zed Books.

Ahmad, A.N. (2008) 'The labour market consequences of human smuggling: "illegal" employment in London's migrant economy', *Journal of Ethnic and Migration Studies*, vol 34, pp 853-74.

Alinsky, S. (1971) *Rules for radicals: a pragmatic primer for realistic radicals*, New York: Random House.

Allain, J., Crane, A., LeBaron, G. and Behbahani, L. (2013) *Forced labour's business models and supply chains*, York: Joseph Rowntree Foundation.

Allamby, L., Bell, J., Hamilton, J., Hansson, U., Jarman, N., Potter, M. and Toma, S. (2011) *Forced labour in Northern Ireland: exploiting vulnerability*, York: Joseph Rowntree Foundation.

Amnesty International UK (2006) *Down and out in London: the road to destitution for rejected asylum seekers*, London: Amnesty International UK.

Amoore, L. (2006) 'Biometric borders: governing mobilities in the war on terror', *Political Geography*, vol 25, pp 336-51.

Anderson, B. (2000) *Doing the dirty work? The global politics of domestic labour*, London and New York: Zed Books.

Anderson, B. (2007) 'A very private business: exploring the demand for migrant domestic workers', *European Journal of Women's Studies*, vol 14, no 3, pp 247-64.

Anderson, B. (2010) 'Migration, immigration controls and the fashioning of precarious workers', *Work, Employment & Society*, vol 24, no 2, pp 300-17.

Anderson, B. (2013) *Us and them? The dangerous politics of immigration control*, Oxford: Oxford University Press.

Anderson, B. and Rogaly, B. (2005) *Forced labour and migration to the UK*, London: Trades Union Congress.

Anderson, B. and Ruhs, M. (2012) 'Reliance on migrant labour: inevitability or policy choice?', *Journal of Poverty and Social Justice*, vol 20, no 1, pp 23-30.

Anderson, B., Ruhs, M., Rogaly, B. and Spencer, S. (2006) *Fair enough? Central and East European migrants in low-wage employment in the UK*, York: Joseph Rowntree Foundation.

Andreas, P. (2004) 'Illicit international political economy: the clandestine side of globalisation', *Review of International Political Economy*, vol 11, no 3, pp 641-52.

Andrees, B. (2008) *Forced labour and trafficking in Europe: how people are trapped in, live through and come out*, ILO Working Paper 57, Geneva: International Labour Office.

Andrijasevic, R. (2010) *Migration, agency and citizenship in sex trafficking*, Basingstoke: Palgrave Macmillan.

Apap, J., de Bruycker, P. and Schmitter, C. (2000) 'Regularisation of illegal aliens in the European Union. Summary report of a comparative study', *European Journal of Migration and Law*, vol 2, pp 263-308.

Asylum Aid (2013) 'Asylum Aid's submission to the Low Commission' (www.asylumaid.org.uk/data/files/publications/205/AsylumAid_LowCommission_Jan2013.pdf).

ATMG (Anti-Trafficking Monitoring Group) (2010) *Wrong kind of victim? One year on: an analysis of UK measures to protect trafficked persons*, London: Anti-Slavery International for ATMG.

ATMG (2012) *All change: preventing trafficking in the UK*, London: ATMG.

Balch, A. (2012) *Regulation and enforcement to tackle forced labour in the UK: a systematic response?*, York: Joseph Rowntree Foundation.

Bales, K. (2004) *Disposable people: new slavery in the global economy*, Berkeley and Los Angeles, CA: University of California Press.

Bales, K., Trodd, Z. and Williamson, A.K. (2009) *Modern slavery: the secret world of 27 million people*, Oxford: Oneworld Publications.

Banaji, J. (2003) 'The fictions of free labour: contract, coercion, and so-called unfree labour', *Historical Materialism*, vol 11, no 3, pp 69-95.

Barbier, J.-C. (2002) *Defining and assessing precarious employment in Europe: a review of main studies and surveys. A tentative approach to precarious employment in France*, Paris: Centre d'Etudes de l'Emploi.

Barbieri, P. (2009) 'Flexible employment and inequality in Europe', *European Sociological Review*, vol 25, no 6, pp 621-8.

Barrientos, S. (2008) 'Contract labour: the "Achilles heel" of corporate codes in commercial value chains', *Development and Change*, vol 39, no 6, pp 977-90.

Barrientos, S., Kothari, U. and Phillips, N. (2013) 'Dynamics of unfree labour in the contemporary global economy', *The Journal of Development Studies*, vol 49, no 8, pp 1037-41.

Bastia, T. and McGrath, S. (2011) *Temporality, migration and unfree labour: migrant garment workers*, Manchester Papers in Political Economy, Working Paper No 6, Manchester: University of Manchester.

Bauder, H. (2011) 'The regulation of labor markets through migration', in N. Phillips (ed) *Migration in the global political economy*, Boulder, CO: Lynne Rienner Publishers, pp 41-60.

BBC (2013a) 'BBC Panorama finds Bangladeshi workers locked in on 19-hour shifts', BBC News, 23 September (www.bbc.co.uk/mediacentre/latestnews/2013/panorama-dying-bargain).

BBC (2013b) 'David Cameron talks tough over European migrants' benefits', BBC News, 25 March (www.bbc.co.uk/news/uk-politics-21921089).

Beck, U. and Beck-Gernscheim, E. (2003) *Individualisation: institutionalized individualism and its social and political consequences*, London: Sage.

Beeks, K. and Amir, D. (2006) *Trafficking and the global sex industry*, Lanham, MD and Oxford: Lexington Books.

Bigo, D. (1994) 'The European internal security field: stakes and rivalries in a newly developing area of police intervention', in M. Anderson and M. den Boer (eds) *Policing across national boundaries*, London: Pinter, pp 42-69.

Blair, T. (2007) 'The shame of slavery', *New Nation*, 27 November.

Blinder, S. (2013) *Migration to the UK: asylum*, Migration Observatory Briefing, Oxford: Centre on Migration, Policy and Society (COMPAS), University of Oxford.

Bloch, A. (2002) *Refugees' opportunities and barriers in employment and training*, DWP Research Report No 179, Leeds: Department for Work and Pensions.

Bloch, A. (2004) *Making it work: refugee employment in the UK*, London: Institute for Public Policy Research.

Bloch, A. (2008) 'Refugees in the UK labour market: the conflict between economic integration and policy-led labour market restriction', *Journal of Social Policy*, vol 37, pp 21-36.

Bloch, A. (2013) 'Living in fear: rejected asylum seekers living as irregular migrants in England', *Journal of Ethnic and Migration Studies*, pp 1-19.

Bloch, A. and Schuster, L. (2002) 'Asylum and welfare: contemporary debates', *Critical Social Policy*, vol 22, no 3, pp 393-414.

Bloch, A. and Schuster, L. (2005) 'At the extremes of exclusion: deportation, detention and dispersal', *Ethnic and Racial Studies*, vol 28, no 3, pp 491-512.

Bloch, A., Sigona, N. and Zetter, R. (2009) *'No right to dream.' The social and economic lives of young undocumented migrants in Britain*, London: Paul Hamlyn Foundation.

Bloch, A., Sigona, N. and Zetter, R. (2011) 'Migration routes and strategies of young undocumented migrants in England: a qualitative perspective', *Ethnic and Racial Studies*, vol 34, no 8, pp 1286-302.

Bondi, L. and Laurie, N. (2005) 'Introduction to special issue on "Working the spaces of neoliberalism: activism, professionalisation and incorporation"', *Antipode*, vol 37, pp 394-401.

Bosniak, L. (2008) *The citizen and the alien: dilemmas of contemporary membership*, Princeton, NJ: Princeton University Press.

Bourdieu, P. (1998) *La précarité est aujourd'hui partout*, Contrefeux, Paris: Liber Raisons d'agir.

Bourdieu, P. (1999) 'Job insecurity is everywhere now', in P. Bourdieu *Acts of resistance: against the tyranny of the market*, New York: New Press.

Bowpitt, G., Dwyer, P., Sundin, E. and Weinstein, M. (2012) *The support priorities of multiply excluded homeless people and their compatibility with support agency agendas*, Salford and Nottingham: University of Salford and Nottingham Trent University.

Brass, T. (1999) *Towards a comparative political economy of unfree labour. Case studies and debates*, London: Frank Cass.

Breman, J. (2007) *Labour bondage in West India: from past to present*, New Delhi: Oxford University Press.

Breman, J. (2010) *Outcast labour in Asia: circulation and informalization of the workforce at the bottom of the economy*, New Delhi: Oxford University Press.

British Red Cross (2010) *Not gone, but forgotten. The urgent need for a more humane asylum system*, London: British Red Cross.

Burnett, J. and Whyte, D. (2010) *The wages of fear: risk, safety and undocumented work*, Leeds and Liverpool: Positive Action for Refugees and Asylum Seekers (PAFRAS) and the University of Liverpool.

Busby, N., McDermont, M., Rose, E. and Sales, A. (2013) *Access to justice in employment disputes: surveying the terrain*, Liverpool: Institute of Employment Rights.

Bush, R. (2007) *Poverty and neoliberalism: persistence and reproduction in the Global South*, London: Pluto Press.

Butler, J. (2004) *Precarious life: the powers of mourning and violence*, London: Verso.

Butler, J. (2009) *Frames of war*, London: Verso.

Buzan, B., Waever, L. and de Wilde, J. (1998) *Security: a new framework for analysis*, Boulder, CO: Lynne Rienner Publishers.

Cameron, D. (2013) 'Immigration speech by the Prime Minister', 25 March (www.gov.uk/government/news/immigration-speech-by-the-prime-minister).

Castles, S. (2002) 'International migration at the beginning of the twenty-first century: global trends and issues', *International Social Science Journal*, no 52, vol 165, pp 269-81.

Castles, S. (2003) 'Towards a sociology of forced migration and social transformation', *Sociology*, vol 37, no 1, pp 13-34.

Castles, S. (2007) 'The factors that make and unmake migration policies', in A. Portes and J. DeWind (eds) *Rethinking migration: new theoretical and empirical perspectives*, New York and Oxford: Berghahn, pp 29-61.

Castles, S. (2013) 'Migration, precarious work and rights: Historical and current perspectives', UNESCO-MOST Conference, Linkoping University, 'Labour rights as human rights? Migration, labour market restructuring, and the role of civil society in global governance', Unpublished.

Castles, S. and Miller, M.J. (2009) *The age of migration: international population movements in the modern world*, Basingstoke: Palgrave Macmillan.

Children's Society, The (2013a) *Report of the Parliamentary Inquiry into asylum support and children and young people* (www.childrenssociety.org. uk/sites/default/files/tcs/asylum_support_inquiry_report_final.pdf).

Children's Society, The (2013b) 'A briefing from The Children's Society highlighting the gap between asylum support and mainstream benefits'.

Citizens Organising Foundation (2007) *'Strangers into Citizens', A campaign by the Citizens Organising Foundation for a pathway into citizenship for thousands of undocumented workers who have made new lives in the UK*, London: Citizens Organising Foundation.

Clark, N. (2013) *Detecting and tackling forced labour in Europe*, York: Joseph Rowntree Foundation.

Clark, N. and Kumarappan, L. (2011) *Turning a blind eye: the British state and migrant domestic workers' employment rights. Summary of findings. Draft report*, London: Working Lives Research Institute.

Clement, W., Mathieu, S., Prus, S. and Uckardesier, E. (2009) *Precarious lives in the new economy: comparative intersectional analysis*, Gender and Work Database (GWD)/Comparative Perspectives Database (CPD) Working Paper Series, York, Canada: GWD/CPD (www.genderwork. ca/cpdworkingpapers/clement-mathieu-prus-uckardesler.pdf).

Clements, J., Rapley, M. and Cummins, R.A. (1999) 'On, to, for, with – vulnerable people and the practices of the research community', *Behavioural and Cognitive Psychotherapy*, vol 27, pp 103-15.

Cohen, R. (1987) *The new helots: migrants in the international division of labour*, Aldershot: Avebury/Gower Publishing Group.

Cohen, S. (2002) *Folk devils and moral panics: the creation of the mods and rockers* (3rd edition), London: Routledge.

Comaroff, J. (1985) *Body of power, spirit of resistance: the culture and history of a South African people*, Chicago, IL: University of Chicago Press.

Cook, I. (2011) *Hierarchies of vulnerability: country report United Kingdom; Labour migration and the systems of social protection*, Prague: Multikulturni Centrum Praha.

Cook, J., Dwyer, P. and Waite, L. (2008) *New migrant communities in Leeds*, Leeds: Leeds Social Sciences Institute, University of Leeds (http://lssi.leeds.ac.uk/projects/11).

Council of Europe (2005) Convention on Action against Trafficking in Human Beings, Warsaw, 16.V.2005.

Craig, G. (2007) '"Cunning, unprincipled, loathsome": the racist tail wags the welfare dog', *Journal of Social Policy*, vol 36, no 4, pp 605-23.

Craig, G., Gaus, A., Wilkinson, M., Skrivankova, K. and McQuade, A. (2007) *Contemporary slavery in the UK: overview and key issues*, York: Joseph Rowntree Foundation.

Crawley, H., Hemmings, J. and Price, N. (2011) *Coping with destitution. Survial and livelihood strategies of refused asylum seekers living in the UK*, Swansea: Swansea University and Oxfam.

Cross, H. (2013a) 'Labour and underdevelopment? Migration, dispossession and accumulation in West Africa and Europe', *Review of African Political Economy*, vol 40, no 136, pp 202-18.

Cross, H. (2013b) *Migrants, borders and global capitalism: West African labour mobility and EU borders*, London: Routledge.

Crossley, S. (2013) *Written out of the picture*, Durham: North East Child Poverty Commission/Regional Refugee Forum North East.

CSJ (Centre for Social Justice) (2013) *It happens here: equipping the United Kingdom to fight modern slavery*, London: CSJ.

Cumbers, A., Nativel, C. and Routledge, P. (2008) 'Labour agency and union positionalities in global production networks', *Journal of Economic Geography*, vol 8, no 3, pp 369-87.

DCLG (Department for Communities and Local Government) (2008) *Review of migrant integration policy in the UK (including a feasibility study of the proposal for an Integration Agency)*, London: DCLG.

Defra (Department for Environment, Food and Rural Affairs) (2012) *Food statistics pocketbook*, London: Defra.

de Genova, N.P. (2002) 'Migrant "illegality" and deportability in everyday life', *Annual Review of Anthropology*, vol 31, no 1, pp 419-47.

Demos (2007) *Recruitment 2020: how recruitment is changing and why it matters*, London: Demos.

Dolan, C. and Humphrey, J. (2000) 'Governance and trade in fresh vegetables: the impact of UK supermarkets on the African horticulture industry', *The Journal of Development Studies*, vol 37, no 2, pp 147-76.

Dorre, K., Kraemer, K. and Speidel, F. (2006) 'The increasing precariousness of the employment society – driving force for a new right-wing populism?', 15th Conference of Europeanists, Chicago, IL, 30 March–2 April.

Drescher, S. (2009) *Abolition: a history of slavery and antislavery*, Cambridge: Cambridge University Press.

Dugan, E. (2013) *Forced labour and human trafficking: media coverage in 2012*, York: Joseph Rowntree Foundation.

Düvell, F. and Jordan, B. (2002) 'Immigration, asylum and welfare: the European context', *Critical Social Policy*, vol 22, no 3, pp 498-517.

Düvell, F., Triandafyllidou, A. and Vollmer, B. (2010) 'Ethical issues in irregular migration research in Europe', *Population, Space and Place*, vol 16, pp 227-39.

Dwyer, P. (2005) 'Governance, forced migration and welfare', *Social Policy & Administration*, vol 39, no 6, pp 622-39.

Dwyer, P. (2008) *Integration? The perceptions and experiences of refugees in Yorkshire and the Humber*, Leeds: Yorkshire and Humber Regional Migration Partnership.

Dwyer, P. and Brown, D. (2005) 'Meeting basic needs? Forced migrants and welfare', *Social Policy and Society*, vol 4, no 4, pp 369-80.

Dwyer, P. and Brown, D. (2008) 'Accommodating "others"? Housing dispersed, forced migrants in the UK', *Journal of Social Welfare and Family Law*, vol 30, no 3, pp 203-18.

Dwyer, P., Lewis, H., Scullion, L. and Waite, L. (2011) *Forced labour and UK immigration policy: status matters?*, York: Joseph Rowntree Foundation.

EHRC (Equality and Human Rights Commission) (2010) *Inquiry into recruitment and employment in the meat and poultry processing sector*, Manchester: EHRC.

Ehrenreich, B. and Hochschild, A. (2003) *Global woman: nannies, maids, and sex workers in the new economy*, New York: Holt Paperbacks.

Esim, S. and Smith, M. (2004) *Gender and migration in Arab states: the case of domestic workers*, Geneva: International Organization for Migration.

Ettlinger, N. (2007) 'Precarity unbound', *Alternatives*, vol 32, pp 319-40.

European Commission (2004) *Report of the Experts Group on Trafficking in Human Beings*, Brussels: European Commission.

European Court of Human Rights (2012) *CN v The United Kingdom*.

Fantone, L. (2007) 'Precarious changes: gender and generational politics in contemporary Italy', *Feminist Review*, vol 87, pp 5-20.

Favell, A. (2008) 'The new face of East–West migration in Europe', *Journal of Ethnic and Migration Studies*, vol 34, no 5, pp 701-16.

Flynn, D. (2007) *Human trafficking and forced labour. What perspectives to challenge exploitation?*, Brussels: Platform for International Cooperation on Undocumented Migrants (PICUM).

Foti, A. (2004) 'Precarity and n/european identity: an interview with Merijn Oudenampsen and Gavin Sullivan (ChainWorkers)', *Mute Magazine* (www.metamute.org/editorial/articles/precarity-and-neuropean-identity-interview-alex-foti-chainworkers).

Foti, A. (2005) 'Mayday Mayday! Euro flex workers, time to get a move on!', European Institute for Progressive Cultural Policies (http://eipcp.net/transversal/0704/foti/en).

Frantz, E. (2008) 'Of maids and madams', *Critical Asian Studies*, vol 40, no 4, pp 609-38.

Friman, R.H. (2011) 'The illegal "migration industry"', in N. Phillips (ed) *Migration in the global political economy*, Boulder, CO: Lynne Rienner Publishers, pp 83-102.

Fryer, P. (1984) *Staying power: the history of black people in Britain*, London: Pluto.

Fryer, P. (1988) *Black people in the British Empire*, London: Pluto.

Fudge, J. (2013) *The precarious migrant status and precarious employment: the paradox of international rights for migrant workers*, Centre of Excellence for Research on Immigration and Diversity Working Paper No 11-15, Vancouver, BC: Metropolis British Columbia.

Fudge, J. and Strauss, K. (eds) (2014) *Temporary work, agencies, and unfree labour: Insecurity in the new world of work*, London: Routledge.

Geddes, A. (2008) *Immigration and European integration: beyond fortress Europe?* (2nd edn), Manchester: Manchester University Press.

Geddes, A. (2011) 'Borders and migration in the European Union', in N. Phillips (ed) *Migration in the global political economy*, Boulder, CO: Lynne Rienner Publishers, pp 193-208.

Geddes, A., Craig, G., Scott, S., Ackers, L., Robinson, O. and Scullion, D. (2013) *Forced labour in the UK*, York: Joseph Rowntree Foundation.

Gibney, M. (2008) 'Asylum and the expansion of deportation in the United Kingdom', *Government and Opposition*, vol 43, no 2, pp 139-43.

Giddens, A. (1984) *The constitution of society: outline of the theory of structuration*, Cambridge: Polity Press.

Giddens, A. (1990) *The consequences of modernity*, Stanford, CA: Stanford University Press.

Giddens, A. (1991) *Modernity and self-identity: self and society in the late modern age*, Cambridge: Polity Press.

Gill, N. (2009) 'Presentational state power: temporal and spatial influences over asylum sector decision makers', *Transactions of the Institute of British Geographers*, vol 34, no 2, pp 215-33.

Gillespie, M. (2012) *Trapped: destitution and asylum in Scotland*, Glasgow: Scottish Poverty Information Unit.

Glidewell Panel, The (1996) *The report from an independent enquiry into the implications and effects of the Asylum and Immigration Bill 1995 and related social security measures*, London: The Glidewell Panel.

Goldring, L. and Landolt, P. (2011) 'Caught in the work–citizenship matrix: the lasting effects of precarious legal status on work for Toronto immigrants', *Globalizations*, vol 8, no 3, pp 325–41.

Gordolan, L. and Lalani, M. (2009) *Care and immigration: migrant care workers in private households*, London and Oxford: Kalayaan and Centre on Migration, Policy and Society (COMPAS), University of Oxford.

Gordon, I., Scanlon, K., Travers, T. and Whitehead, C. (2009) 'Economic impact on London and the UK of an earned regularisation of irregular migrants in the UK', London: London School of Economics (www. lse.ac.uk/collections/LSELondon/pdf/irregular%20migrants%20 full%20report.pdf).

Guardian, The (2005) 'Cocklers' gangmaster "showed gross negligence"', 19 September.

Gubbay, J. (1999) 'The European Union role in the formation and, legitimation and implementation of migration policy', in G. Dale and M. Cole (eds) *The European Union and migrant labour*, Oxford: Berg, pp 23-35.

Guild, E. (2009) *Security and migration in the 21st century*, Cambridge: Polity.

Gupta, R. (2007) *Enslaved: the new British slavery*, London: Portobello Books.

Hardt, M. and Negri, A. (2004) *Multitude: war and democracy in the age of empire*, London: Penguin Press.

Harrod, J. and O'Brien, R. (2002) *Global unions? Theory and strategies of organized labour in the global political economy*, London and New York: Routledge.

Harvey, D. (2005) *A brief history of neoliberalism*, Oxford and New York: Oxford University Press.

Head, E. (2009) 'The ethics and implications of paying participants in qualitative research', *International Journal of Social Research Methodology*, vol 12, no 4, pp 335-44.

Herbert, J., Datta, K., Evans, Y., May, J., McIlwaine, C. and Wills, J. (2006) *Multiculturalism at work: the experiences of Ghanaians in London*, London: School of Geography, Queen Mary, University of London.

Herlihy, J., Scragg, P. and Turner, S. (2002) 'Discrepancies in autobiographical memories: implications for the assessment of asylum seekers: repeated interviews study', *British Medical Journal*, vol 324, pp 324-7.

Herod, A. (2000) 'Workers and workplaces in a neoliberal global economy', *Environment and Planning A*, vol 32, no 10, pp 1781-90.

Hodkinson, S. (2005) 'Is there a new trade union internationalism? The International Confederation of Free Trade Unions' response to globalization, 1996-2002', *Labour, Capital and Society*, vol 38, no 1 & 2, pp 36-65.

Holgate, J. (2011) 'Temporary migrant workers and labor organization', *Working USA: The Journal of Labor and Society*, vol 14, pp 191-9.

Hollander, J. and Einwohner, R. (2004) 'Conceptualizing resistance', *Sociological Forum*, vol 19, no 4, pp 533-54.

Hollifield, J.F. (2004) 'The emerging migration state', *International Migration Review*, vol 38, no 3, pp 885-911.

Home Office (2013a) *Draft Modern Slavery Bill*, December, London: HMSO.

Home Office (2013b) 'Immigration Bill: overview factsheet' (www.gov.uk/government/uploads/system/uploads/attachmentdata/file/249251/Overview_Immigration_Bill_Factsheet.pdf).

Home Office (2013c) *Tables for immigration statistics, April to June 2013*, London: Home Office.

Hondagneu-Sotelo, P. (2001) *Doméstica: immigrant workers cleaning and caring in the shadows of affluence*, Oakland, CA: University of California Press.

Hugman, R., Pittaway, E. and Barolomei, L. (2011) 'When "do no harm" is not enough: the ethics of research with refugees and other vulnerable groups', *British Journal of Social Work*, vol 41, no 7, pp 1271-87.

Hurstfield, J., Pearson, R., Hooker, H., Ritchie, H. and Sinclair, A. (2004) *Employing refugees: some organisations' experience*, London Institute for Employment Studies.

Hynes, P. (2003) *The issue of 'trust' or 'mistrust' in research with refugees: choices, caveats and considerations for researchers*, New Issues in Refugee Research, UNHCR Working Paper No 98, Geneva: United Nations Refugee Agency.

Hynes, P. (2010) 'Global points of "vulnerability": understanding processes of the trafficking of children and young people into, within and out of the UK', *The International Journal of Human Rights*, vol 14, no 6, pp 952-70.

Hynes, P. (2011) *The dispersal and social exclusion of asylum seekers*, Bristol: Policy Press.

IAC (Independent Asylum Commission) (2008) *Safe return. How to improve what happens when we refuse people sanctuary. The Independent Asylum Commission's second report of conclusions and recommendations*, London: IAC.

ILO (International Labour Organization) (1930) Forced Labour Convention (No 29), Geneva: ILO.

ILO (1949) Migration for Employment Convention (Revised) (No 97), Geneva: ILO.

ILO (1957) Abolition of Forced Labour Convention (No 105), Geneva: ILO.

ILO (1975) Migrant Workers (Supplementary Provisions) Convention (No 143), Geneva: ILO.

ILO (2005) *Human trafficking and forced labour exploitation. Guidelines for legislation and law enforcement*, Geneva: ILO.

ILO (2011) *Hard to see, harder to count. Survery guidelines to estimate forced labour of adults and children*, Geneva: ILO.

ILO (2012a) *ILO indicators of forced labour*, Geneva: ILO.

ILO (2012b) *ILO global estimate of forced labour: results and methodology*, Geneva: ILO.

IOM (International Organization for Migration) (2009) *The impact of the global financial crisis on migrants and migration*, Policy Brief, March, Geneva: IOM.

Jeffreys, S. (2002) 'Australia and the traffic in women into sexual exploitation', *Arena Magazine*, April.

Joint Committee on Human Rights (2007) *The treatment of asylum seekers. Tenth report of the session 2006-07. Volume 1*, London: House of Commons.

Joint Committee on the Draft Modern Slavery Bill (2014) *Draft Modern Slavery Bill report*, London.

Joppke, C. (1998) 'Why liberal states accept unwanted immigration', *World Politics*, vol 50, no 2, pp 266-93.

Jordan, B. and Brown, P. (2007) 'Migration and work in the United Kingdom: mobility and the social order', *Mobilities*, vol 2, no 2, pp 255-76.

Jordan, B. and Düvell, F. (2002) *Irregular migration: the dilemmas of transnational mobility*, Cheltenham: Edward Arnold.

JRCT (Joseph Rowntree Charitable Trust) (2007) *Joseph Rowntree Charitable Trust inquiry into destitution among refused asylum seekers. Commissioner's report. From destitution to contribution*, York: JRCT.

Kagan, C., Lo, S., Mok, L., Lawthom, R., Sham, S., Greenwood, M. and Baines, S. (2011) *Experiences of forced labour among Chinese migrant workers*, York: Joseph Rowntree Foundation.

Katungi, D., Neale, E. and Barbour, A. (2006) *People in low-paid informal work: need not greed*, York: Joseph Rowntree Foundation.

Katz, C. (2004) *Growing up global: economic restructuring and children's everday lives*, Minneapolis, MN: University of Minnesota Press.

Kay, K. (2009) *Portrait of Yorkshire and the Humber*, London: Office for National Statistics.

Kaye, M. (2003) *The migration-trafficking nexus: combating trafficking through the protection of migrants' human rights*, London: Anti-Slavery International.

Khosravi, S. (2010) 'An ethnography of migrant "illegality" in Sweden: included yet excepted?', *Journal of International Political Theory*, vol 6, no 1, pp 95-116.

Kibreab, G. (2009) 'Forced labour in Eritrea', *The Journal of Modern African Studies*, vol 47, no 1, pp 41-72.

Kofman, E. (2002) 'Contemporary European migrations, civic stratification and citizenship', *Political Geography*, vol 21, no 8, pp 1035-54.

Lalani, M. (2011) *Ending the abuse: policies that work to protect migrant domestic workers*, London: Kalayaan.

Lalani, M. and Metcalf, H. (2012) *Forced labour in the UK: the business angle*, York: Joseph Rowntree Foundation.

Lerche, J. (2007) 'A global alliance against forced labour? Unfree labour, neo-liberal globalization and the International Labour Organization', *Journal of Agrarian Change*, vol 7, no 4, pp 425-52.

Lever, J. (2012) *No return no asylum. Destitution as a way of life?*, Bradford: Destitution Concern Bradford.

Levinson, A. (2005) *Why countries continue to consider regularization*, Washington, DC: Migration Information Source/Migration Policy Institute.

Lewis, H. (2007) *Destitution in Leeds: the experiences of people seeking asylum and supporting agencies*, York: Joseph Rowntree Charitable Trust.

Lewis, H. (2009) *Still destitute: a worsening problem for refused asylum seekers*, York: Joseph Rowntree Charitable Trust.

Lewis, H., Dwyer, P., Hodkinson, S. and Waite, L. (2014: forthcoming) 'Hyper-precarious lives? Migrants, work and forced labour in the Global North', *Progress in Human Geography*, DOI: 10.1177/0309132514548303.

Lewis, H., Dwyer, P., Scullion, L. and Waite, L. (2012) 'From restrictions to the cap: trends in UK immigration policy', *Poverty and Social Justice*, vol 20, no 1, pp 87-91.

Longhi, V. (2013) *The immigrant war: a global movement against discrimination and exploitation*, Bristol: Policy Press.

Lopes de Souza, M. (2009) 'Social movements in the face of criminal power. The socio-political fragmentation of space and "micro-level warlords" as challenges for emancipative urban struggles', *City*, vol 13, no 1, pp 26-52.

Lutz, H. (2010) 'Gender in the migratory process', *Journal of Ethnic and Migration Studies*, vol 36, no 10, pp 1647-63.

Lynn, N. and Lea, S. (2003) '"A phantom menace and the new apartheid": the social construction of asylum-seekers in the United Kingdom', *Discourse & Society*, vol 14, pp 425-52.

Mackenzie, C., McDowell, C. and Pittaway, E. (2007) 'Beyond "do no harm": the challenge of constructing ethical relationships in refugee research', *Journal of Refugee Studies*, vol 2, no 2, pp 219-319.

MacKenzie, R. and Forde, C. (2009) 'The rhetoric of the "good worker" versus the realities of employers' use and the experiences of migrant workers', *Work, Employment & Society*, vol 23, no 1, pp 142-59.

Macleod, C. (2000) 'My son and the lorry of death', *The Independent*, 23 July.

McDowell, L. (2008) 'Thinking through work: complex inequalities, constructions of difference and trans-national migrants', *Progress in Human Geography*, vol 32, no 4, pp 491-507.

McDowell, L., Batnitzky, A. and Dyer, S. (2009) 'Precarious work and economic migration: emerging immigrant divisions of labour in Greater London's service sector', *International Journal of Urban and Regional Research*, vol 33, no 1, pp 3-25.

McGrath, S. (2012) 'Many chains to break: the multi-dimensional concept of slave labour in Brazil', *Antipode*, vol 45, no 4, pp 1005-28.

McIntyre, P. and Mogire, E. (2012) *Between a rock and a hard place: the dilemma facing refused asylum seekers*, London: Refugee Council.

McKay, S., Markova, E., Paraskevopoulou, A. and Wright, T. (2009) *The relationship between migration status and employment outcomes*, London: Undocumented Worker Transitions.

McLaughlin, J. and Hennebry, J. (2010) 'Pathways to precarity: structural vulnerabilities and lived consequences for migrant farmworkers in Canada', in L. Goldring and P. Landolt (eds) *Producing and negotiating non-citizenship: precarious legal status in Canada*, Toronto: University of Toronto Press, pp 175-94.

Mahdavi, P. (2013) 'Gender, labour and the law: the nexus of domestic work, human trafficking and the informal economy in the United Arab Emirates', *Global Networks*, vol 13, no 4, pp 425-40.

Mai, N. (2011) 'Tampering with the sex of "angels": migrant male minors and young adults selling sex in the EU', *Journal of Ethnic and Migration Studies*, vol 37, no 8, pp 1237-52.

Malkki, L. (1995) 'Refugees and exiles: from "Refugee Studies" to the national order of things', *Annual Review of Anthropology*, vol 25, pp 495-523.

Malkki, L. (1997) 'National geographic: the rooting of peoples and the territorialization of national identity among scholars and refugees', in A. Gupta and J. Ferguson (eds) *Culture, power, place: explorations in critical anthropology*, Durham, NC and London: Duke University Press, pp 52-74.

Marfleet, P. (2006) *Refugees in a global era*, Basingstoke: Palgrave Macmillan.

Marshall, L.W. (2011) 'Toward a new definition of "refugee": is the 1951 Convention out of date?', *European Journal of Trauma and Emergency Surgery*, vol 37, pp 61-6.

Martin, A. and Ross, G. (eds) (1999) *The brave new world of European labor: European trade unions at the millennium*, New York and Oxford: Berghahn Books.

Marx, K. (1976 [1867]) *Capital, Volume 1*, Harmondsworth: Penguin.

Marx, K. and Engels, F. (1848) *The Communist manifesto* (1998 edn), New York: Signet Classics.

Maul, D.R. (2007) 'The International Labour Organization and the struggle against forced labour from 1919 to the present', *Labor History*, vol 48, no 4, pp 477-500.

May, T. (2013) 'Speech of the Home Secretary to the Conservative Party Conference', Conservative Party Annual Conference, 30 September 2013.

Migration Yorkshire (2013a) Personal correspondence, 6 August.

Migration Yorkshire (2013b) *Trafficking for labour exploitation*, Leeds: Migration Yorkshire.

Migration Yorkshire (2013c) *Yorkshire and the Humber local migration profile, June 2013. Summary document*, Leeds: Migration Yorkshire.

Migration Observatory, The (2011) *Commentary: a loose fitting cap: why is the limit on skilled non-EU workers undersubscribed?*, Oxford: The Migration Observatory.

Migration Observatory, The (2013) *Evidence and values – the UK migration debate 2011-2013*, Oxford: The Migration Observatory.

Miles, R. (1987) *Capitalism and unfree labour: anomaly or necessity?*, London and New York: Tavistock Publications.

Mitchell, D. (2011) 'Labor's geography: capital, violence, guest workers and the post-World War II landscape', *Antipode*, vol 43, no 2, pp 563-95.

Mittelman, J.H. (2000) *The globalization syndrome: transformation and resistance*, Princeton, NJ: Princeton University Press.

Model, S. (2002) 'Immigrants' social class in three global cities', in M. Cross and R. Moore (eds) *Globalization and the new city: migrants, minorities and urban transformations in comparative perspective*, Basingstoke and New York: Palgrave Macmillan, pp 88-118.

Mohapatra, P.P. (2007) 'Eurocentrism, forced labour and global migration: a critical assessment', *International Review of Social History*, vol 52, pp 110-15.

Moore, L.W. and Miller, M. (1999) 'Initiating with doubly vulnerably populations', *Journal of Advanced Nursing*, vol 30, no 5, pp 1034-40.

Morgan, J. and Olsen, W. (2009) *Unfreedom as the shadow of freedom: an initial contribution to the meaning of unfree labour*, Manchester Papers in Political Economy, Working Paper 02/09, Manchester: University of Manchester.

Morris, L. (2001) 'Stratified rights and the management of migration. National distinctiveness in Europe', *European Societies*, vol 3, no 4, pp 387-411.

MRN (Migrants' Rights Network) (2008) *'Papers please'. The impact of the civil penalty regime on the employment of rights of migrants in the UK*, London: MRN.

Müller, M. (2007) 'What's in a word? Problematizing translation between languages', *Area*, vol 39, no 2, pp 206-13.

Munck, R. (2010) 'Slavery: exception or rule?', in G. Wylie and P. McRedmond (eds) *Human trafficking in Europe: character, cases and consequences*, Basingstoke: Palgrave Macmillan, pp 17-29.

Munz, R., Straubhaar, T., Vadean, F. and Vadean, N. (2007) *What are the migrants' contributions to employment and growth? A European approach*, Hamburg: Hamburg Institute of International Economics.

Neilson, B. and Rossiter, N. (2005) 'From precarity to precariousness and back again: labour, life and unstable networks', *The Fibreculture Journal*, issue 5 [online] (http://five.fibreculturejournal.org/fcj-022-from-precarity-to-precariousness-and-back-again-labour-life-and-unstable-networks).

Neilson, B. and Rossiter, N. (2008) 'Precarity as political concept, or, Fordism as exception', *Theory, Culture & Society*, vol 25, no 7-8, pp 51-72.

O'Connell Davidson, J. (2010) 'New slavery, old binaries: human trafficking and the borders of "freedom"', *Global Networks*, vol 10, no 2, pp 244-61.

O'Connell Davidson, J. (2013) 'Troubling freedom: migration, debt, and modern slavery', *Migration Studies*, vol 1, no 2, pp 176-95.

O'Neill, J. (2011) *Varieties of unfreedom*, Manchester Papers in Political Economy, Manchester: University of Manchester (www.socialsciences.manchester.ac.uk/PEI/publications/wp/documents/ONeillunfreepaper.pdf).

Ong, A. (1987) *Spirits of resistance and capitalist discipline: factory women in Malaysia*, New York: Suny.

Oxfam and Kalayaan (2008) *The new bonded labour? The impact of proposed changes to the UK immigration system on migrant domestic workers*, London: Oxfam and Kalayaan.

Pai, H.H. (2008) *Chinese whispers*, Harmondsworth: Penguin.

Parreñas, R. (2008) *The force of domesticity: Filipina migrants and globalization*, New York: New York University Press.

Peck, J., Theodore, N. and Ward, K. (2005) 'Constructing markets for temporary labour: employment liberalization and the internationalization of the staffing industry', *Global Networks*, vol 5, no 1, pp 3-26.

Pettitt, J. (2013) *The poverty barrier: the right to rehabilitation for survivors of torture in the UK*, London: Freedom from Torture.

Peutz, N. and de Genova, N. (2010) 'Introduction', in N. Peutz and N. de Genova (eds) *The deportation regime*, Durham, NC: Duke University Press, pp 1-32.

Phillips, D. (2006) 'Moving towards integration: the housing of asylum seekers and refugees in Britain', *Housing Studies*, vol 21, no 4, pp 539-53.

Phillips, N. (2013a) 'Lessons from California: why compliance is not enough', *The Guardian*, 19 September (www.theguardian.com/global-development-professionals-network/2013/sep/19/why-compliance-isnt-enough).

Phillips, N. (2013b) 'Unfree labour and adverse incorporation in the global economy: comparative perspectives on Brazil and India', *Economy and Society*, vol 42, no 2, pp 171-96.

Phillips, N. and Mieres, F. (2010) 'Fielding the wrong ball? A critique of global policy approaches to "forced labour"', presented at: 'Ten years of war against poverty: what we have learned since 2000 and what we should do 2010–2020', Chronic Poverty Research Centre, University of Manchester, 8-10 September.

Phillips, N. and Mieres, F. (2013) 'The governance of forced labour in the global economy', Unpublished.

Piper, N. (2008) 'Political participation and the empowerment of foreign workers: gendered advocacy and migrant labour organising in Southeast and East Asia', in N. Piper (ed) *New perspectives on gender and migration. Livelihoods, rights and entitlements*, New York and Abingdon: Routledge, pp 247-73.

Platform on Forced Labour and Asylum (2014), http://forcedlabourasylum.wordpress.com

Pollard, N., Latorre, M. and Sriskandarajah, D. (2008) *Floodgates or turnstiles? Post EU enlargement migration flows to (and from) the UK*, London: Institute for Public Policy Research.

Radice, H. (2000) 'Responses to globalisation: a critique of progressive nationalism', *New Political Economy*, vol 5, no 1, pp 5-19.

Rao, J.M. (1999) 'Freedom, equality, property and Bentham: the debate over unfree labour', *Journal of Peasant Studies*, vol 27, no 1, pp 97-127.

Rapport, N. and Dawson, A. (eds) (1998) *Migrants of identity: perceptions of home in a world of movement*, Oxford: Berg.

Refugee Action (2006) *The destitution trap: research into destitution among refused asylum seekers in the UK*, London: Refugee Action.

Renton, D. and Macey, A. (2013) *Justice deferred: a critical guide to the Coalition's employment tribunal reforms*, Liverpool: Institute of Employment Rights.

Richmond, A. (1994) *Global apartheid*, Oxford: Oxford University Press.

Rodney, W. (1972) *How Europe underdeveloped Africa*, London: Bogle-L'Ouverture Publications.

Rogaly, B. (2008) 'Migrant workers in the ILO's global alliance against forced labour report: a critical appraisal', *Third World Quarterly*, vol 29, pp 1431-47.

Royle, T. (2005) 'Realism or idealism? Corporate social responsibility and the employee stakeholder in the global fast-food industry', *Business Ethics*, vol 14, no 1, pp 42-55.

Ruhs, M. and Anderson, B. (2010) *Who needs migrant workers? Labour shortages, immigration and public policy*, Oxford: Oxford University Press.

Schuster, L. (2003) *The use and abuse of political asylum in Britain and Germany*, London: Frank Cass.

Scott, J. (1985) *Weapons of the weak: everyday forms of peasant resistance*, New Haven, CT: Yale University Press.

Scott, S., Craig, G. and Geddes, A. (2012) *The experience of forced labour in the UK food industry*, York: Joseph Rowntree Foundation.

Scullion, L., Lewis, H., Dwyer, P. and Waite, L. (2014) 'Exploring the link between forced labor and immigration status in the UK', in K.K. Hoang and R. Parreñas (eds) *Human trafficking reconsidered: rethinking the problem, envisioning new solutions*, New York, London and Amsterdam: International Debate Education Association, pp 247-73.

Shelley, T. (2007) *Exploited: migrant labour in the new global economy*, London and New York: Zed Books.

Shutes, I. (2011) 'Welfare-to-work and the responsiveness of employment providers to the needs of refugees', *Journal of Social Policy*, vol 40, no 3, pp 557-74.

Sigona, N. (2012) '"I have too much baggage": the impacts of legal status on the social worlds of irregular migrants', *Social Anthropology*, vol 20, no 1, pp 50-65.

Sigona, N. and Hughes, V. (2012) *No way out, no way in. Irregular migrant children and families in the UK*, Oxford: Centre on Migration, Policy and Society (COMPAS), University of Oxford.

Skeldon, R. (2011) *Unfree labour, migration and mobility: contested outcomes*, Manchester: University of Manchester.

Skřivánková, K. (2006) *Trafficking for forced labour: UK country report*, London: Anti-Slavery International.

Skřivánková, K. (2010) *Between decent work and forced labour: examining the continuum of exploitation*, York: Joseph Rowntree Foundation.

Smart, K. (2009) *The second destitution tally: an indication of the extent of destitution among asylum seekers, refused asylum seekers and refugees*, Asylum Support Partnership.

Smart, K. and Fullegar, S. (2008) *The destitution tally: an indication of the extent of destitution among asylum seekers and refugees*, The Asylum Support Programme Inter-Agency Partnership.

Solidar (2010) *International migration: the search for decent work*, Brussels: Solidar.

Sparke, M. (2006) 'A neoliberal nexus: citizenship, security and the future of the border', *Political Geography*, vol 25, no 2, pp 151-80.

Standing, G. (2011) *The precariat: the new dangerous class*, London and New York: Bloomsbury Academic.

Standing, G. (2014) *A precariat charter: from denizens to citizens*, London: Bloomsbury Academic.

Steinfeld, R. (2009) *Coercion/consent in labour*, Oxford: Centre on Migration, Policy & Society (COMPAS), University of Oxford.

Stepnitz, A. (2012) 'A lie more disastrous than the truth: asylum and the identification of trafficked women in the UK', *Anti-Trafficking Review*, vol 1, pp 104-19.

Stewart, E. (2004) 'Deficiencies in UK asylum data: Practical and theoretical challenges', *Journal of Refugee Studies*, vol 17, no 1, pp 29-49.

Stiglitz, J.E. (2002) *Globalization and its discontents*, London: Penguin.

Strauss, K. (2012a) 'Coerced, forced and unfree labour: geographies of exploitation in contemporary labour markets', *Geography Compass*, vol 6, no 3, pp 137-48.

Strauss, K. (2012b) 'Unfree labour and the construction of legal categories in the UK', presented at 'Vulnerable workers, forced labour, migration and ethical trading' Conference, 14 December, University of Leeds.

Strauss, K. (2013) 'Unfree again: social reproduction, flexible labour markets and the resurgence of gang labour in the UK', *Antipode*, vol 45, no 1, pp 180-97.

Stronger Together (2014), http://stronger2gether.org

Suebsaeng, A. (2014) 'Steve McQueen dedicated his "12 Years a Slave" best pic Oscar to victims of modern-day slavery', *Mother Jones*, 2 March.

Tambini, D. (2001) 'Post-national citizenship', *Ethnic and Racial Studies*, vol 24, no 2, pp 195-217.

Taran, P. (2009) 'The impact of the financial crisis on migrant workers', first presented at the 2nd Preparatory Meeting for 17th OSCE (Organization for Security and Cooperation in Europe) Economic and Environmental Forum in Tirana.

Taran, P. (2011) *Crisis, migration and precarious work: impacts and responses: focus on European Union member countries*, Geneva: Global Migration Policy Associates.

Taran, P. and Geronimi, E. (2003) *Globalization, labour and migration: protection is paramount*, Perspectives on Labour Migration, 3E, Geneva: ILO.

Taylor, D. (2009) *Underground lives: an investigation ito the living conditions and survival strategies of destitute asylum seekers in the UK*, Leeds: Positive Action for Refugees and Asylum Seekers (PAFRAS).

Taylor, D. (2013) 'Home Office accused of "fixing" asylum figures', *The Guardian*, 26 October.

Temple, B. and Moran, R. (2006) *Doing research with refugees. Issues and guidelines*, Bristol: Policy Press.

Thomson, D. and Larson, R. (1978) *Where were you, brother? An account of trade union imperialism,* London: War on Want.

Triandafyllidou, A. and Maroukis, T. (2012) *Migrant smuggling*, London: Palgrave Macmillan.

TUC (Trades Union Congress) (2008) *Hard work, hidden lives. The full report of the Commission on Vulnerable Employment* (www. vulnerableworkers.org.uk/files/CoVE_full_report.pdf).

TUC (2010) 'A bad seven days for health and safety' (www.tuc.org. uk/workplace/tuc-18703-f0.cfm).

Turner, V. (1969) *The ritual process: structure and anti-structure*, London: Routledge and Kegan Paul.

Turton, D. (2003) *Conceptualising forced migration*, Refugee Studies Centre Working Paper No 12, Oxford: Refugee Studies Centre, University of Oxford.

UKBA (United Kingdom Border Agency) (2008) 'Living and working in the UK. The rights and responsibilities of nationals from Bulgaria and Romania from 1 January 2007' (www.ukba.homeoffice.gov.uk/ sitecontent/documents/workingintheuk/livingandworkinga2.pdf).

UKBA (2013) 'Working in the UK' (www.ukba.homeoffice.gov.uk/ visas-immigration/working).

UN (United Nations) (1948) The Universal Declaration of Human Rights, New York: UN (www.un.org/en/documents/udhr/).

UN (1990) International Convention on the protection of the rights of all migrant workers and members of their families (www2.ohchr. org/english/bodies/cmw/cmw.htm), New York: UN.

UN DESA (United Nations Department of Economic and Social Affairs) (2009) *Trends in international migrant stock: the 2008 revision*, New York: UN DESA.

UNDP (United Nations Development Programme) (2009) *Human development report 2009: overcoming barriers, human mobility and development*, New York: UNDP.

UNHCR (United Nations Refugee Agency) (2007) *Refugee protection and mixed migration: a 10-point plan of action*, Geneva: UNHCR.

UNHCR (2011) *UNHCR resettlement handbook. Country chapters – UK*, Geneva: UNHCR.

UNHCR (2012) *Asylum trends 2012. Levels and trends in industrialized countries*, Geneva: UNHCR.

UNHCR (2013) *Facts and figures about refugees*, Geneva: UNHCR.

UN General Assembly (2000) *Protocol to prevent, suppress and punish trafficking in persons, especially women and children, supplementing the United Nations Convention against transnational organized crime*, Geneva: United Nations.

UNODC (United Nations Office on Drugs and Crime) (2013) *Abuse of a position of vulnerability and other 'means' within the definition of trafficking in persons*, New York: UNODC.

Valentine, R. (2010) *Hope costs nothing: the lives of undocumented migrants in the UK*, London: Migrants Resource Centre and Barrow Cadbury Trust.

van den Anker, C. (2009) 'Rights and responsibilities in trafficking for forced labour: migration regimes, labour law and welfare states', *Web Journal of Current Legal Issues*, vol 1 (http://eprints.uwe.ac.uk/12725/).

van Hear, N. (1998) *New diasporas: the mass exodus, dispersal and regrouping of migrant communities*, London: UCL Press.

Vertovec, S. (2006) *The emergence of super-diversity in Britain*, COMPAS Working Paper No 25, Oxford: Centre on Migration, Policy and Society (COMPAS), University of Oxford.

Vine, J. (2012) *An inspection of the UK Border Agency's handling of legacy asylum and migration cases. March-July 2012*, London: Independent Chief Inspector of Borders and Immigration.

Waite, L. (2009) 'A place and space for a critical geography of precarity?', *Geography Compass*, vol 3, no 1, pp 412-33.

Walters, W. (2004) 'Secure borders, safe haven, domopolitics', *Citizenship Studies*, vol 8, no 3, pp 237-60.

Waterman, P. (2001) 'Trade union internationalism in the age of Seattle', *Antipode*, vol 33, no 3, pp 312-36.

Weitz, R. (2001) 'Women and their hair: seeking power through resistance and accommodation', *Gender & Society*, vol 15, no 5, pp 667-86.

Wilkinson, M., Craig, G. and Gaus, A. (2009) *Forced labour in the UK and the Gangmasters Licensing Authority*, Hull: The Wilberforce Institute, University of Hull.

Williams, E. (1944) *Capitalism and slavery*, Richmond, VA: University of North Carolina Press.

Williams, R. and Kaye, M. (2010) *At the end of the line: restoring the integrity of the UK's asylum system*, Still Human Still Here.

Willis, P.E. (1977) *Learning to labour: how working class kids get working class jobs*, Aldershot: Saxon House.

Wills, J. (2005) 'The geography of union organising in low paid service industries in the UK: lessons from the T&G's campaign to unionise the Dorchester Hotel', *Antipode*, vol 37, pp 139-59.

Wills, J., Datta, K., Evans, Y., Herbert, J., May, J. and McIlwaine, C. (2010) *Global cities at work: new migrant divisions of labour*, London: Pluto Press.

Wilson, R. and Lewis, H. (2006) *A part of society. Refugees and asylum seekers volunteering in the UK. A report based on case studies of ten organisations*, Leeds: Tandem Communications and Research Ltd.

Woolfson, C. and Likic-Brboric, B. (2008) 'Migrants and the unequal burdening of "toxic" risk: towards a new global governance regime', *Debatte: Journal of Contemporary Central and Eastern Europe*, vol 16, no 3, pp 291-308.

World Development Movement (2007) *200 years on: the legacies of enslavement and abolition*, London: World Development Movement.

Zetter, R. (2010) 'Forced migration in an era of global financial crisis – what will happen to refugees?', online paper for 'Migration and the Global Financial Crisis – A Virtual Symposium', *The Age of Migration* Update 1B, 26 January 2010 (www.age-of-migration.com/uk/financialcrisis/updates/1b.pdf).

Zimmermann, S. and Zetter, R. (2011) *Reconsidering the role of conflict in the lives of refugees: the case of Somalis in Europe*, Oxford: Queen Elizabeth House, University of Oxford.

Zolberg, A. (1989) 'The next waves: migration theory for a changing world', *International Migration Review*, vol 23, no 3, pp 403-30.

Index

Note: The following abbreviations have been used – *f* = figure; *n* = note; *t* = table

W

Y

Z